A. 467

C. 467

E.C. 467

E.C. 443

BUNGALOW DETAILS: EXTERIOR

JANE POWELL &
LINDA SVENDSEN

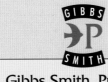

Gibbs Smith, Publisher
Salt Lake City

PAGE 6: Taking the idea of building with local natural
materials and running with it, a shingled bungalow in
Memphis, Tennessee, features not only tapered columns
made of stacked logs but also log-facing on the chimney
and tree branches used as brackets in the gable as well
as under the porch roof. By the back door on the left, a
screen constructed of saplings divides the porch from
the backyard. The rusticity of the logs is balanced by the
delicate tracery of the window muntins in the upper
floor's casement windows. Local stone forms the bases
for the columns and porch.

First Edition
08 07 06 05 04 5 4 3 2 1

Text © 2004 Jane Powell
Photographs © 2004 Linda Svendsen

Published by
Gibbs Smith, Publisher
P.O. Box 667
Layton, Utah 84041

Orders: 1.800.748.5439
www.gibbs-smith.com

Designed by Maralee Lassiter, Lassiter Design, Inc.
Printed and bound in Hong Kong

Library of Congress Control Number: 2004107213

ISBN 1-58685-306-6

CONTENTS:

7 Acknowledgments

9 Foreword

12 Chapter 1: **What Is a Bungalow?**
History of the Bungalow ▪ *The Reader's Digest Condensed Arts and Crafts Movement* ▪ *Bungalow Spotting*

28 Chapter 2: **Good House Keeping**
Erik's Bungalow Manifesto

32 Chapter 3: **Take It from the Top**
Roofing It ▪ *Thatch Entertainment* ▪ *Vinyl Straw* ▪ *Shake It Up* ▪ *Swinging Shingles* ▪ *Viscous Rumors* ▪
Perfect Pitch ▪ *Coal Incidence* ▪ *Concrete Evidence* ▪ *A Tile Told by an Idiot* ▪ *Terne It Up* ▪ *Clean Slate* ▪
Icicle Built for Two ▪ *Dormer Vous?* ▪ *Got the Blues* ▪ *Flue Shot* ▪ *Mind in the Gutter* ▪
Take Me to Your Leader ▪ *All About Eaves* ▪ *Turret Syndrome* ▪ *Squab the Deck*

74 Chapter 4: **The Envelope, Please**
Side Show ▪ *Stud Service* ▪ *Log Off* ▪ *Thick as a Brick* ▪ *Bond, James Bond* ▪ *Stone Face* ▪ *Mudslinging* ▪
Concrete Evidence ▪ *Hollow, My Name Is . . .* ▪ *Sympathy for the Bevel* ▪ *Barking Up the Wrong Tree* ▪
Plaster than a Speeding Bullet ▪ *Let Us Spray* ▪ *Foam at the Mouth* ▪ *Brick-a-Brac* ▪ *Veneer Real Disease* ▪
Bad Form ▪ *Cement the Deal* ▪ *White (Trash) Sidewalls* ▪ *Aluminum Wage* ▪ *Vinyl Conflict* ▪
Veneer of Civilization ▪ *House Blend* ▪ *Stain Alive* ▪ *Gable TV* ▪ *Vent Elation* ▪ *Well-Padded* ▪
Jekyll and (Formalde) Hyde ▪ *Vapor or Plastic?*

102 Chapter 5: **Grand Openings**
Pane Threshold ▪ *Scam, Scam, Scam, Scam, Scam, Scam, Lovely Scam!* ▪ *Scorn on the Cob* ▪ *Bar Hopping* ▪
Block Party ▪ *Steel Away* ▪ *The Perfect Storm* ▪ *In Space, No One Can Hear You Screen* ▪ *Blank Canvas* ▪
Shutter to Think ▪ *More Door* ▪ *Gone Door* ▪ *Barad-Door* ▪ *Area Door* ▪ *Casing the Joint*

136 Chapter 6: **The Foundation of All Knowledge**
Motivated Cellars ▪ *Footing the Bill* ▪ *Pier Intently* ▪ *Joist the Facts, Ma'am* ▪ *Wriggle Room*

140 Chapter 7: **Let's Porch the Place**
Veranda Rights ▪ *A Front to Decency* ▪ *Pillars of the Community* ▪ *Long Walk Off a Short Pier* ▪
Railing Against Fate ▪ *Floor and Aft* ▪ *Tread Lightly* ▪ *Accessibility Issues* ▪ *Screening Room* ▪ *An Exercise in
Utility* ▪ *To Air Is Human* ▪ *Balcony Scene* ▪ *Ruling from the Bench* ▪ *It Don't Mean a Thing If It`Ain't Got
That Swing* ▪ *Do You Urn a Lot?* ▪ *Illuminating Conversation* ▪ *Mail Bonding* ▪ *Figure Skating* ▪ *Chime In* ▪
Knocking Around ▪ *Built to Latch* ▪ *Knob Hill* ▪ *Pivot Hedge*

182 Chapter 8: **Outside Chances**
Coupe Up ▪ *Drive to Succeed* ▪ *Any Porte Cochere in a Storm* ▪ *Walk Like an Egyptian* ▪ *Shack Up* ▪
Pool Your Resources ▪ *If You Picket It'll Never Heal* ▪ *Beyond the Pale* ▪ *Thrown for a Loop* ▪ *Chain of Fools* ▪
Percentage of the Gate ▪ *Wall Street* ▪ *Cutting Hedge* ▪ *Overwrought Iron*

204 Epilogue: **Final Confusion**
A Bungle-Ode

208 Bibliography

O LD BUILDINGS ARE NOT OURS. THEY BELONG, PARTLY TO THOSE WHO BUILT THEM, AND PARTLY TO THE GENERA-TIONS OF MANKIND WHO ARE TO FOLLOW US. THE DEAD STILL HAVE THEIR RIGHT IN THEM: THAT WHICH THEY LABORED FOR . . . WE HAVE NO RIGHT TO OBLITERATE.

WHAT WE OURSELVES HAVE BUILT, WE ARE AT LIBERTY TO THROW DOWN. BUT WHAT OTHER MEN GAVE THEIR STRENGTH, AND WEALTH, AND LIFE TO ACCOMPLISH, THEIR RIGHT OVER IT DOES NOT PASS AWAY WITH THEIR DEATH.

— *John Ruskin*

ACKNOWLEDGMENTS

A finished book, especially one as complex as this, is the result of collaboration by many people, of whom I am only one. As always, I have to thank my co-author, Linda Svendsen, for her fabulous photography, and my editor, Suzanne Taylor, for keeping the spirit of my words intact. My friend Melanie Hofmann spent a long day helping me scan books and magazines, as did Tim Counts of the Twin Cities Bungalow Club in Minneapolis. The support of everyone at Gibbs Smith, Publisher, is something I can always count on. And I want to thank the numerous anonymous homeowners whose bungalows we photographed from sidewalks all over the United States and Canada—to track you down would have been impossible, but we are still grateful.

We are also thankful to the many people who graciously allowed us to photograph their homes; provided us with leads and referrals; lent books, magazines, and catalogs; or provided information. They are in no particular order (of importance, alphabet, or anything else, though I have tried to group them by geography). In Vancouver, British Columbia: Jo Scott-B, John Atkin, Heather and Bill Andrews. In Victoria, British Columbia: Jennifer Barr of the Victoria Heritage Foundation, Suzanne and Patrick Bulmer, Sheila and Jim Colwill, Paul and Marilynne Convey, Judith and Richard Andersen. In Seattle: Laurie Taylor of Ivy Hill Interiors, Larry Kreisman of Historic Seattle, Clint Miller, Larry Johnson, Pamela and Gerard Zytnicki, Carrie Schnelker and Michael Sobieck, Olivia Dresher, Mary Fields and John Aylward, Shelley and Michael Clair, Mary Casey and Bob Welland, Jessie Jones and Matt Johnson, Barbara Griffin and Judy Cherin. In Berkeley: Tim Hansen, Terry Geiser, John Ribovich. In Ventura, California: Cynthia Thompson at the Pierpont Inn, Richard Gould, Jean Gould Bryant, and Celia Orozco at the Gould House. In Los Angeles: Adam Janeiro and Colleen Davis, Kathy and Bill Couturie, Tom and Annie Goepel. In Eagle Rock, California: Suzanne and Dennis Prieur, Patty Saris. In Pasadena: Bob Kneisel of the Bungalow Heaven Neighborhood Association, Kristopher Doe and Susan Halpin, Tom and Nancy Reitze. In San Diego: Erik and Ingrid Hanson. In Denver: Robert Rust and Pam McClary, Steve Ciancio. In Chicago: Allison Freedland at the Historic Chicago Bungalow Association, Jim and Margaret De Lauria, Nancy Jane Lauren and Frank Pokorny, Lisa Klein, Marty and Ron Thomas. In Milwaukee: Denise and Keith Hice, Carlen Hatala, Diane Campion. In Memphis: Sue Williams, Janey Outlan, Rip and Nicole Haney, Genevieve Posey, Carole Raiford, Meridith Starling, Michael Wayt, Sean and Jitka McGivney, Sam and Charlotte Cantor, Edith Heller, Margareta Boyd. In New Jersey: Beth Ann MacPherson at Craftsman Farms, Ray Stubblebine. In Massachusetts: David Liberty at windowrepair.com. In New Hampshire: Alan Rumrill of the Historical Society of Cheshire County. And I have no doubt there are many others whom I have forgotten, for which I apologize profusely and blame the complexity of the task and my lack of brain cells.

Last, and maybe even least, given that two of them weigh less than ten pounds each, the furry feline beings who give me joy every day—tiny Zoe and Ubu, and the rather larger Milo. And Emma (10/31/92–9/28/02), the tiniest tortie in the world. I still miss her every day.

— JANE POWELL

Contact the author:
P.O. Box 31683
Oakland, California 94604
(510) 532-6704
www.bungalowkitchens.com

Contact the Photographer:
3915 Bayview Circle
Concord, California 94520
(925) 676-8299
www.lindasvendsen.com

E.C. 2

S.B. 2

C. 2

E.C.K. 2

P.B. 2

D.D. 2 × H.1

FOREWORD:

I can't tell you how many times in my life I've been accused of not being able to see the forest for the trees. This is my revenge. I can actually see the forest; it's just that I'm way more interested in the trees. So I wrote a book that is, in more ways than one, about the trees.

I bought my first bungalow in 1987. I didn't set out to buy a bungalow. It's not that I didn't know what they were, or that I had never heard of the Arts and Crafts Movement, but I was just looking for an old house. I looked at anything in my price range that was built before World War II: Victorians, Colonial Revivals, Spanish Revivals, Romantic Revivals, Moderne houses, brown shingles (the local term for a shingled house, whether Arts and Crafts or Colonial Revival, usually two-story), and bungalows. Of the 150 houses I looked at, I'll bet 100 of them were bungalows. Partly that's because I was looking here in the lovely East Bay, where it's pretty much Bungalow Central, and partly because bungalows, because of their smaller size, were the most affordable. By the time I walked into the one I eventually bought, bungalows had already begun to work their magic on me. Every day I lived there, I came to appreciate the subtle elements of the house more and more.

After my first television appearance on HGTV's *Curb Appeal* a couple of years ago, I got a letter from a woman in a small town somewhere in southern California. She sent me a picture of her house and said that until she saw the show, she didn't know that her house was a bungalow—all she knew was that she liked it. Bungalows are like that. They're like a pair of shoes that are immediately comfortable and don't have to be broken in.

It was a slippery slope, though. Since that first bungalow, I've owned and restored seven more, plus a Prairie-style house, and my current (and permanent) home, the fabulous 1905 Sunset House. I loved every one of them, and they were all different, yet they were all Arts and Crafts houses. The smallest was 857 square feet, and the fabulous bunga-mansion (as Paul Duchscherer has named my house, "It's not a bungalow—it's a bunga-mansion!") is 3,800 square feet, yet they all have the same mysterious hold on me, and charms that still reveal themselves daily. It's not that I don't like other kinds of houses—I do—but these are the only houses that speak to me.

Linda and I traveled the country (and Canada) to photograph bungalows for this and upcoming books. She took well over six hundred pictures, which are not all represented here, and yet we barely scratched the surface of what bungalows in North America have to offer. (Also, given that there are so many pictures, I hope I can be forgiven if I can't remember exactly where each one was taken and am forced to resort to vague allusions in the captions, like "the Jersey Shore" or "southern California.") I was amazed at the beauty, the variety, the sheer inventiveness of these houses. Given the philosophy of simplicity, natural materials, and expressed structure, it is absolutely amazing what was done within this framework.

And I need to address one other thing. In our travels, we often encountered people who would utter some variation on the following: "Oh, you're from California. You have the really good bungalows there. Ours aren't really that great." Now, I'm as provincial as the next person, and

California gets unfairly maligned enough that I'm all ready to stick up for it, and, yes, we took the bungalow idea and ran with it, and yes, we have fabulous bungalows here. But there are fabulous bungalows everywhere, and I want to stop this lack of "bungalow self-esteem" in its tracks. Be proud of your bungalow, no matter how modest, and no matter where it is. And think about this: in California we have no basements, and therefore nowhere to put our junk except the garage, and our gentle weather (which I wouldn't give up for anything) nonetheless means this: twelve months of weeding.

For a simple house, bungalows can be immensely complex, as I found out by writing this book. Just when I would think I was done with a section, and would even have gone on to something else, I would realize that I'd left something out and have to go back and insert it. I've tried to be thorough (I know there will be some who think I've been a little too thorough), but I guarantee there are some things I missed. And I'm warning you ahead of time—I have opinions. Strong opinions. Says that right on my business card: Strong Opinions, Obscure Knowledge, Bad Puns. If this is the first of my books you've ever read, just be prepared. I have a particularly bad opinion of things that are toxic, because I'm a cancer survivor, so you can expect to find condemnation of vinyl, formaldehyde, pressure-treated wood, and such in the text.

I've tried to make this a practical book, and like my previous books, *Bungalow Kitchens* and *Bungalow Bathrooms* (which you should rush out and buy immediately if you don't have them, as well as my other book, *Linoleum*), this book includes both "Obsessive Restoration" and "Compromise Solution" sidebars and a resource guide as comprehensive as I could make it. As always, I urge everyone to deal locally if possible, and I know I couldn't possibly include everyone who's out there. Many of the companies I've listed may also carry things that are inappropriate for a bungalow. I hope that this book will arm you with enough knowledge to do right by your bungalow, to stand up to those who say it can't or shouldn't be done, that "they don't make those anymore," or that the modern replacement thing is better than the time-tested thing of which your bungalow was made.

Lastly, I would like to dedicate this book to my father, who taught me that the details matter.

— **JANE POWELL**

Another bungalow in Memphis, Tennessee, shows the complexity that can be achieved while still remaining within the parameters of the style. The elaborate stonework of the porch—arched openings filled in with ashlar (rectangular stones with rough-cut faces), surrounded by rubble stone for the railing and columns, and topped with limestone slabs—supports double beams with shaped ends. On top of these, more sets of shaped double beams support two more intricately pierced beams that span the width of the porch. Shaped rafter tails decorate the eaves of the side-gabled roof, and the curved profile of the fascia board at the gable's edge is held up by numerous pierced brackets. On the upper floor, a gabled dormer with arched windows and built-in planter boxes features similar brackets that appear to pierce the fascia board.

CHAPTER ONE

WHAT IS A BUNGALOW?

"I can't bear it—I'm going upstairs."
"There isn't an upstairs, dear—it's a bungalow."

— *Monty Python*

HISTORY OF THE BUNGALOW

A bungalow is difficult to define. Charles White wrote in the 1923 *Bungalow Book* that the word *bungalow* was "a curious example of how we Americans overwork a word that is euphonious and the meaning of which, because of the word's recent assimilation into the language, is somewhat uncertain."

Looking up *bungalow* in various dictionaries provides these definitions: "A low house having only one story or, in some cases, upper rooms set in the roof, typically with dormer windows"; "a usually one-storied house with a low-pitched roof"; "a small house all on one level"; "a small house or cottage usually having a single story and sometimes an additional attic story"; "a thatched or tiled one-story house in India surrounded by a wide verandah"; "a usually one-storied house of a type first developed in India and characterized by low sweeping lines and a wide veranda." Okay, there seems to be general agreement on "small" and "one or one-and-a-half stories," but that's about it. The kind of house that is thought of as a bungalow is different depending on where you are in the world.

Perhaps a little history will throw some light on the subject—or confuse things even more. It is generally agreed that bungalows (called variously *banggolo*, *bangala*, or *bangla* depending on who's translating) descended from thatched Bengali peasant huts in India, and were possibly crossed with a hip-roofed peasant hut called a *chauyari* (literally meaning "four sides"), further crossed with the standard British Army tent. It's pretty easy to see how it was Anglicized to "bungalow." (The modern spelling of "bungalow" was first recorded in 1784.) The original huts could be movable, in which case they were made of a bamboo frame and covered in thatch or leaves, or they could be permanent, in which case they were raised up on a plinth made of several layers of dried mud, with walls also made of dried mud, put on in layers about 18 inches thick, each layer being allowed to dry before the next was added. Bamboo rafters were laid on top of the wall, projecting a foot or more beyond the wall. A bamboo grid was laid over the rafters and the thatch was attached to it. The roof could be hipped (pyramidal) or curvilinear, as described by nineteenth-century traveler Francis Buchanan, " . . . a hut with a pent roof constructed of two sloping sides which meet in a ridge forming the segment of a circle so that it has a resemblance to a boat when overturned . . ." Because the plinth was wider than the actual hut, combined with the roof overhangs it formed a porch or verandah on four sides of the hut. Later the thatched roofs

OPPOSITE: Gustav Stickley used logs and shingle siding, as well as stone for a massive chimney, to build his home at Craftsman Farms in Parsippany, New Jersey. The diamond-pane casements harken back to English buildings. The green Dutch door is a side door, lit in the evenings by a hanging lantern with amber slag glass.

Sizeable concrete block piers (unfortunately painted) "pierced" by the large timbers of the porch railing, as well as the openwork in the gable, beam ends, rafter tails, and low roof pitch, place this home in the West Adams district of Los Angeles firmly within the bungalow category. The home next door is also a bungalow, in spite of the neoclassical dentil molding along the side of the porch.

were replaced by tile, as some of the locals didn't subscribe to Mahatma Gandhi's nonviolence concept. Because of the verandah and the necessity of cross-ventilation, bungalows rarely had corridors.

The British altered the native dwelling into something that conformed better to their idea of what a house should be. They built these Anglo-Indian bungalows in compounds outside of the cities and towns, as well as in hill stations where the Europeans would go in the summer to get away from the heat. Eventually the bungalow was exported to all corners of the British Empire as being the proper sort of house for Europeans in the tropics. By the nineteenth century, it was understood to be a one-story house of Indian origin. In England, the first structure that was called a bungalow, rather than a cottage, was built in 1869 at a seaside resort on the English coast. At this time, industrialization had increased the wealth and leisure time of the middle and upper classes, and seaside resorts catered to people's desire to get away from the city and have a simpler and healthier

life for a while. A contemporary account noted, " . . . people at the seaside are, for the most part, intent on doing nothing, and the object is to do this in as great a variety of ways as possible." (Well, that part hasn't changed much.) This 1800s-style bungalow was no small cottage—there were several bedrooms, a 15- by 23-foot dining room, numerous service rooms, stables, and a coach house. But the architecture was stunningly simplified by Victorian standards.

The simplicity of bungalows was both an aesthetic choice and a reaction to the increasing "servant problem." It was also bound up with bohemian ideals about a simple, rustic life, which were, in large part, a reaction to the societal changes brought on by the Industrial Revolution. Although advancements in technology and manufacturing resulted in many beneficial products, like the cook stove, the sewing machine, and indoor plumbing, the other side of the coin was pollution, sweatshops, overcrowding, social unrest, and the mass production of shoddy goods that were poorly designed. Most middle- and upper-class people merely wanted to get away from the cities and their problems, but a few actually wanted to do something about these matters, and some of them were the founders of the Arts and Crafts Movement. Although Arts and Crafts is often thought of nowadays as a style or an aesthetic, it was also a philosophical, political, and social movement.

The Arts and Crafts reformers believed that a return to handcraftmanship would restore the dignity of labor that had been lost in mass production, and that good design in homes and furnishings would result in an improved society. They believed that nature was the proper source for inspiration and design motifs. The most famous of them was William Morris, a gifted designer whose textile and wallpaper designs have been in continuous production since the nineteenth century. He was one of many calling for a simpler life. Edward Carpenter wrote in a book called *The Simplification of Life*: "No doubt immense simplifications of our daily life are possible, but this does not seem to be a matter which has been much studied. Rather hitherto the tendency has been all the other way, and every additional ornament to the mantelpiece has been regarded as an acquisition and not as a nuisance, though one doesn't see any reason, in the nature of things, why it should be regarded as one more than the other. It cannot be too often remembered that every additional object in a house requires additional dusting, cleaning, repairing: and lucky you are if its requirements stop there . . ." Interestingly enough, the British Arts and Crafts Movement didn't particularly embrace the bungalow, though certainly many of its architects designed some

The E. W. Stillwell Company of Los Angeles advertised their "California Bungalow Books" in the 1912 *House Beautiful* using this photo of a sprawling bungalow that manages to combine Oriental-looking gable ornaments and a large picture window with a set of four Moorish windows in a front-facing bay. The yard is landscaped with fan palms just to make the California location obvious. For fifty cents you would receive "a book of one-story Bungalows of four to six rooms costing $500 to $2,000."

Typical of Anglo-Indian bungalows, this nineteenth-century planter's house is made of whitewashed brick, sitting on a low plinth, and surrounded by verandahs on all four sides. On either side, the verandahs have been enclosed (usually for bathrooms and the like), the house is topped with a thatched hip roof, and the whole is surrounded by gardens. A low house in the midst of a garden has been the bungalow ideal ever since.

The September 1918 issue of *House Beautiful* ran this advertisement by the California Redwood Association, extolling the virtues of redwood by featuring an English-influenced bungalow with redwood shingled walls and a faux "thatch" roof with shingles.

By 1925, bungalows had moved to the back pages of the Lewis Homes ready-cut catalog, the front being devoted to Colonial Revival homes, but bungalows were still popular enough to be included. This particular model, the Pasadena, a classic side-gabled model with a shed-roof dormer, was touted as "one of the most popular semi-bungalow designs Lewis architects have ever produced." The copy went on to say, "the fact that it is a semi-bungalow with practically all ceilings upstairs full height, is one reason." They must have been right about its popularity, since some version of this bungalow is found in practically every city and town in North America.

The Radford Architectural Company, based in Chicago, offered this modern-looking bungalow in their 1908 Radford's Artistic Bungalows catalog. While many of the Radford designs were awkward and not artistic at all, their Prairie School–influenced designs were cutting edge and, like much Prairie School architecture, still seem contemporary today. Note the sinuous ornament on the corners, showing the influence of Chicago architect Louis Sullivan, who was a mentor to many of the Prairie School architects.

houses that fit the description. The British movement looked back to the Gothic period, or to vernacular architecture, for inspiration. It wasn't until the bungalow arrived in North America that it really became associated with the Arts and Crafts Movement. Most bungalows in Britain were built after World War I, long after the demise of the Arts and Crafts Movement there, and are viewed in the same way we might view the cheap tract houses thrown together after World War II in the United States.

In America as in Britain, seaside, lakeside, or mountain resorts were built with hotels and summer cottages for the upper classes. Some of the "cottages," such as those built at Newport, Rhode Island, were not cottages at all; they were ostentatious mansions. The first named bungalow in America was built on Cape Cod in 1879. Designed by William Gibbons Preston, a Boston architect, it was two and a half stories tall—not really a bungalow—though it had a simple structure and broad verandah. In 1884, architect Arnold Brunner featured a bungalow as the frontispiece in his catalog Cottages or Hints on Economical Building. Though that design cost $4,000, he also included designs costing between $500 and $1,000, aimed at a growing middle class. Brunner wrote, " . . . during the last few years, our conception of what a country house should be has entirely changed. Simplicity, elegance, and refinement of design are demanded and outward display, overloading with cheap ornamentation, is no longer in favour." Of course, he was wrong about that, as outward display and cheap ornamentation continued in fashion for quite

some time. In fact, it's still quite popular in some circles.

The bungalow's initial use as vacation architecture meant that it came to be associated with leisure and informality in a natural setting. This association continued even as bungalows began to be built in cities. Architectural styles used for resort houses in the nineteenth century, such as the Shingle style on the East Coast (so called because of the shingle siding used) and the rustic Adirondack style in the mountains (featuring rustic wood and log detailing) had a lasting influence on bungalow architecture.

By the turn of the twentieth century, the Arts and Crafts Movement had spread to America through periodicals, lectures, books, and travel. In the last few years of the nineteenth century and the early years of the twentieth, Arts and Crafts societies were set up in many major cities. Even so, it is doubtful the movement would have taken off had it not been promoted in national magazines like *The Craftsman, House Beautiful,* and *Ladies' Home Journal.* Although these magazines publicized bungalows and other Arts and Crafts house styles, one of the main reasons for the bungalow's widespread popularity in all parts of the United States and Canada was house plan books and mail-order houses.

The hope of plan book publishers was that people would buy the actual plans from them at a price generally between five and twenty-five dollars, so plan books were inexpensive, or even sometimes given away. Some were nothing more than a black-and-white catalog, while others

American Carpenter and Builder was a publication aimed at builders and each issue featured home plans that could be purchased (for $7.00, in this case). Many bungalows were built by individual builders who purchased plans in this way. This particular plan, published in November 1915, was for a five-room, 1,150-square-foot home with a very typical layout: living room, dining room, and kitchen on the right side, two bedrooms with a bath in between on the left side. This one had the added attraction of a sleeping porch off the back bedroom. The massive brick pillars and low piers of the porch were combined with a concrete railing supported by brick balusters. The copy mentioned that "the unusual railing around the window in the gable is a sample of doing things a little different (sic) from the ordinary way. Anybody that can get past this house, without noticing it, is blind."

books without actually purchasing the plans. There is also evidence that many of the plan book publishers copied the designs of well-known architects and published them as their own, maybe with slight alterations. In the fashion business, this is rationalized with the phrase, "It's an original—I changed the buttons."

Sears Roebuck published their first book of house plans in 1908 and would also supply almost everything necessary to build the house. A few years later, they began to offer ready-cut home kits. They were not the first company to offer pre-cut buildings—that honor goes to the Aladdin Company of Bay City, Michigan, which offered its first pre-cut building, a boathouse, in 1906. By the 1910s, the company was publishing a hundred-page catalog of bungalows and other house styles, as well as garages, barns, and even small apartment buildings.

were lushly illustrated with color. Usually a photo or illustration of each house was accompanied by a simplified floor plan and often a lot of purple prose describing the house. A 1920s catalog from the Henry L. Wilson Company reports: "Here is a little gem that will appeal to every lover of inexpensive, artistic homes. Its irregular but harmonious lines will at once win a place in the heart of seekers of something pleasing. This bungalow does not cost any more, but it 'looks like more' and that is what most of us want, our money's worth; and for a comfortable, homelike bungalow to fit the ordinary purse it has few equals and no superiors. Cleverly arranged and indicative of ability in artistic designing this bungalow speaks for itself." (Although if the bungalow spoke for itself, perhaps it would make more sense than Mr. Wilson, who called his catalog A Short Sketch of the Evolution of the Bungalow: From Its Primitive Crudeness to Its Present State of Artistic Beauty.)

There were many plan books and mail-order house books, published by architects, lumber companies, builders, real estate syndicates, and, of course, the national mail-order companies Sears Roebuck and Montgomery Ward. Gustav Stickley's *Craftsman* magazine also published two plan books of designs. No doubt there were people who just took the photo and floor plan to a builder and had it copied, or builders would build from plan

Jud Yoho's Craftsman Bungalow Company in Seattle was the source of the plans for this home in Vancouver, British Columbia. The unusual pillars are made of notched 4- by 4-inch timbers stacked like cordwood, culminating in two side-by-side 6-inch timbers supporting the beam that holds up the porch roof. Under the eaves is a glimpse of the skip-sheathing used as a base for the wood-shingle roofing; the spaces between the sheathing boards allow for air circulation around the shingles.

Other ready-cut companies followed suit, such as Lewis Homes and Sterling Homes, also of Bay City; Bennett Homes of North Tonawanda, New York; Gordon Van-Tine Homes of Davenport, Iowa; California Ready-Cut Bungalows and Pacific Ready-Cut Homes of Los Angeles; Robinson's Money-Saving Mill-Made Cut-to-Fit Houses of Providence, Rhode Island (a real tongue-twister and hyphen-happy to boot); Ready-Built House Company and the Rice-Penne Company of Portland, Oregon; the Ainslie-Boyd Company of Seattle, Washington; and the Thayer Portable House Company of Keene, New Hampshire. There were probably others even more obscure than some of these.

Plan books evolved from the "carpenter's handbooks" of the eighteenth and nineteenth centuries. By the early twentieth century, there were probably hundreds of plan books, including Gustav Stickley's *Craftsman Homes* and *More Craftsman Homes,* which featured houses taken from the pages of the magazine. Other plan books available at the time included *Our Book of Attractive Small Homes* by the Beatty Lumber Company of Morris, Illinois; *Central's Book of Homes* by the Central Lumber Company of Reading, Pennsylvania; *Radford's Artistic Bungalows* by the Radford Architectural Company of Chicago, Illinois; *California Homes Book of Houseplans* by Dixon and Hillen of Oakland, California; *Loizeaux's Plan Book No. 7* by the Loizeaux Lumber Company of Plainfield, New Jersey; *Building With Assurance* by the Morgan Woodwork Organization of Chicago, Illinois; *One Hundred Bungalows* by the Building Brick Association of America in Boston, Massachusetts; *Artistic Homes* by Herbert Chivers of St. Louis, Missouri; *Attractive Homes* by J. W. Lindstrom of Minneapolis, Minnesota; *Little Bungalows* by Stillwell and Company of Los Angeles, California; *The Bungalow Book* by Charles E. White Jr. of New

BELOW: A photo montage of bungalows in the 1912 catalog of the Pacific Hardware Manufacturing Company of Los Angeles shows some of the variety of California bungalows, though the two in the center are a bit questionable. Mission Revival gables are found on bungalows, but the model on the left goes a little beyond what I would consider to be a bungalow, being purely Mission Revival, and the overly-decorated half-timbered home on the right is disqualified by virtue of being two stories tall, though it is extremely amusing.

RIGHT: Massive timbers like these at the Gould House in Ventura, California, were cut from trees that had lived thousands of years, then skillfully shaped by craftsmen working for architect Henry Greene. But even the simplest bungalows were built of old-growth timber, and numerous trees were killed for even the smallest house. Every stud, every piece of siding, was once a living thing. That should be honored.

Though they were losing popularity to the simpler styles, even in 1925, the more rustic and complex California type of bungalow was still being recommended. This model, Lewis Homes LaVitello, was noted for the "overhanging roof without pillars or columns to obstruct the view" on the front, though the porch on the left-hand side has pillars supporting its pergola. Notice how the window trim is wider at the bottom, echoing the tapered shape of the pillars and chimney. This is the sort of bungalow often called "Craftsman," though technically only homes featured in Gustav Stickley's *The Craftsman* magazine should be called that. There is much regional nomenclature pertaining to bungalows. In my part of the world, this sort of bungalow would be called "craftsman," which usually refers to a wood-sided bungalow with lots of brackets and rafter tails and stone and clinker brick, while a "California bungalow" would refer to a simpler stucco type with massive pillars.

Lewis Homes 1925 Vallejo bungalow model (pronounced Vah-láy-ho) of 1925 features massive tapered pillars resting on a shingled base, dwarfing the foot-high railing. The copy announces, "The massive structure, and low, wide eaves of the Vallejo are distinctive among much costlier homes."

BELOW: By the 1920s, many bungalows were simplified to a basic form, such as this model, the La Veta, from Lewis Homes, which retains only the square pillars supporting the porch roof and knee-braces in the gables. The shape of the porch roof is unusual, with a gable and valley on either side, but everything else is much simplified. Still, a good-sized living room and dining room, small kitchen, two upstairs bedrooms, and a 6- by 6-foot bath were squeezed into a house of less than a thousand square feet.

York; *Artistic Bungalows* by the Architectural Construction Company, *Allen Bungalows* by the W. E. Allen Company, *The Bungalow Book* by the Standard Building and Investment Company, and *Bungalows* by Edward E. Sweet, all of Los Angeles; (see below) as well as plan books by The Bungalowcraft Company, Ye Planry, Stillwell and Company, all of Los Angeles, California; The Craftsman Bungalow Company and the Long Building Company of Seattle, Washington; Harris Bros. of Chicago, Illinois, and the aforementioned Henry L. Wilson, who called himself The Bungalow Man. Wilson also published *Bungalow Magazine* from 1907 to 1912. In 1912, he sold it to Jud Yoho of the Craftsman Bungalow Company in Seattle, where it continued to be published until 1916.

There is much evidence that the bungalow's popularity spread from the West Coast to the East, contrary to the way architectural styles had traveled across America in the past. The bungalow even made its way

The notched timbers of these pillars have a good deal of exposed end-grain, which soaks up water easily and is likely to rot if the timbers are not kept sealed, especially in the rainy climate of Vancouver, British Columbia, where this bungalow is located. Old-growth timber of this quality is not easily replaced, so it would make more sense to maintain the pillars.

A pillar composed of four 6- by 6-inch timbers that seem to be connected by gold tenons (tabs) that pass through mortises (slots) in the timbers and protrude from the other side is most likely a fake that is merely held together with nails. Nonetheless, it gives this Memphis bungalow a lot of style.

A simplified hip roof bungalow called the Ferndale, with square porch columns and a shingled railing, was offered in the 1925 Lewis Homes catalog. Ready-cut companies bragged of their machine-driven efficiency. "Lewis standardization allows us to use huge power-driven machines, doing the work of hundreds of carpenters."

A cross-gabled bungalow, the Alameda, "has been erected a great many times in all parts of the country and with many combinations, and has never failed to be charming to look upon," according to the Lewis catalog. Standardization of floor plans allowed bungalows to be dressed in different "skins" that made each one unique. Square lattice beneath the porch is framed by wide moldings in this model, and a row of large corbels decorates the porch gable.

to Australia via California rather than via Britain, and the style there is called "Californian Bungalow." Certainly, the West Coast, particularly California, embraced the ideal of the bungalow, and we unquestionably ran with it. There are those who believe the California bungalow represents the acme of the style, but I'm not taking sides. (I did enjoy being able to use the word "acme" though. Beep, beep!)

Because of plan books and pre-cut houses, bungalows in the United States and Canada share stylistic similarities even though there are regional differences in climate, locally obtainable building materials, the skills of available workmen, and the innate preferences of builders and owners.

The real heyday of bungalows lasted from the turn of the twentieth century until the end of World War I, pretty much corresponding to the demise of the Arts and Crafts Movement. After the war, bungalows continued to be built, but in a simplified style, and the growing popularity of the Romantic Revival styles (Tudor, Normandy, Spanish) cut into their popularity. Nonetheless, bungalows continued to be built well into the 1930s, though by that time they were no longer trendy. Yet the plan books and pre-cut house companies continued to offer them even as their popularity declined. (In a similar vein, ranch houses continue to be built, long after *their* heyday in the 1950s and '60s.) "The author hopes by this series that he may do a service to many people who contemplate erecting a bungalow for

themselves, and who wish their little house to embody the most convenient and economical arrangements, while at the same time attaining definite architectural character, so being redeemed from the vulgar appearance which, unfortunately, so many bungalows display." Thus wrote R. Randal Phillips in *The Book of Bungalows* in 1920. Personally, I embrace the vulgar appearance, if by that he meant the exuberance of bungalow architecture. But I expect that even after all that history you're still confused. And this is probably why: Architecture isn't simple. Any given house represents the convergence of plan or type (how the house is arranged—types include foursquare, I-house, shotgun, hall-and-parlor, etc.), time period (for instance, Victorian is a time period, not a type of house), and decorative style (the shape of the box and the stuff that's on it and in it—a house of the Victorian time period might be Italianate, Second Empire, or Queen Anne in style). Complicated enough for most things. But bungalows add a fourth dimension, and that is philosophy. Although bungalows have an informal plan, are of a certain time period, and come in different styles with names like Craftsman, California, Japanesque, Swiss Chalet, Prairie, Rustic, and so forth, they are also based on a philosophy that is the foundation for how they are built and furnished, for how people expected to live in them, and how their residents related to the larger society of which they were a part.

Even a small bungalow like the 660-square-foot Milton was given a little style with a pergola over the porch and shingled sides that flared near the ground. And while the dining room that bumps out on the left is small (about 9 feet by 10 feet), it was not left out, and two small bedrooms and a decently sized bath were part of the plan as well.

The Home, a yearly supplement to the magazine *Women's Weekly*, showed this "bungalowette" as "The Last Word in Compact Comfort" in 1923. Though it was only 440 square feet, it still had many features of larger bungalows, including large timbers holding up the porch roof, beam ends that appeared to penetrate the fascia board, shaped rafter tails, and attached trellises for the all-important climbing roses.

THE READER'S DIGEST CONDENSED ARTS AND CRAFTS MOVEMENT

So now for the Reader's Digest Condensed Arts and Crafts Movement. There are many fine books that explore the Arts and Crafts Movement in depth, and I do suggest that you read those as well. But it is impossible to discuss bungalows without at least some understanding of the movement. The Arts and Crafts Movement began in Britain in the nineteenth century as a reaction to the Industrial Revolution. It was both a reaction against shoddy mass-produced goods, overwrought decorating, and the appalling social conditions brought on by industrialization. The upside of the Industrial Revolution was the emergence of a large middle class, who were of course the purchasers of the mass-produced doodads, because previously only rich people could afford to have lots of stuff. Unfortunately, the widespread availability of stuff was only possible because of exploitation of the lower classes in factories and sweatshops. (A tradition that continues today as production is moved offshore to various third world countries where the wages are cheap and the labor and environmental regulations nearly non-existent.) And the stuff was lavishly ornamented because machines made it possible to produce ornament that previously required a great deal of expensive handwork. And frankly, because they could. This was the world that Charles

Dickens was writing about. It's easy to think of Arts and Crafts as a style, which it is, but it was also a political movement that hoped to better the lot of the lower classes at the same time that it improved the design of both buildings and the things that went in them. Many of them, including William Morris, were socialists. The proponents of the movement wanted to restore the dignity of hand labor that had been lost to factory work, and they believed a return to hand craftsmanship, as had been a tradition in English villages since medieval times, was the way to go about it. Morris said, " . . . I believe the day is not so far distant when the best of men will set to work trying to simplify life on a new basis—when the organisation of labour will mean something else than the struggle of the strong to use, each one to his best advantage, the necessities and miseries of the weak." (Morris was a little long-winded, and that was only part of the sentence.) They were preservationists, too, and fought against the ill-advised "restoration" of medieval churches and other buildings. The movement proponents included architects, artists, designers, and writers. They were bohemians who advocated things like Rational Dress (because Victorian clothes, especially women's clothes, were irrational to say the least. Morris once commented about women's clothing, "I beg of you fervently do not allow yourselves to be upholstered like armchairs, but drape yourselves like women"). But possibly their most radical idea was

Buff-colored bricks were used to construct this hip-roofed bungalow in Milwaukee, Wisconsin. Though the eight-sided tower that holds the front door is unusual, the hip roof with its double dormers, the three-part front window, and the simple construction all fit comfortably within the bungalow milieu. The boxed-in eaves are typical of Prairie School architecture, which was influential in Milwaukee as well as Chicago. The modern wrought-iron railing likely replaced one originally made of wood.

the idea that craft, or "the lesser arts," was just as important and should be accorded the same respect as "the fine arts" like painting and sculpture. It is hard to conceive, from a twenty-first century viewpoint, just how radical their ideas were.

The unfortunate reality, however, was that handcrafting made the wares produced by Morris and others prohibitively expensive. This doesn't mean that Morris and others were wrong, or that the movement was a failure; it just means that theory isn't the same as practice.

The Arts and Crafts Movement was in many ways more successful in North America. When the ideas reached these shores around 1900, they were taken up by progressive idealists in many cities, and popularized by people like Gustav Stickley (through his magazine *The Craftsman*), Elbert Hubbard at the Roycrofters, and Edward Bok at the *Ladies' Home Journal*. Most cities had Arts and Crafts societies

ABOVE: In harsher climates such as those of the Midwest, the large open porch that was typical of California bungalows was often replaced with a large bay window to serve as a sunroom. This brick bungalow has a semi-circular bay with projecting corbels designed to hold planters. The square pillar near the front door, as well as the low brick retaining wall on either side of the front walkway show some Prairie School influence. Bungalows such as this were built by the thousands in and around Chicago in what is now known as the "Bungalow Belt."

BELOW: Although the canopy over the front door of this home veers dangerously close to being a neoclassic pediment, the exposed beam ends of the gables and the square brick piers of the front porch push this from being a mere cottage into the realm of bungalows.

or guilds, and the movement was aligned with various progressive political causes. There was just one small problem with the movement as imported from Britain—Americans had no medieval tradition to look back to, because we hadn't been here that long. So instead we had to opt for incorporating various alternative ideas either involving traditional ways of building (though technically those had been imported as well) like log cabins, Spanish missions, and Native American dwellings, or things considered exotic, such as architecture and decorative arts from Japan, which had only recently opened up to the outside world.

The other thing that distinguished the American movement was a more practical and democratic approach. Rather than throwing the machines out with the bathwater, so to speak, we viewed machines as useful tools that could be used to relieve drudgery and do tedious and repetitious parts of work, freeing up time and thought for the artistic part, and allowing hand labor to be devoted to artistry. We opted to celebrate simplicity, natural (especially local) materials, and honesty of structure. Of course much of this was lip service, because a lot of things promoted as handcrafted or handmade were actually made entirely by machine, and honesty of structure, especially on houses, was often a sham, as we will see later. (Honesty of structure, by the way, was known as "expressed structure" in architectural terms, and basically means that you're not hiding how the house was actually built, which is why bungalows have all the exposed rafters and beam ends and such.) This hypocritical aspect of the movement in no way diminishes the beauty of both the objects and the houses. In fact, it probably allowed the movement to succeed and allowed the middle and working classes, for the first time, to own houses that were both economical (so they could afford them), artistic (they were beautiful), and practical (bungalows and other Arts and Crafts–era houses were the first truly "modern" houses with indoor plumbing, central heating, and electricity). Before bungalows, at least in the nineteenth century, no one had made a virtue of simplicity, low cost, or ease of construction—these things had merely been viewed as cheap but not desirable. But there was more to bungalows than that. The Arts and Crafts advocates believed that design could change people's lives. They believed that the design of objects mattered, they believed that the built environment mattered, and they believed that people living in these houses, having these objects, raising their children there, would result in a wholesome life, upstanding citizens, and a peaceful and prosperous country. That it didn't quite work out that way doesn't mean they were wrong. It just means that the problem was a bit larger and more complex than they thought it was.

BUNGALOW SPOTTING

Okay, that's all well and good, but it still doesn't tell you what a bungalow is. At least part of the problem is that it's a "know one when you see one" kind of thing. Of course, the good thing about being the author is that you get to make up your own definition. So here's mine: a bungalow is a one- or one-and-a-half story house of simple design, expressed structure, built from natural or local materials, with a low-slope roof, overhanging eaves, and a porch, built during the Arts and Crafts period in America (approximately 1900–1930).

Although many books allow for things like one-story Spanish Revival or Colonial Revival houses as bungalows, I'm drawing the line there. Well, sort of. Because everything in the above definition has an exception—for instance, the dates. There were bungalows built after 1930, and in fact, the National Park Service maintained the style for park buildings long after the bungalow era was technically over. And here's the other thing—there's no such thing as architectural purity. So a bungalow may have some classical detailing normally found on a Colonial Revival house—things like neoclassical columns or dentil molding. Or a bungalow may have arched windows or a Mission-style gable that would normally be found on a Spanish Revival house. Many bungalows have a medieval English influence, as reflected in half-timbering or diamond-pane windows. And don't even get me started about the cognitive dissonance between the outside architecture of a house and the interior style. So I'm going with the legal requirement in a civil suit: a preponderance of the evidence. The house needs to have a critical mass of bungalow "details" (thus the name of the book) in order to qualify as a bungalow. After you see enough bungalows, and learn to recognize the details that make a house a bungalow, you, too, should be able to "know one when you see one."

RESOURCES

Aladdin Built In A Day House Catalogs online
http://clarke.cmich.edu/aladdin/Aladdin.htm

The Arts and Crafts Society
www.arts-crafts.com
(734) 358-6882

Craftsman Farms
www.stickleymuseum.org
(973) 540-1165

OPPOSITE: Elaborate plaster brackets and arched plaster decoration in the porch gable, as well as the arched windows of this home in Milwaukee, might indicate that it isn't a bungalow; but the square porch columns, the massiveness of the beam ends, the twin front gables, and the deep overhangs nudge it into the bungalow category.

CHAPTER TWO

·GOOD HOUSE·KEEPING

Before I get into anything else, I have to address the apparently pervasive belief in Western culture that everything is disposable and nothing should require maintenance. Some homeowners seem stunned to discover that houses actually require something beyond paying the mortgage and the property taxes.

And there are many, many companies out there just waiting to take money from people who can be conned into believing that there is such a thing as no-maintenance siding, or windows, or roofing, or gutters, or any of the other myriad items on the outside of a house. THERE IS NO SUCH THING AS NO MAINTENANCE! For instance, vinyl siding requires a large amount of caulking to seal it—around windows and doors, at corners, and anywhere there is a J-channel at the end of a run of siding. Because vinyl siding expands and contracts so much, the caulking fails in just a few years. If you don't re-caulk (and caulking is a pain—a job that can't be done that well even after years of practice), then water will get behind the siding, leading to mold and rot and expensive repair bills. Never forget that the goal of these companies is to part you from large amounts of hard-earned cash! All building materials have to be maintained! If you want no maintenance, then buy a condominium. Traditional building materials can last hun-

dreds or even thousands of years if they are properly maintained. And traditional materials have already undergone hundreds or thousands of years of rigorous real-life testing in actual buildings—that's how they became traditional.

American culture, and advertising in particular, has done an excellent job of convincing consumers that THEY are the center of the universe, and that THEIR needs and desires should be more important than anything else. This has led to a huge sense of entitlement, including the idea that one's time is so valuable that it couldn't possibly be spent maintaining the house. Here's some news you may find distressing. YOU are not the center of the universe. I am not the center of the universe, either. We are temporary. We are not playing Monopoly, and there is no "get-out-of-maintenance-free" card. (Those who are elderly or disabled get slack.) A house comes with responsibilities, and a historic house comes with more responsibilities. We are only the caretakers of these houses, which were here before we owned them and which will be here after we are gone. They contain the wood from the old-growth forests, they are monuments to the skill of those who labored to build them, they represent our cultural heritage. To destroy them, or allow them to be destroyed by neglect, to remove their original fabric in the pointless pursuit of "no maintenance" is profoundly

OPPOSITE: An exuberant bungalow in Vancouver, British Columbia, displays wacky porch columns, a slotted fascia board, massive uprights in the open-work porch gable, and shingled sidewalls flared at the base. Interesting window muntins complete the picture. And this might as well be said now: just because numerous bungalows in this book belong to people who have chosen to paint their trim white, doesn't mean it's the right thing to do.

disrespectful both to the trees that gave their lives and to the labor and skill of those who built the houses—with hand tools, I might add.

There are two ways to do maintenance: you can do it yourself or you can pay someone else. Believe it or not, doing your own maintenance can be rewarding. It can give you a feeling of accomplishment, and it allows you to know the house intimately and understand it on a more profound level. It's often good exercise too. Regular maintenance also keeps small problems from turning into big expensive problems. Doing things yourself is also much cheaper than hiring someone.

You may not choose to do everything yourself. Cleaning the gutters might not be a good job for someone who doesn't like heights. I usually pay someone else to do exterior painting because it's mostly prep work, and I hate prepping for painting. But I'm perfectly happy to reglaze windows or trim the shrubbery. The problem with doing some things yourself is that the learning curve can be quite steep, and then you may never have to do that particular thing again. But some maintenance tasks have to be done every year, so you can get better at those.

Hiring someone else to do things has its own set of problems. For one thing, most contractors are set in their ways, and a lot of them don't understand old houses. And even people in the trades have bought into the "no-maintenance" crap to some extent, and like many people they are motivated by money, so the guy you hire to clean the gutters will try to talk you into replacing them instead (more money for him), or whoever you call to fix the windows will try to sell you replacement windows (also more money for them). And people just seem to have gotten out of the habit of fixing things. Partly that's because a lot of modern products, from cars to computers, are either not meant to be fixed or are no longer fixable by ordinary humans. People of my generation (yes, the dreaded baby boomers) can still remember when the hardware store had a tube tester, and if the TV wasn't work-

ing, you took the suspect tubes down to the hardware store and tested them to see which ones were bad, and then you bought new ones to replace those, put them back in the TV, and then it worked again. Recently I had a problem with the fax machine, and when I called the company to tell them everything I faxed arrived with a black line down the middle, they told me to buy a new machine, because that would be cheaper than having it fixed. Bungalows, on the other hand, don't generally involve electronics. But finding someone to do maintenance or small repairs can be difficult. That's still no excuse.

In either case, it's important to educate yourself, whether you plan to do any work yourself or not. Armed with information about the way things used to be done, or ought to be done, on the house will be useful when you are told, "Nobody does that any more" or "Nobody makes those now—you need to get X, it's a new product, and it's completely maintenance-free!" (If someone tells you that, continue to call around until you find someone who doesn't.) Also, you'd be amazed what you can do yourself using only some simple directions and maybe a diagram.

This isn't really a how-to book, more like a "what-to" book, so I recommend a subscription to *Old House Journal* combined with a general fix-it book like the *Reader's Digest Do-It-Yourself Manual.*

RESOURCES

Old House Journal
www.oldhousejournal.com
(800) 234-3797

American Bungalow
www.ambungalow.com
(626) 355-1651

Old House Interiors
www.oldhouseinteriors.com
(800) 462-0211

Reader's Digest
www.rd.com

Fine Homebuilding
www.taunton.com
(800) 477-8727

Erik Hanson's Web site
www.irvinggill.com

ERIK'S BUNGALOW MANIFESTO

Even though the stucco porch gable of this redbrick home in Memphis, Tennessee, is graced by a neoclassical plaster swag, the square pillars, tripartite front window, exposed rafters, and wide eaves still mark it as a bungalow.

by Erik Hanson (with editorial comments)

Remove your window bars and security doors; nothing you own is worth having a pitiful home.

Gustav Stickley did not make kitchen hardware for your bungalow. *(Or cabinets.)*

Keep interior walls dark; white walls are for bathrooms, do you want your dining room to look like a bathroom?

Your roof should be red or green unless you have specific proof to the contrary.

Most of the generic furniture and accessories we collect were made by teenagers: teach your kids to create and save a bundle.

A house without a porch is like a woman without a nose.

Anything over two cats is mental illness. *(I'm in big trouble.)*

If your house is too small, you have too much stuff.

Almost every bungalow, when new, was decorated by someone who hadn't ever heard of the Gamble House. Use places such as this as an inspiration to quality, not as a motif.

If a tradesman says, "It can't be done," fire him for his lack of vision.

Plant climbing roses.

Good restoration is a series of modest projects done well; more history was destroyed by spending too much money than by not enough.

There is a special place in hell reserved for those who remove wood windows. *(Right next door to the special place in hell reserved for those who paint over sash locks.)*

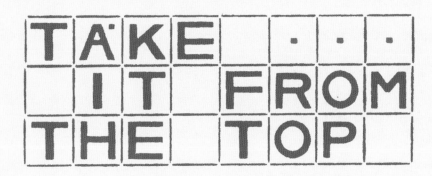

CHAPTER THREE

"Everything is more complicated than anybody knows."
— Fred Allen

ROOFING IT

Let's take it from the top, so to speak, and work our way down. The roof is a major feature of many bungalows; indeed, some may appear to be almost all roof.

Although bungalows in India generally had *hipped* (pyramidal) roofs, many different rooflines are found on bungalows in America. The *gable,* or *triangular,* roof is probably the most common, consisting of two sloping sides that meet at a ridge. Bungalows may feature one, two, or more gables. A single gable might have its ridgeline parallel to the street (known as *side-gabled*) or perpendicular to the street *(front-gabled).* Multiple gables facing different directions *(cross-gabled)* are also common. Often the front porch may have a separate gabled roof of its own. A gabled roof may have its point clipped, known as a *clipped gable,* or *jerkinhead,* roof. Another type of gable roof is the *gambrel* (often found on barns), which has a lower slope that is steeply pitched and an upper slope that is less steep, allowing for more headroom on the upper story. The opposite of the gambrel, in which the top slope is steeper and the bottom slope less so, is commonly known as a *saltbox,* or *"catslide,"* roof. Less common are various kinds of shaped gables, such as the *Dutch gable,* which was more often featured as a decorative porch roof. A one-sided gable roof is known as a *shed* roof and can be attached either to the roof or to the side of the building. Shed roofs are popular for porches and dormers.

A hipped roof may be either pyramidal (comes to a point) or have a ridge along the top, resulting in two triangular slopes and two trapezoidal slopes. Many gable or hipped roofs may also have what are called "kicked," or flared, eaves.

One roof rarely seen on bungalows (which doesn't mean there isn't one somewhere) is the *mansard* roof. Named after François Mansart, a French architect (who used them a lot, though he didn't invent them), a mansard roof is kind of a cross between the gambrel (double-pitched) roof and the hipped roof. A mansard roof has a double-pitched slope on each of the four sides of the building, with the lower slope so steep as to be near-vertical, and the upper slope flat or nearly so.

Occasionally seen is a flat roof with a parapet (low wall), which is kind of like putting a shallow swimming pool on your roof. A flat roof is generally a bad idea, given that water runs downhill, and putting a wall around a flat roof is a worse idea. This kind of roof needs to be checked often for leaks and potential leaks.

Just to confuse things even further, many bungalows

OPPOSITE: On this very English-looking bungalow in Milwaukee, the hip roof extends over the front door and windows, with the cutaway corners making the roof overhangs look almost like awnings. Meanwhile, a gabled dormer with a vent and a tiny gabled dormer surrounding the chimney add interest to the rest of the roof. The overhangs are supported by huge curved brackets and beams that are entirely too large for the small amount of weight they are bearing. This is part of what makes bungalows so interesting.

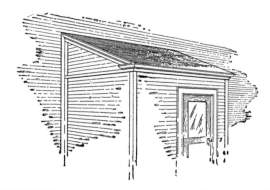

An *American Carpenter and Builder* illustration shows a gable roof (above) and a gambrel roof (below). A gambrel roof provides more headroom in the attic.

Another illustration from *American Carpenter and Builder* shows a shed (or lean-to) roof attached to the side of a building. A shed roof can also be attached to another roof and is commonly used for dormers.

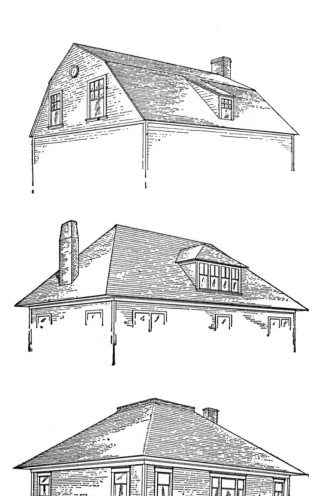

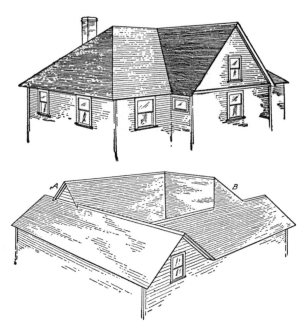

In the top illustration, a gable roof is combined with a hip roof. The area where the two meet is known as a valley. The bottom drawing shows a complex set of hip and gable roofs around a courtyard. No, I don't know why the plural isn't "rooves"—it seems it should be.

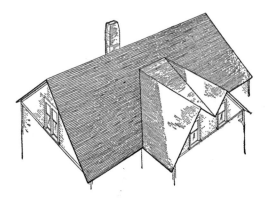

These illustrations show two different variations on a hip roof, one with a ridge (top) and one that culminates in a flat roof deck (bottom). A third kind which is not shown is the pyramid roof, in which the four sides come to a point.

A drawing showing double gables attached to the side of a gable roof. Double gables were often used for dormers.

have combinations of roof styles—a gabled porch roof with a gambrel roof for the rest of the house, a hipped roof with shed roofs for dormers or porches, gable-roofed dormers set into a hipped roof, etc. The number of possible combinations is mind-boggling.

Bungalows commonly have low-pitched roofs. Roof pitch (or angle) is calculated by the number of inches it rises vertically for every foot it extends horizontally. For instance, a roof that rises 6 inches in every foot has a 6-in-12 pitch, and might be found on a bungalow. A 1-in-12 pitch would be nearly flat, and a 10-in-12 pitch would be really steep. Roof pitch not only affects the look of a house, but may have a bearing on what kind of roof coverings can be used.

THATCH ENTERTAINMENT

The purpose of the roof, obviously, is to keep out the elements, so various coverings are employed for that purpose. Original roof covering choices depended on many factors, including budget, local availability, and what was fashionable at the time. The original *banggolos* used thatch, a roof

The Creo-Dipt Company showed a "thatch roof" using their shingles in an ad in the June 1918 *House Beautiful*. Steam bending allowed for the curving roof over the porch as well as bending the shingles over the eaves for a soft edge. The upper floor dormer is a combination of shed and gable roofs. Although this house is sort of a bungalow, it is definitely closer to a Period Revival cottage.

AN EASY WAY TO FIGURE YOUR ROOF PITCH WITHOUT CLIMBING ON YOUR ROOF

Go into the attic, accompanied by a 2-foot level, a tape measure, and a pencil. A light would be useful as well. Make a mark 12 inches from one end of the level. Place one end of the level against the bottom face of a roof rafter, and hold it perfectly level (for those unfamiliar with levels, that would be when the air bubble in the vial is exactly between the two lines). Then measure straight up from the 12-inch mark on the level to the underside of the rafter—that measurement is the number of inches that the roof rises in a foot.

This information is useful if you are installing a dormer or a skylight, or planning an addition. You can also use it as a factoid to impress people at parties.

R. Randal Phillips pointed out in *The Book of Bungalows* that "room for room the bungalow must cover double the area of a two-story house, and the spreading out of the accommodation on one floor means a corresponding increase in roofing. As against this there is a saving in the cost of walling; also the elimination of the staircase, and the cost of the scaffolding needed in the case of a two-story house has to be included to the credit of the account in building a bungalow; but if the rooms are spread out in an extravagant manner and involve a complex roof, there is every likelihood that these savings will be outbalanced to a considerable extent by the roofing cost."

covering which has mostly fallen from favor, at least in North America. Thatch can be defined as any vegetation used for roofing on a structure, although various kinds of grasses or reeds are the most popular. *Thatch* is beginning to enjoy somewhat of a comeback as a "green" building material. Though it may seem counterintuitive, thatch is a long-lasting roof material that is easily repaired, and new technology has allowed it to be made fire-retardant as well. A new thatch roof is easily a foot thick and has an insulation value of R-40. Although thatch isn't common, it would make for a very authentic Indian-style bungalow.

VINYL STRAW

Believe it or not, there is such a thing as synthetic thatch. Some of it is made of PVC (vinyl), which should be avoided because it is toxic. But there is a product made from

WOODEN SHINGLES

OBSESSIVE RESTORATION

Assuming wood shingles are not banned in your area, they really do look right on a bungalow that was meant to have them. Even if asphalt shingles have been put on top, a look in the attic may confirm whether the house originally had wood shingles. (Even if the shingles are gone, there is a tendency to nail the new plywood right over the old skip sheathing.) If the shingles are still there underneath other roofing, it will be easy to figure out the exposure, and if they were stained, possibly some will be left on the underside to give a clue as to the color. Creosote stains are no longer being made, because although it is a fine wood preservative, it is also carcinogenic. But modern oil base stains can be tinted in custom colors, so it should be possible to match an existing color if need be. The shingles you find on the roof may not be the original ones—even if the originals lasted fifty years, they may have been removed and what is there now could be the second or third set, probably with a couple of layers of asphalt shingles on top as well.

It's brutal on the roof—there's rain, snow, ice, hail, sun, wind, dirt, leaves, branches, insects, and more. But the various forms of water are the worst. Because the exposed portion of the shingles absorbs water, they need to be able to dry out (thus the skip-sheathing). Wood shingles can also be installed over solid plywood sheathing and roofing felt, but there will need to be battens or furring strips on the plywood to keep an airspace underneath. Or you can use a product called Cedar-breather, a kind of nylon mesh akin to a dish scrubber, that can be installed over the plywood for an airspace.

It's important to keep a wood shingle roof clear of moss, lichen, leaves, and other debris that can hold moisture in the wood. Even so, a wood roof is still subject to weathering. The softer sapwood erodes from exposure to water, wind, grit, and ultraviolet light. Stains or clear finishes made for roof shingles usually contain UV-filtering ingredients as well as fungicides. The best way to apply stain is by dipping the shingles in it before they are applied to the roof. Obviously that can only be done the first time—once the shingles are installed, the stain will have to be renewed by brushing or spraying them every five years or so—might be something to think about before planning that three-color, variegated roof.

The lack of snow in southern California allows for the very low pitch on the twin gables and "pop-top" of a bungalow in Eagle Rock, California. The upswept gables have a slight Japanese influence, and the shingle pattern on the side walls is typical of many southern California bungalows. The pop-up has its own inset porch accessed from a French door, while the front porch features a simple pattern of open beams in the gable.

Of course, for hundreds of years no one bothered to apply anything to the roof—it was just left to weather naturally until it was time to get a new one.

There are some environmental issues to consider when re-roofing with wood, the first one being whether to consume any more old-growth timber for the purpose. Certainly if the house is a museum or a landmark of some sort it can be justified. And one could make the argument that re-roofing a 900-square-foot bungalow doesn't use that much wood anyway. It's a good idea to keep some extra shingles around to use for repairs later on.

COMPROMISE SOLUTION

There are roofing materials that mimic the look of wood fairly successfully, especially composite products such as fiber-cement and concrete, as well as metal. These will not weather like wood and will retain a more uniform appearance that may lack the charm of a real wood roof. On the other hand, they don't rot, burn, or fall prey to termites. The new fiber-cement shingles, which use cellulose fiber rather than asbestos, have not been produced long enough to have a clear idea of their longevity. Concrete roofing is heavy, so the roof structure may have to be beefed up. There is also a product made from vinyl and cellulose, but since vinyl is toxic and hopefully will soon be banned as asbestos and lead paint have been, vinyl shingles are not a good option.

polyolefin that is less toxic and looks fairly authentic. Aluminum thatch is also available. Thatch can also be imitated using wood shingles cut, bent, and installed in an undulating pattern. A similar treatment can be accomplished with asphalt shingles.

SHAKE IT UP

In keeping with the emphasis on the natural, wood shakes or shingles were an obvious choice for bungalow roofing. Traditionally, both wood shakes and shingles were split by hand from a block of wood using a sharp blade called a froe and a mallet. *Shake* is a modern term referring to the split version, usually implying a thicker shingle, but it's still a shingle. Most shingles are now sawn rather than split. Some shakes are still made by hand, but power equipment has taken over the splitting. Shakes can be split straight (with parallel sides) or at an angle (thicker on one end). Sometimes straight split shakes are then resawn from end to end on an angle, creating a shake with one split and one sawn face, known as "handsplit and resawn." A shake can be anywhere from about 18 to 30 inches long and about $5/8$ to $3/4$ inch thick at the butt end. Handsplitting results in an uneven face on the shake, giving it a rustic look. Shakes are usually laid with about $7 1/2$ inches exposed on each shake. There are also sawn shakes, made the same way as shingles but thicker at the ends.

SWINGING SHINGLES

Shingles, on the other hand, are sawn on both sides and are thinner than shakes, about a half-inch thick at the butt. Shingles are normally laid with less exposure than shakes, about 5 inches to the weather. Shingles can also be laid in decorative ways, such as undulating and steam-bent shingles that mimic thatch. Decoratively cut shingles, where the butts are cut into shapes that provide an interesting pattern when laid up, were much more common in the Victorian period and are not often found on bungalow roofs.

Many kinds of wood were used for shingles and shakes, but the most popular were (and are) eastern white cedar, western red cedar, Alaskan yellow cedar, redwood, and cypress, although white oak, shingle oak (*Quercus imbricana*—imbricana means "overlapping") and chestnut were also popular in some parts of the country. Unfortunately, most of the chestnut trees in America were killed by a blight introduced from China in 1904, and only a few dozen are left. Most chestnut lumber now is salvaged from historic barns and other buildings, although efforts to breed a blight-resistant tree are continuing.

All of it was old-growth tight-grained wood, which made wood shingles fairly durable. Some wood roofs have lasted 75 to 100 years (oak shingles), but 30 years is about average. As old-growth wood has become scarce, second growth or fast-

The waves of a wood roof on a bungalow in Denver show the artistic effects that can be created with shingles . . . and money, because this sort of roof doesn't come cheap.

growing woods such as Southern yellow pine are being pressure-treated and used for shingles. Even when using premium wood shingles, a modern wood roof has a life expectancy of 15 to 30 years.

The roof pitch must be 3-in-12 or greater for wood shingles. Wood shingles require ventilation, so they were traditionally laid on *skip-sheathing* (sheathing boards with large spaces left between them) or *battens* (narrow boards) without building felt (tar paper). Sometimes you can see this in the attic, even if the house has since been re-roofed with something else. Laying the shingles with only about a third of their length exposed to the weather meant that the roof ended up being three shingles thick, enough to keep out water. The shingle joints were staggered for the same reason. In fact, most roof detailing has to do with keeping out water, which is the roof's job after all.

Shingles were often stained, using creosote oil stains

COMPOSITION ROOFING

OBSESSIVE RESTORATION

Built-up roofs were traditionally "hot-mopped"—that is, the felt was laid down, then coated with hot asphalt to waterproof it and adhere the next layer of felt. Minerals were embedded in the top coat of asphalt to protect it from deterioration, or it was covered with aluminum paint or another coating of asphalt. (But this is ugly—stick with the gravel.) This also meant you could walk on it without getting stuck. Composition roofs are still done this way—you've probably smelled one being installed. The minerals used were in small pieces ($1/8$ inch or less) and tended to be gray, so don't do that mid-century thing and use white gravel or red lava rock.

A more recent process is the cold-applied built-up roofing system. Similar in application to the hot system, the difference is that the asphalt is dissolved in solvents rather than heated.

Another composition roof system uses felt sheets saturated with modified bitumen—asphalt or tar with added polymers that modify the tar to give it better weathering characteristics. There are two flavors of modified bitumen: APP (atactic polypropylene) and SBS (styrene butadiene styrene). No, it does not come in chocolate. In APP, the polymer encapsulates the asphalt molecules, and in SBS, the rubber-like polymer becomes part of the asphalt mole-cule and changes its characteristics. SBS products generally have a granular surface, while APP products are smooth and require some sort of coating. APP sheets are usually "heat-welded" (sometimes known as "torch-down"), which melts the bitumen on the back of the sheet so it will adhere to the substrate. SBS products can be applied with hot or cold asphalt, or by heat welding. There is also a self-adhesive version, used mainly for flashing.

Any of these methods are acceptable for a built-up roof. A composition roof can last anywhere from 12 to 30 years. Coal tar is preferable on a flat roof where water might pond, as it is more impervious to water than asphalt. Coal tar also has a low melting point, causing it to become fluid in the summer, which allows it to self-heal. On the other hand, you might not want to be walking on it then. Asphalt is used on roofs with a slope of more than $1/4$ inch per foot, where the low melting point of coal tar might cause slippage.

There is some concern about hot asphalt or tar fumes being carcinogenic, but studies so far have been inconclusive. Of course, several of the studies have been sponsored by the Asphalt Institute, an industry trade group. The short exposure from having a house re-roofed is probably insignificant, though the fumes can certainly cause nausea.

COMPROMISE SOLUTION

Metal is still an option, though an expensive one. Probably best left for small roofs such as over an oriel or bay window. Several new membrane materials, including EPDM (ethylene propylene diene monomer), TPO (thermoplastic polyolefin), and PVC, are now available for flat or low-slope roofs. These are useful in certain applications, for instance, on two-story porches where the roof forms the floor of the upstairs porch. EPDM has a life expectancy of 40 or 50 years. And I hate to keep harping on this, but no PVC. Ever.

Another option is SPUF (sprayed polyurethane foam)—you've gotta like the acronym. It can be sprayed on top of existing roofs, and adds insulation to boot. It has to be covered with an elastomeric coating to prevent degradation by ultraviolet light, although gravel can also be used. Using gravel might help make it look better, because frankly, it makes me think of trailer parks or Santa's house at the North Pole. If the coating is maintained, it can last a long time, but no one really knows how long, because it's only been used since the 1960s. Twenty years seems to be the average length of the guarantees offered by various companies, though.

The numerous flat roofs and parapet walls of this Los Angeles home make it an ideal candidate for composition roofing. Many types of composition roofing can be walked on, making it useful for the porch area on the left. In spite of its Mission Revival characteristics, this home still has enough Arts and Crafts elements (brackets, square pillars, ribbon windows) that if it were one story instead of two, it would be a Prairie-style bungalow.

(invented by Samuel Cabot in 1877) in shades of brown, green, red, and gray. Using one stain color gave a uniform appearance, but occasionally two or more colors were combined on a roof for a striped or variegated effect. The ridges and valleys of the roof could also be highlighted by using different-colored shingles on those areas. Even if no stain was used, various protective coatings such as boiled linseed oil were often applied, as it was believed they would add to the roof's durability.

Wood shingles are flammable, and this has led to them being banned in some areas. They can be treated to reduce flammability, though this generally shortens their lifespan. The chemicals used in pressure-treating shingles made of fast-growing woods are toxic, and no one knows how long they will hold up, so that doesn't seem like a good environmental choice.

VISCOUS RUMORS

Composition, or built-up roofing, is a multi-ply roof system of felt or paper combined with a viscous waterproofing substance and covered with a mineral aggregate. Composition roofing first made an appearance in the early nineteenth century when pine tar was applied to a canvas roof covering at the Octagon House in Washington, D.C. In the mid-nineteenth century, brothers Samuel and Cyrus Warren started a roofing business using a method of applying pine pitch to layers of heavy paper, the whole then being sprinkled with sand. A few years later, they replaced the pine pitch in the system with coal tar, a by-product created when coal was refined to obtain illuminating gas, and later with petroleum tar. By the 1870s, there were numerous patents for various types of composition roofing, as there were more flat or low-slope roofs due to changing architectural styles. Previously, these roofs had to be covered with metal, which was expensive. Composition roofs were cheap and are still favored for commercial buildings.

Many bungalows, due to their shallowly pitched roofs, were candidates for composition roofing that is usually known as tar-and-gravel. It was and is an inexpensive roofing method, so it was perfect for modest bungalows. Asphalt shingles can't be applied to a roof with a pitch of less than 2-in-12, and even that's pushing it, leaving built-up roofing as one of the few options.

PERFECT PITCH

Asphalt-saturated felt with mineral granules was introduced in the late nineteenth century, a natural progression from built-up

roofing. Instead of felt, asphalt, and gravel layered on-site, the components were assembled in a factory in the form of long strips. Initially called "ready-roofing," this product is now known as "roll roofing." It was usually applied in overlapping horizontal strips. Inexpensive at the time (and it still is), it was often used for garages and other outbuildings. On the other hand, architects Charles and Henry Greene of Pasadena were fond of it and used it on many of their buildings. Because it is only one layer when applied, it doesn't last as long as asphalt shingles.

A less expensive way to get a thatch look is shown on a Denver bungalow, which uses asphalt shingles bent around the roof edges. The soft edges emphasize the curving roof of the "saddlebag dormer/pop-top" that straddles the ridge of this cross-gabled bungalow as well as the clipped gable of the porch. Stucco insets in the brickwork of the porch pillars and chimney emphasize the vertical nature of those elements, while horizontal stucco inserts in the brick of the porch railing echoes the half-timbered stucco in the gables.

COAL INCIDENCE

Asphalt shingles were introduced in 1903 as a by-product of the manufacture of the tar and asphalt-impregnated felt used on flat roofs, often called tar paper. Asphalt is a hydrocarbon obtained from natural beds (think the La Brea Tar Pits) or as a residue from petroleum or coal tar refining, which had been used for centuries as a cement or for waterproofing. Initially the felt used for shingles had high proportions of cotton and wool fibers (from rags), but in the twentieth century, that changed to cellulose fibers derived from waste paper and wood fiber. In the late 1970s, fiberglass matting was introduced, though the cellulose product continues to be available. For shingles, the felt was saturated with asphalt and then covered with crushed limestone, slate, or other rock. The minerals add

The Patent Vulcanite Roofing Company advertised their asphalt shingles in a 1915 issue of *American Carpenter and Builder*. Although the shingles on the right-hand bungalow (with its "catslide roof") aren't all that interesting, check out the two-tone checkerboard pattern on the left. Since a side-gabled bungalow has a lot of roof showing, one might as well make the roof interesting.

color, protect the underlying mat from ultraviolet light, and increase fire resistance. Later on, ceramic materials such as crushed brick were also used, allowing a wider variety of colors. During the bungalow era, asphalt shingles were sold as individual shingles, measuring about 12 by 16 inches, as well the now typical 12- by 36-inch strips (commonly called 3-tab shingles) that are sold today. Although square-cut tabs were popular, there were many other shapes, including hexagons, diamonds, dog-eared, interlocking (T-shaped), and even shingles with undulating bottom edges that vaguely resembled thatch. Many of the more interesting shapes were discontinued in the late twentieth century because they could not meet new building code requirements having to do with the amount of overlap between rows of shingles. The early shingle colors were limited and monochromatic, usually red, green, or black. Not until the introduction of ceramic coatings in the 1930s did asphalt shingles acquire the blended colors

they often have today. Asphalt shingles then became popular, and are still the most prevalent roof covering. Because of that, asphalt shingles removed in re-roofing projects are one of the largest components of landfills. There has been a small effort to recycle asphalt shingles for use in paving, but very few are diverted to that end. Some older asphalt shingles also contained asbestos, although tests conducted on asphalt shingle debris at various landfills found asbestos content at one percent or less on average.

CONCRETE EVIDENCE

In 1824, a British stonemason named Joseph Aspdin obtained a patent for a new kind of cement he produced in his kitchen by combining finely ground limestone and clay, heating it in his oven, then grinding it into a powder. He called it portland cement because it resembled a kind of stone found on the Isle of Portland off the British coast. Combine portland cement with sand, aggregate, and water, and the result is concrete. By the 1840s, a German concrete manufacturer developed a process for pressing concrete tiles that resembled shingles. In 1900, Austrian Ludwig Hatschek invented a way to manufacture rolled and pressed asbestos-cement sheets. The asbestos fibers were used for

New T-lok shingles add textural interest to the roof of a Berkeley, California, bungalow. This kind of shingle is less prone to blow off and is used in high-wind areas.

SHINGLE SHAPE AND COLOR

Diamond-shaped, asbestos-cement shingles cover the roof of a side-gabled bungalow in Vancouver, British Columbia. This type of shingle lasts a long time, and these red shingles might be original to this 1920s home.

OBSESSIVE RESTORATION

Replacing square-tab shingles with new ones in a solid color won't be that difficult, except for the argument you'll have with the roofer who wants you to get the blended colors. Other shapes will be a bit more difficult. Only a few companies make shaped shingles these days, and shapes are limited to dog-eared, diamond, T-shaped, and undulating. Most companies are concentrating on laminated (called "architectural") shingles, which have a pattern unlike anything available when bungalows were being built, so these are best avoided. They weren't as afraid of color then as we are now, so not all roofs were in tasteful browns and greens and grays. Red was big, and can be a good choice if it works with the surroundings, but it has to be real red, not the blended red (which is basically pink). Sometimes they used to use a different color shingle on the ridges. As with

wood shingles, sometimes three or more shingle colors were blended on the roof. This can be done with modern three-tab shingles as well, if you do it yourself or talk the roofer into it. Because of the landfill issue, try to buy the longest-lasting asphalt shingles you can afford (that are still appropriate for the house). Most jurisdictions limit the number of layers of roofing on a house to three. It will be a better roofing job if the previous shingles are removed down to the sheathing—this also allows the sheathing to be inspected for damage or rot and for repairs to be made. On the other hand, a roof with three layers of shingles on it is less likely to leak, even if the top layer is starting to go. But it may be more weight than the rafters were engineered to bear and can cause sagging, or even cause rafters to break.

COMPROMISE SOLUTION

Most people won't notice if the shingle color is solid or blended. Try to stay away from colors like blue and blended red (it looks pink). Although light colors are recommended for hot climates, they make the roof look like it's going to float away. As stated above, it's best to remove the previous layers of roofing before putting the new one on, though that often isn't done.

Laminated shingles are thicker, which means they can last longer than some other types. Some are guaranteed for as long as forty years, but since they've only been around for about ten years, it's hard to say. The length of the guarantee offered by the roofing manufacturer has nothing to do with how long the shingles will actually last. Weather conditions and maintenance have a greater bearing on shingle life.

ASBESTOS

Asbestos is a naturally occurring mineral. At the time it first began to be used, no one was aware of the health effects of the product. Inhaled asbestos fibers lodge in the lungs and stay there, causing scarring and, eventually, asbestosis and cancer. When the industry became aware of this, early in the twentieth century, they did everything they could to cover it up, which is why asbestos was not (sort of) banned until 1989. (The first case of asbestos-related lung disease was reported in 1906.) The original Environmental Protection Agency ban was overturned by a federal appeals court in 1991. Thus, while corrugated paper, flooring felt, and new uses of asbestos are still banned, asbestos-cement shingles, vinyl-asbestos floor tiles (two toxics for the price of one!), pipe wrap, brake pads, roofing felt, and roof coatings containing asbestos are not. As with many things that have been found to be toxic, asbestos continued to be utilized because it was a really good filler and reinforcement, it was fireproof, and, of course, there was money to be made. Besides roofing and siding, it was also used in flooring, duct insulation, flues, joint compound, plaster, and the dreadful "cottage cheese" or "popcorn" ceilings. In fact, it continues to be mined and used in products. Many of the companies that used asbestos in the U.S. are now mired in class-action lawsuits, as well they should be. While asbestos is not to be taken lightly, so far there have not been any reported cases of asbestos-related disease stemming from residential exposure.

There is likely to be asbestos somewhere in a bungalow—if not as roofing or siding, then possibly as a flue for the furnace, as duct insulation, or as the lining for the fusebox. The general rule for asbestos is to leave it alone unless it is friable (crumbling). In roof shingles and siding, the asbestos is encapsulated, meaning fibers can't escape into the air unless the shingles are cut, crumbled, sanded, or pressure-washed. Asbestos on ducts and flues can be encapsulated in various ways—painting, wrapping, etc. Asbestos removal is best done by experts, although in some jurisdictions homeowners are allowed to remove a certain amount themselves. Check with the city or county to see what the rules are. If they allow it, they can probably also give you instructions as to the best way to go about it. The main thing is to get it wet so the fibers don't escape. All removed asbestos has to be double-bagged and sent to special landfills. And a note from personal experience: if you want it removed from your ducts, they don't do that—they just take the whole thing, and then you have to replace all the ductwork.

There may also be asbestos in the plaster or flooring, so it is a good idea to send some samples to a local testing lab before doing any demolition. Don't be cavalier about this stuff—there hasn't been a residential exposure case yet, but you don't want to be the first.

OBSESSIVE RESTORATION

If it's in good shape, existing asbestos-cement roofing should probably be left alone. It can also be repaired. There are even sources for new and used asbestos-cement tiles. It is better to repair the roof and leave it in place than to remove it. Asbestos-cement tiles should not be walked on—hairline cracks can form that will admit water. If the roof has to be removed, precautions have to be taken to keep the fibers from becoming airborne—this means no tossing the shingles off the roof into the dumpster! Start at the highest point of the roof and look for exposed nail heads—pry them up or cut them off so the shingle can be removed without breakage. Once the first row is removed, the nailheads of the next row will be exposed. If you're doing it yourself, be responsible and don't just take them to the dump—bag them up and dispose of them properly. Sometimes old asbestos-cement roofing looks bad, but resist the urge to pressure-wash it and try to think of it as patina.

New fiber-cement shingles can mimic the look of the old ones, though some of the old shapes are no longer being made. The jury is still out on the longevity of fiber-cement shingles—some of the early ones had problems like swelling up and retaining water.

Concrete tiles should be good for some years, and if the building paper is on its last legs, the tiles can be removed (carefully) and reused. Concrete tiles are still being made and are popular in regions where hurricanes are common, because they don't blow off in a high wind.

COMPROMISE SOLUTION

Both new concrete and new fiber-cement tiles are being made. If the roof is being replaced, these are a good option. The old shape may not be available in new shingles or tiles, but try to get something similar. Metal tiles that resemble shingles or tiles may also be an option. Asphalt shingles may be available in an appropriate shape, although the texture will be different.

reinforcement, just as the Romans had used horsehair for reinforcement in their concrete. Color could be added during the process, and though initially it was promised that the colors wouldn't fade, as it turned out, that was not the case, and many a red asbestos-cement roof faded to pink. Asbestos-cement tiles became popular as roofing for seaside bungalows in Britain. After 1907, asbestos-cement shingles began to proliferate rapidly in America. They were lightweight, economical, and fireproof, and were promoted as substitutes for traditional roofing materials such as slate, wood, and clay tile. (Unfortunately, they were also promoted as a fireproof siding, and way too many bungalows were re-sided with asbestos shingles.) Many styles and sizes were made, which allowed for roofs laid with various methods including American, Dutch Lap, and French (hexagonal, honeycomb, or diamond). The French patterns were particularly popular. As a roofing material, asbestos-cement shingles or tiles are remarkably long-lived, which is why they continued to be produced into the 1980s. (An asbestos-cement roof can last up to 100 years.) The asbestos has since been replaced with cellulose or other fibers in what are now called fibercement roofing products. As with other long-lasting roof coverings like tile, usually the tar paper underneath fails before the roofing does.

of clay over their thighs. Ceramics last pretty much forever—that's why archaeologists are always finding potshards. As a roof, tiles also last pretty much forever, although the building paper underneath usually gives out, so every hundred years, give or take, all the tiles have to be taken off so the building paper can be replaced. Tiles are heavy, so a tile roof

Green glazed ceramic S-tiles top the roof and clipped gable dormer of a Chicago bungalow. A special ornamental tile accents the end of the ridge. Unfortunately, this home's wooden eaves have been replaced with the dreaded aluminum soffit, though the decorative limestone inserts in the brick work remain.

Concrete roofing tiles without asbestos were also made. These were also fireproof, though they weighed more. Concrete tiles were more likely to be shaped like traditional tile roofing rather than shingles, such as barrel tiles, S-shaped tiles, etc. Unlike asbestos-cement tiles, which were nailed in place, concrete tiles were interlocking and were laid using hanger strips. Only the hip and ridge tiles were nailed, then the holes were filled with matching mortar.

A TILE TOLD BY AN IDIOT

Although tile roofs are commonly viewed as a roof covering reserved for Spanish or Mediterranean houses, or possibly Chinese temples, the fact is that quite a few bungalows have (or had) tile roofs. Tile roofs are ancient, dating to the time when humans first learned to bake clay into pottery. Clay tiles that date to 10,000 B.C. have been found in China, and tiles in the Middle East appeared only a short time later. Barrel tiles were originally made by workers bending a slab

needs a beefy structure to hold it up. Tiles are not good in earthquake country, as they tend to go flying off during a quake, possibly injuring innocent bystanders, although steps can be taken to avoid this. Tiles are expensive initially, though they last so long that the amortized cost is low. Special care or arrangements are required to walk on a tile roof without breaking the tiles.

Tile shards have been found at the 1585 settlement at Roanoke Island in North Carolina. Clay tile was also used at Jamestown, Virginia, at St. Augustine in Florida, and in New Orleans. Dutch settlers imported clay tiles from Holland until 1650, when they built their own tile works in the upper Hudson Valley. By the time of the American Revolution, several tile manufacturing companies were offering glazed and unglazed tile. On the West Coast, clay tile was first manufactured in 1780 at Mission San Antonio de Padua in California.

Initially tiles were formed by hand, later by machine extrusion (introduced in the 1870s), and fired at a high

ROOFING TILES

OBSESSIVE RESTORATION

Clay tile never wears out—it only breaks. For that reason, much salvaged historic roof tile is still available. And many historic shapes are still being produced. Late-nineteenth- and early-twentieth-century tiles were often marked on the back with the company name, the size of the tile, and the name of that particular shape. Many of the companies are still in business and may still be making that shape. But sometimes the name of the pattern will have remained the same, but the size, shape, thickness, or profile may have been altered slightly so that it won't quite match. Sometimes it is possible to scrounge up enough original tiles for the prominent parts of the roof, and use the ones that don't quite match on the back, behind a chimney, or somewhere else where they are less visible.

Even if a particular tile is no longer being made, the company

Gustav Stickley chose flat green clay tiles from the Ludowici Company for the roof of his home at Craftsman Farms. If you look closely, you can see the round snow guards on the first few rows of tiles.

may still have the molds and be willing to make some up if the order is large enough. There are also companies that specialize in custom reproduction of historic tiles, though this will not be cheap. But then, none of it will be cheap. Historic tiles were glazed by hand, so the color is not uniform, giving interest to the roof. On modern glazed tiles the glaze is sprayed on, providing a uniform glaze that doesn't have the color range of historic tiles. If it is necessary to use these, they should be on a

roof slope by themselves, not mixed with historic tiles, and hopefully not visible from the street.

Sometimes a tile roof has been removed altogether by a previous owner who decided it was too expensive to fix and replaced it with asphalt shingles or some other inappropriate roof. Often elements of the roof are overscaled to stand up to the tile, and without it the proportions are all wrong. I can only urge you to put the tile back, even if it means your children will have to attend the local community college instead of Stanford. You could do it in sections—start with the most visible parts, and do one roof face each year.

COMPROMISE SOLUTION

Concrete, fiber-cement, or metal tiles may be able to substitute for unglazed roofing tiles, but there is really not a good substitute for glazed roofing tiles. Modern glazed tiles are uniform and don't give quite the look that historic tiles offer. Some of the metal tiles have to be painted, so that becomes a maintenance issue. Any of the look-alike tiles are still a better bet than switching to asphalt shingles or some other roofing.

temperature. They could be textured or glazed. Unglazed tiles were the color of the clay, ranging from terra-cotta to brown, buff, or pale pink. Pouring a manganese solution over the tiles before firing resulted in brown or nearly black tiles. Glazed tiles came into wide use around the end of the nineteenth century, and popular colors included greens, blues, and even purples. Pantiles (S-curved tiles, sometimes called Flemish tiles) and flat tiles were popular, especially in crowded cities, where they were used as a precaution against fire. Mid-eighteenth-century Moravian settlements in Pennsylvania used tiles that resembled German tiles—about 14 inches long, with a curved butt and scored with

grooves to promote drainage. A lug on the back allowed the tiles to hang from lath or battens without nails—in other words, there was nothing holding them up but gravity. The flat rectangular tiles in use then measured about 10 by 6 inches and had two holes at the top for nails. Sometimes mortar was applied between the courses to secure the tiles further.

Tiles may be either *interlocking* or *overlapping*. Interlocking tiles come in pairs so that an extrusion or lip on one tile hooks over the other tile, locking the two together. They are also nailed to the roof. Overlapping tiles can also function in pairs, but don't have a lip, and have to be nailed in place.

The tiles that cover the majority of the roof are called field tiles. Different roof shapes also require specialty tiles for finishing ridges, corners, valleys, dormers, etc. There are also tiles for the edge of the eaves, which are solid on one end to keep birds from nesting in the voids under the bottom row of curved tiles.

Up until the mid-nineteenth century, tiles were traditionally installed on battens or lath nailed directly to the roof rafters, with no sheathing or building paper (tar paper). This method made it easy to find leaks and make repairs but meant depending entirely on the tiles to keep out water. Gradually, tiles began to be nailed directly to wood sheathing or hung on lath that was nailed to the sheathing horizontally. Some kinds of tile, especially barrel tile, was nailed to vertical battens, or sometimes attached with copper wire. Some tile shapes are not completely water-repellent when used on a low-pitched roof, so these require an additional waterproof layer of tar paper, or sometimes are laid in mortar. Modern roofing practices require tiles to be laid on 1-inch-thick sheathing with 30-pound building paper or built-up roofing underneath.

Often the fastening system is the part that gives out—if iron nails were used they can rust out, which is why copper nails are recommended. And the flashings and gutters must be the best quality metal: copper or lead-coated copper, if they are to last as long as the roof tiles.

Spanish-style barrel tiles are not that common on bungalows, but many of the flatter kinds of tile are. Green seems to be a favored color, though terra-cotta was also popular. Chicago bungalows almost always had tile roofs, but tile was used in all parts of the country. Like concrete roofing, tile is popular in hurricane areas, though additional fastening is required.

TERNE IT UP

Metal roofing didn't become popular until the nineteenth century. Before that, the only metals used were lead and copper or sheet iron, principally for roofs where wood, tile, or slate was inappropriate due to the roof's pitch or shape. That's why the roofs on domed buildings are often made of copper. The process for corrugating iron was patented in England in 1829. Corrugating stiffened the sheets, which allowed them to be thinner and to span greater distances (and that's why we have corrugated cardboard). Of course they rusted, which was a drawback, until galvanizing was invented in France in 1837. In galvanizing, the iron is coated with zinc to protect it from rust. Iron could also be coated with tin for the same purpose, and this is commonly called tin roofing. Tin roofing was already being used extensively in Canada in the eighteenth century but took longer to catch on in the U.S., even though Thomas Jefferson was a big fan, having installed a standing seam tin roof on Monticello.

Terne metal came in various forms, including these S-tiles by the Edwards Manufacturing Company (top). They could be ordered either galvanized or "dip" painted. The lower right corner shows their "patented interlocking device" that protected the nailheads from the weather. Cortright metal shingles (lower left) were tin shingles applied individually in the same way as wood or slate (note in the illustration that they are applied over solid sheathing rather than the skip-sheathing used for wood or slate).

Eventually rolling mills were set up in the States, and the low cost and light weight of tin plate made it the most popular roofing material of the nineteenth century. It was available in sheets or in embossed shingles. It had to be painted, and red was a popular color, although architect Andrew Jackson Davis suggested using a green color to imitate the patina of copper.

A similar kind of roofing was terne plate, which differed in that the iron was coated with an alloy of lead and tin. The two are often confused, "tin plate" having become a generic term rather like linoleum, which is used to refer to any kind of resilient sheet flooring.

In the twentieth century, corrugated aluminum replaced much of the galvanized iron or tin plate, since it didn't rust. Galvanized, tin, and terne plate roofs became associated primarily with rural buildings, particularly barns, and also, unfortunately, with poverty, as in "tin shack." Terne metal is currently making somewhat of a comeback.

Sheet metal roofing was commonly installed with "standing seams," where the edges of the sheets are bent and interlocked in such a way as to prevent water intrusion, so obviously the seams have to be vertical. Corrugated sheets would be overlapped by a couple of corrugations for the same purpose. Copper or lead roofs, if they were small, would have overlapping sheets that were soldered along the seams, although larger roofs were installed with standing seams. Metal shingles, of course, were nailed like any other kind of shingle.

Metal shingles were and still are molded to look like other roof coverings, including wood shingles, tile, and probably even thatch. They can also be coated with granules to look like asphalt. Nowadays metal shingles are usually steel, sometimes aluminum or lead, and there are copper shingles if you have the money. These would be unlikely to be found on a modest bungalow.

Metal roofs can last a very long time if they are maintained. Tin and terne plate have to be painted every so often.

One reason that red was and is popular for metal roofs is that the iron oxide pigment it contains is long-lasting and inexpensive. Other kinds of metal roofing will oxidize and don't need painting. There is some concern that runoff from copper roofs will pollute the groundwater, causing harm to aquatic life, but the jury is still out. Studies so far show that copper runoff molecules usually combine with other metals in the ground before the water reaches the storm drain system. Contrary to what one might think, a lead roof quickly develops a patina that is insoluble in water. Because lead is malleable at low temperatures (about 70 degrees Fahrenheit) and easily bent into complex shapes, it is often used for flashing. Sometimes lead-coated copper is used for flashing, roofing, or gutters because it is lighter than pure lead, and also because lead acts as a lubricant for the copper, making it easier to bend. Currently, the Environmental Protection Agency has no regulations restricting or prohibiting the use of lead or lead-coated copper in roofing systems, although some states have their own rules, so it is a good idea to check with your state's environmental protection agency before using lead or lead-coated copper products.

If not heavily insulated, metal roofing can be noisy dur-

METAL ROOFING

The unusual roof covering on this building in Denver uses overlapping metal-barrel lids, a good example of a creative use of locally available materials. This building is part of a compound of bungalows and outbuildings in a semi-industrial part of town.

OBSESSIVE RESTORATION

Some bungalows did have metal roofs, and if so, the roof should be retained or replaced in kind. Most historic roofing metals, whether sheets or shingles, are still being manufactured, and improvements have been made in some of them, especially in paint coatings for terne metal. The low pitch of some bungalow roofs can cause problems with metal roofing when water runoff is not sufficient and causes ponding. This water quickly finds its way into seams and penetrations. Generally, metal roofing needs a slope of at least 2 1/2-in-12, if not more, for effective water runoff.

A standing seam roof being replaced by a new one should retain the same spacing as the old roof. It should not be replaced by corrugated metal or metal shingles, as it is likely the seams were part of the bungalow's design. This is also true in reverse. And modest bungalows were unlikely to have full copper roofs—at best, there might have been a copper roof over a bay window or porch.

Maybe this is obvious, but I'll say it anyway—if the bungalow didn't have a metal roof to begin with, don't add one.

ing rainstorms or hailstorms. Some people find the noise annoying, while others like it. Some manufacturers offer metal roofing with insulation already attached.

CLEAN SLATE

Slate is one of the most durable of all roofing materials. Properly installed, a slate roof requires little maintenance and will last 60 to 125 years or longer, depending on the type of slate, roof slope, and geographical location of the house. Some slate roofs have lasted over 200 years. In areas where slate was quarried, it was used even on utilitarian buildings such as barns.

Slate was used in the United States as early as 1625, with most of it being imported from Wales. The first quarry in the U.S. opened in Pennsylvania in 1785 but supplied only the local markets. In the nineteenth century, improvements in quarrying technology and the extension of the railroad system led to greater availability and market demand. The immigration of Welsh slate workers may also have had something to do with it. Slate roofing was promoted in architectural pattern books as well. By 1899, there were more than 200 slate quar-

ries in operation, primarily in Vermont, New York, Virginia, and Pennsylvania. The peak period of slate roofing production in the U.S. was 1897–1914. After 1914, competition from substitute materials such as asphalt shingles and a decline in the skilled labor required for fabricating and installing slate resulted in the decline of the industry. The Romantic Revival in the 1920s and '30s helped a little, as slate was a popular roof for Tudor and Normandy Revival houses.

The use of natural slate was consistent with Arts and Crafts principles that called for local, natural materials. The variety of colors and textures in the slate fit in well with the earthy Arts and Crafts palette.

A slate roof requires, at minimum, a 4-in-12 pitch, and that requires special slate sizes, exposure, and underlayment. Steeper pitches are better, which rules out a lot of bungalows.

Gustav Stickley often called for slate roofs on the house plans featured in his magazine *The Craftsman*. Slate roofs were expensive, so are more likely to be found on larger, impressive bungalows. Slate roofs are also more likely to be found in cities and towns around the major slate-quarrying regions, chiefly in the Northeast.

COMPROMISE SOLUTION

If cost is an issue, replacement of deteriorated metal roofing with a less expensive metal (aluminum instead of terne metal, for example) would be an acceptable compromise, though it would be good to try to match the color. There are various kinds of galvanized metal— some are more corrosion-resistant than others and are priced accordingly. Copper roofing is quite expensive but very long-lasting, so it would probably be better to repair it than replace it. Some kinds of metal roofing require more skill in installation than, say, asphalt shingles, so make sure the roofing company is experienced with metal roofing.

These granule-covered metal shingles have been laid in a very random pattern, mimicking what might be done with wood shingles and giving this home a very rustic-looking roof.

SLATE ROOFING

OBSESSIVE RESTORATION

Many original slate roofs may be coming to the end of their useful lives. Different kinds of slate have varying life spans, depending on where they were quarried. More often, the underlayment, roof structure, fasteners, or flashings may have deteriorated to the point where replacement is necessary. If enough of the slate is in good condition, it can be removed; the underlying sheathing, building paper, and flashing repaired or replaced, and the good slates reused on the most visible parts of the roof.

Used roofing slates are available, and it's important to try to match the existing roofing by using slates quarried in the same area as the originals. If new slates are to be used, they should also be from quarries in the same area and should be used on the less visible roof areas, as they will not be as weathered as the old slates and so will not match.

Some varieties of slate may be at the end of their useful life—stone from different quarries may have different life spans. It will be expensive to replace the whole roof with new slate, but you didn't really need that new European sports car anyway, did you?

Because slate is a long-lasting roof, the flashings, gutters, and fasteners must last as long as the roof, and that means copper, lead-coated copper, and stainless steel or copper nails for attaching the slates. Slate roofs also use *snow guards* or *snow brakes,* which keeps the snow from sliding off the roof onto your head.

COMPROMISE SOLUTION

There are various kinds of faux slate made in various materials, including concrete, fiber-cement, rubber, asphalt, clay tile, and even vinyl. These will not have the color variation or richness of the real stone, and some may cost almost as much as the real thing. Vinyl is to be avoided at all costs. The asphalt products don't really fool anyone. Some of the others look pretty good and can be an acceptable and less expensive substitute.

Multicolored green slate covers the swooping roof curves and clipped gables of a stone bungalow in New Jersey. The walls of local brown stone would be better complemented by something other than bright white trim, and the arched front door is probably a modern replacement, though the clipped hedges surrounding the house do a good job of tying it into the landscape.

ICICLE BUILT FOR TWO

Icicles hanging from the edge of a snowy roof in winter are beautiful and kind of romantic. Unless you know what they mean. And what they mean is the dreaded ice dam, a phrase that awakes fear in the hearts of homeowners in cold winter climates.

An ice dam is a ridge of ice that develops at the edge of a roof and prevents melting snow from draining off the roof. The water that backs up behind the dam can find its way underneath the roof covering and leak into the house, damaging walls, ceilings, insulation, and other areas. Ice dams are formed by a complex interaction between heat loss from the house, outside temperatures, and the amount of snow cover on the roof. For an ice dam to form, there must be snow on the roof, and the lower portion of the roof must be below 32 degrees Fahrenheit while the upper portion is warmer than 32 degrees—this can be caused by sunshine or heat loss from the house. The snow on the upper portion where it is warmer will melt and run down the roof to the colder part where it will refreeze, forming the ice dam. The more snow melts from the top and runs down, the larger the ice dam becomes. Some of the water gets over the edge and freezes, producing icicles, which get larger and larger like hand-dipped taper candles.

There's still a lot of argument about ways to prevent ice dams, but there seems to be agreement on the following principles: insulate the attic, and seal penetrations into the attic, such as light fixtures, exhaust fans, chimneys, etc., to keep heated air from escaping the heated areas of the house into the attic; remove snow from the roof; when re-roofing, include a waterproof membrane (usually a self-adhesive bituminous product) that extends at a foot above the point where the outside wall of the house meets the roof, to prevent water intrusion if an ice dam does form. There is less agreement about whether attic ventilation (usually comprising soffit and ridge vents) or mechanical ventilation (fans) is a good idea or not. Me, I'm a Californian—I just laugh and skip this part.

DORMER VOUS?

Dormer comes from a French word meaning "sleeping room." A dormer is a smaller roof form projecting from the main roof slope, usually containing one or more windows, or sometimes a door leading to a porch. On a one-story bungalow, dormers may be used to provide light and/or ventilation for the attic, and if the roof is steep enough, to provide more headroom in the attic. In a one-and-a-half-

Two knee braces and a decorative beam end support a cross beam on a twin-gabled dormer. The dormer windows are plain, while the lower windows have a muntin pattern with a central diamond motif. Sturdy six-by-six timbers, tripled at the outer corners, hold up the edge of the side gabled roof. The T-lok shingle roof covering is popular in Vancouver.

An unusually shaped overhang and wood trim distinguishes the clipped gable dormer on this Denver bungalow.

The tapered shingle walls of a shed-roof dormer on a bungalow in Eagle Rock, California, are echoed by the tapered trim around its three horizontal windows.

RIGHT: A large gable dormer with massive brackets and an interesting drop ornament in the peak is flanked by two small eyebrow dormers (one missing its window) on a Milwaukee bungalow. The porch gable repeats the brackets and ornament on a somewhat smaller scale. The lower portion of the home is brick, but the dormer appears to be covered with asphalt siding made to resemble ashlar (rectangular rough-face stone blocks).

BELOW: The battered (wider at the bottom) pillars supporting the porch roof of a Milwaukee bungalow are reflected in the similarly tapered walls of the home's hip-roofed stucco dormer. The earthy rust and brown tones of the trim and window sashes harmonize with the brick and stucco better than the white paint usually chosen for this purpose.

story bungalow, dormers provide additional ceiling height in the attic space so it can be used as living area, generally for bedrooms. Sometimes dormers are just there for architectural interest. Ventilation dormers may not have windows at all, only louvers or latticework. This should have screening behind it to prevent insects or animals from getting into the attic. Dormers were frequently used instead of skylights to bring light from the attic to the lower rooms.

Dormers are found in all the roof shapes used for main roofs: gable (sometimes called "doghouse" dormers), clipped gable (jerkinhead), hipped, flat, flat with parapet, gabled with parapet, curved (depending on the curve, sometimes called "eyebrow" dormers), arched (a more pronounced curve than an eyebrow), shed, and inset (set into the roof—often combined with an upstairs porch). The roof style of the dormer may not necessarily match the roof style of the house, and there may be more than one kind of dormer style on the same house.

Inset dormers—now there's a bad idea. Yes, they look very cool, and yes, it's lovely to have an upstairs porch if that is included with the dormer. Let's review: cut a potential swimming pool INTO the roof, oh yes, that makes so much sense. These might have a metal (steel or copper) pan with sides that run up under the siding, sometimes with an integral gutter on the outer edge, and a wooden deck sitting on top of that. Or possibly the whole thing would merely be lined with rolled roofing. Worse yet, they may have used only painted or rubberized canvas, which was popular for outdoor porches. Suffice it to say that an inset dormer should be obsessively flashed, caulked, and maintained.

SKYLIGHTS

OBSESSIVE RESTORATION

Old skylights may leak, the wood may be rotten, or the steel in a metal skylight may have rusted through. The glass may need reglazing as well. Stained-glass skylights may have sagged if there was not sufficient support for the leading. Epoxy consolidants may be used to rebuild the rotted parts of a wood skylight. If it is too far gone, it should be replicated with new wood. Steel skylights can also be rebuilt if only small parts are rusted through, otherwise, they should also be replaced in kind. All skylights should be carefully flashed and sealed and some method put in place to deal with condensation from inside the house. Most new skylights have this as part of the design, but old ones may not.

GOT THE BLUES

Skylights or roof windows are not common in bungalows, but they are not unheard of. A decorative skylight might use art glass and be installed over a dining room, entry hall, or stairway. A more utilitarian skylight would be made of wood or metal and probably utilize wire glass for strength. Historically, skylights were likely to have been flat- or pyramid-shaped. Other shapes, such as domes, barrel vaulted, etc., are far less likely on a bungalow, although no doubt there is at least one of these types installed somewhere. Most sky-

INSET DORMERS

OBSESSIVE RESTORATION

Put in a new metal pan. Use copper. If there was canvas, put it on top of something more waterproof.

COMPROMISE SOLUTION

Can you say EPDM? I knew you could.

Asymmetry rules the day on this set of gabled dormers on a Vancouver, British Columbia, bungalow. The larger dormer lets in plenty of light with bands of windows on three sides, while the smaller one possibly lights a closet. X-shaped decorations combined with classic knee braces highlight the large dormer, while the porch below features a slightly different brace with a central element where the porch intersects with the exterior wall of the house.

COMPROMISE SOLUTION

Sometimes a strategically placed skylight can add to the livability of a bungalow, bringing light to the end of a dark hallway or stairwell. Often new, taller buildings built next to a bungalow may cut off the light from the windows the house had when it was new; a skylight can be a good solution for that problem. This does not mean it's okay to put a row of five skylights in your kitchen, and don't go crazy putting them in the attic either—consider dormers instead, unless that will change the roofline too drastically.

As above, put a skylight on a secondary roof, not visible from the street, if possible. Glass is preferable, but acrylic is okay provided that it is FLAT. Bubble skylights and solar tubes are out.

Possibly a bit large for the average bungalow, a smaller version of the Willis Hipped Turret Skylight might have been just the thing. Pivoting windows on the sides could be opened for ventilation.

lights were fixed, although occasionally an operable skylight is found.

Skylights are useful for bringing light (in the daytime, anyway) to areas of the house that might otherwise be dark. Sometimes art-glass skylights would have lighting above the glass to illuminate them after dark as well. Unlike today, skylights were not typically installed in kitchens or bathrooms.

A skylight was generally placed on a secondary roof that was not visible from the street, and this is a good rule to follow if adding a new skylight to a bungalow. New skylights should be as small as possible, rectangular or square, and if there is more than one, lined up in an even row. Acrylic bubble skylights should NOT be used, nor should the round "sun tunnel" type of skylights.

FLUE SHOT

Misshapen clinker bricks give a spiky aspect to this narrow chimney in Vancouver, British Columbia.

Since the hearth was regarded by the Arts and Crafts Movement as the very soul of the home, there is almost always going to be a chimney or two in a bungalow. Depending on the location of the fireplace, the chimney may be on an outside wall, or come up through the middle of the house. The kitchen usually had its own chimney, serving the stove and the water heater, and possibly the furnace. Or the furnace might share the main chimney. Each chimney could have more than one flue. Although stove and furnace chimneys could be made of metal or asbestos (usually referred to now as "transite," after one particular brand), the main chimney was always masonry. It might be brick, stone, river rock, clinker brick, concrete block, or some combination of these. If the house had stucco siding, the masonry of the chimney might be covered with stucco as well, or it might not. Some chimneys were quite plain, but others gave the mason a chance to show off. Square or rectangular chimneys were more common, but round wasn't unheard of, and asymmetry provided the natural look that the movement embraced. Chimneys sometimes had decorative chimney pots, which had the added bonus of making the chimney taller, which can improve the draw. Bungalow chimneys are often shorter than what is required by modern building codes, which dictate a certain height above the roof surface for the chimney top, but the good news is that if you don't mess with it, it's grandfathered in. (Minimum is three feet above the highest point where the chimney penetrates the roofline, or

A whole selection of chimneys built from local stone decorates the rolled roof of a tiny bungalow in a town on the New Jersey shore. The chimney on the left has three separate flues and looks to have been increased in height at some point, probably to improve the draw.

Scalloped parapet walls surround a flat roof on a home in Denver, Colorado. The swastika on the chimney was once a legitimate design motif before certain parties put it to bad use.

A rectangular chimney with a slight taper emerges from the roof of a Denver bungalow. The lighter bricks, flecked with iron, are set off by a band and ornamental cap of maroon bricks.

Rounded rocks from Lake Michigan combine with chunks of limestone plus a row of bricks to form a substantial chimney for a log bungalow in Milwaukee, Wisconsin. The rounded dormers are unusual and are sided in a wave-like shingle pattern, suggesting that at one time the roof may have worn a similar wood shingle "thatch." The logs are stepped out at the top of the wall to form a "bracket" supporting a small log beam at the edge of the roof. And while it may be a good idea to seal the end grain on a log, white paint is not the optimum choice for that purpose.

A fairly random-looking pile of rocks with a lot of mortar in between looks as though it could topple momentarily, though it's probably been a part of this Denver bungalow for quite some time.

A massive chimney largely composed of rounded granite rocks keeps this Eagle Rock, California, bungalow firmly rooted to the earth. The rocks decrease in size as the chimney tapers rather significantly toward the top, and indeed, above the roofline the chimney is quite small.

two feet higher than any portion of the structure within ten feet of the chimney.) You can see how this means the steeper the roof, the higher the chimney has to be. Chimneys may be lined with terra-cotta flue liners, though some are just brick. Flue liners often fail at the joints. Retrofit flue liners of stainless steel and/or concrete can be used to strengthen existing chimneys.

The top of the chimney should have a cap, usually made of concrete, that is sloped to shed water, which is known (at least in Britain) by the amusing term *flaunching*.

All chimneys should have a spark arrester on top and a damper (which can be retrofitted into chimneys that don't have them—and you might as well get an energy-saving damper that has a gasket like a refrigerator) that will keep all your heated air from escaping out the chimney in winter. It will also keep birds and squirrels from nesting in your chimney and has the additional benefit of keeping water out, which keeps the chimney from deteriorating.

Chimneys often need re-pointing (removing deteriorated mortar and replacing it, especially above the roofline where the chimney is exposed to the weather the most). Old chimneys should not be re-pointed with modern portland cement-based mortars—they are too hard. Mortar is supposed to be sacrificial—the mortar is supposed to crack, not the bricks. With modern mortar, the softer bricks, stones, etc., will crack instead.

The joint where the chimney meets the roofline is a likely place for roof leaks if the chimney flashing has failed or has not been installed properly. (Flashing is Z-shaped metal that slides under the shingles and into the mortar joints to prevent water from getting in. Chimneys need *step-flashing,* where separate pieces of flashing are lapped like shingles.) Often roofers will just slap some black goop (roofing cement) on the joint. Not only does this look bad, but the roofing cement will crack in a couple of years and allow water to get in. Chimney flashing should be made of a material that will last as long as the roofing, whatever the roofing happens to be.

Masonry chimneys can fail in an earthquake, and there are differing points of view on what to do about this. Some advocate bracing the chimney above the roofline with metal braces, while others think the entire chimney should be replaced with a stainless-steel triple-wall flue and the visible parts faced with brick or other masonry veneer. At the very least, installing plywood on the attic floor all around the chimney will keep it from crashing down into the living space below should it fail in an earthquake. All of the above is also true of hurricanes and other major windstorms. Or, as Bill Porter of the Mobile, Alabama, newspaper *Mobile Register* wrote, "There's nothing more annoying than a flying brick."

OPPOSITE: An asymmetrical chimney built using two shades of textured brick (sometimes called "reptile" brick) features an unusual top with the flues turned at various angles. Left, just above the gutter and also at the right near the roof edge, the metal step-flashing can be seen. The downspout at the left is capped with a decorative leader head.

At the time that bungalows were being built, furnaces were so inefficient that a lot of heat went up the chimney, so the water vapor created by combustion was burned off. Modern furnaces and water heaters should not be vented into masonry chimneys. Their more efficient combustion means that the flue gases are at a much cooler temperature when they enter the chimney, which causes them to con-

CHIMNEYS

OBSESSIVE RESTORATION
Chimneys are important to the roofline of a house, so even a chimney that is no longer in use should be left in place. A chimney liner can be installed without compromising the exterior integrity of the chimney. (Although a concrete flue liner is irreversible, so give that some serious thought before committing to one.)

COMPROMISE SOLUTION
If the chimney is going to be replaced, at least salvage the original bricks, stones, or whatever, and use them to face the new chimney. If the existing chimney was covered with stucco, match the design and profile, since stucco chimneys often had details such as recessed panels or molded decoration. If the kitchen chimney is to be removed (due to a kitchen redo), at least leave the visible part on the roof in place, though this may require some engineering, or fake it with a plywood box faced with the original chimney material. DO NOT cover the plywood box that covers a new metal flue with wood siding or shingles, or any other kind of siding that does not involve masonry or concrete.

dense into water and corrosive sulfuric and hydrofluoric acids, which can eat through metal flue liners and leak through the joints of clay tile flue liners, and really do a number on the masonry of unlined chimneys. A 150,000 BTU furnace produces a gallon of acid-laced water every hour it is running. Some of that will exit the chimney as vapor, but the larger the flue, the more condensation. Typically a new furnace, which should have a four-inch vent, is exhausted into an 8- or 12-inch flue at about 200 degrees Fahrenheit. It promptly condenses, the corrosive liquid eats away at the flue, gets into the masonry, and begins to destroy the chimney. This can cause damage to both the interior and exterior of the house. Sometimes interior water damage thought to be from roof leaks or failing chimney flashing is actually due to excess moisture in the chimney. It can also allow carbon monoxide to enter the house, particularly if the chimney goes through the house instead of up an outside wall, or if there are thimbles for stoves or other appliances. The solution is to install a smaller flue inside the existing chimney, or reroute the flue out through a sidewall or up through the roof by a different route that doesn't involve the chimney.

MIND IN THE GUTTER

Gutters and downspouts exist to catch water from the roof and carry it to the ground, hopefully away from the house, thus saving the foundation and keeping water out of the basement. Gutters first began to be used in America in the eighteenth century. These were either V-shaped gutters made by fastening the long sides of two boards together, or gutters made from a hollowed-out half log. Downspouts were made from four long boards fastened together to form a long rectangular box. These had a tendency to leak and were soon replaced by metal downspouts. Lead was also used for gutters and downspouts, though it was a bit on the heavy side. Possibly this is why copper, tinplate, and terne plate eventually became more popular as gutter materials. Downspouts might lead to a rain barrel or cistern, or might merely dump onto some gravel or a strategically placed stone used as a splashblock.

Built-in gutters were introduced in the eighteenth century—these were box gutters integrated with the roof edge or cornice, and were usually made of wood and lined with metal. Built-in gutters might also take the form of a trough in the roof a few inches from the roof edge. (Just for clarity, I'm going to call these *trough gutters* and the kind that are built into the edge of the roof *box gutters.*) Sometimes built-in gutters are called *Yankee gutters.* Another type of gutter was the *pole,* or *stop,* gutter—a piece of metal folded so that one edge would be perpendicular to the roof, fastened near the eaves to direct water off the roof or over to a downspout. A piece of wood fastened to the roof directly below it helped support the metal. Sometimes THESE are called Yankee gutters too.

In the nineteenth century, hanging gutters became popular and were made in different styles, from half-round to imitations of classical moldings. These hung from the edge of the roof or from the fascia board. Hanging gutters were made of wood or various kinds of metal. In the mid-twentieth century, the classical profiles were whittled down to just one: the *ogee* (kind of a backwards "S"), which, for reasons that are not clear, is known as a *K-style gutter.* Yes, it should be an O-style or S-style, but it isn't. In any case, it didn't become the standard until the 1960s, so it doesn't generally belong on a bungalow.

Bungalows used all these kinds of gutters plus another type, which may be exclusive to bungalows because of their low-pitched roofs, so I'm just going to call them *bungalow gutters.* Often found on built-up or tar and gravel roofs, these are akin to box gutters, except much shallower—not much more than a slight depression running along the edge of the roof, angled slightly toward holes drilled through the eaves leading to downspouts. In theory, because of the low slope of the roof, water won't be moving that fast and can just pool up in the depression and make its way in a leisurely fashion over to the nearest downspout. It works pretty well, too, until there's a serious downpour—then the water shoots straight off the edge of the roof. Some bungalows have no gutters at all, a bit optimistic, perhaps. If that's the case, it might be a good idea to put some gravel along the ground where the water will

A photo from the July 1918 issue of *Keith's Magazine* shows an inset dormer with a porch. At the bottom of the shingled porch railing is a slot which ostensibly drains water from the porch floor, which is generally angled a bit so this will occur. Whenever water goes through a wall, there is always the potential for trouble. Although this sort of upstairs porch is charming, it should be aggressively maintained and checked often for leakage.

American Carpenter and Builder showed this shingled bungalow with a shed dormer and inset porch with a pergola in the March 1915 issue. It also has an interesting roof edge which has been notched back over the casement windows, perhaps to let in more light. The horizontal ridge parallel to the roof edge is called a stop gutter. The side entrance is not as typical as a front facing entrance, although the accompanying prose suggested that "a home of this character is supposed to be built on a rather wide lot, where it is exposed to the air and sunshine from all sides."

Quite an elaborate leader box tops a downspout of equally interesting design, all attached to the half-timbered wall of a Vancouver home. The underside of the boxed-in cornice is ornamented with applied wooden strips forming a simple design.

Wooden gutters with diamonds applied to the ends are attached to the edge of boxed-in cornices supported by beams. The complex roof's crossed gables give the appearance of being supported by the brackets underneath the fascia board as well as by the beams (barely seen) that seem to penetrate the fascia board, anchored by four wedges (probably fake) in the same way that pegged through-tenons were a prominent feature of Arts and Crafts furniture. It is likely that much of this Milwaukee bungalow's "expressed structure" is merely nailed on.

hit, and make sure the ground is sloped away from the foundation.

What kinds of gutters are used and how they are attached will depend on the detailing of the roof edge. If the rafter tails extend beyond the eaves, they will be notched to hold the gutter, or a stop or trough gutter will be used instead. If the rafter tails do not extend beyond the roof edge, then the gutter may be attached directly to the ends of the rafters, or there may be a fascia board attached to the ends and the gutter attached to that; or box gutters may be used instead. Metal gutters attached to rafter ends or fascia boards traditionally were attached with spikes (big honkin' nails that go through both edges of the gutter trough and into the wood) or sometimes with brackets that slide under the roof covering to attach to the roof deck or sheathing. Wood gutters in notched rafters are generally toe-nailed (the nail goes in at an angle) to the rafters with finishing nails, or nailed through the back of the gutter if they are attached to the ends of the rafters or to a fascia board.

The wood gutters manufactured today are primarily made of redwood, a highly rot-resistant wood that is well suited for gutters. A well-maintained wood gutter can last 50 to 100 years. The main thing with wood gutters is that they have to be able to dry out—this means cleaning them at least twice a year, because rotting leaves, asphalt roof

debris, etc., will hold moisture in the wood, and that's how rot starts. There is debate about whether wood gutters should be oiled periodically or not. Here are the various points of view: don't oil them at all; oil them, but only with non-drying oils like mineral oil or shingle oil (made by Chevron); oil them, but use drying oils like tung oil or linseed oil (diluted with turpentine or paint thinner so it soaks in); paint the insides with clear oil stain or oil-base primer; or soak the whole thing with liquid epoxy consolidant. About the only thing everyone seems to agree on is NOT to line them with metal, plastic, EPDM membranes, etc., because that will trap moisture underneath and guarantee rot. The other thing NOT to do is to paint them with asphaltic roof paint or roofing cement (the aforementioned "black gunk"). Another option is to not do anything at all except keep them clean so the wood can dry out.

Any joints in wood gutters should be scarf (diagonal) joints that are sealed with butyl caulk. End caps should have mitered returns. At the time bungalows were built, joints were usually covered with pieces of metal, but this caused the wood to rot underneath. The caulk may have to be renewed periodically. Wood gutters ordinarily use metal drop outlets and downspouts, though sometimes the drop outlet is underneath rather than inside the gutter.

GUTTERS AND LEADERS

OBSESSIVE RESTORATION

If the original gutters are still there, they should be restored (if possible) or replicated if they are too far gone. Different gutter profiles are available, and custom profiles can also be manufactured. Wood gutters can last 50 to 100 years if they are maintained, so don't feel that longevity is compromised if you don't switch to metal. (For example, the average life span of a galvanized gutter is about 15 years.) Wooden gutters that have areas of rot may be candidates for epoxy consolidants rather than complete replacement.

Metal gutters that are too far gone should be replaced with a matching profile, rather than just slapping up a modern K-style gutter. This being "obsessive restoration," that also means galvanized, terne metal, etc., should be replaced with the same metal. These gutters can last a long time if properly maintained, the same as wood gutters. It's very tempting to fancy up the house with copper gutters, and copper gutters do last a very long time, but the average bungalow did not have them.

It's also important to keep and repair trough or box gutters in order to maintain the integrity of the roof edge. These were often lined with metal, and if the metal has rusted out or corroded, water can leak into the overhang or even into the house. Depending on how extensive the corrosion is, (matching) metal patches can be soldered or riveted into place. If all the metal needs to be replaced, some roof repair may be involved as well, because the new metal needs to go underneath the roofing. It is suggested that a strip of rosin paper (paper impregnated with rosin—it's pink) be placed underneath, so any moisture trapped beneath the gutter will not get to the wood underneath. Obviously the ideal time to do this is while getting a new roof. Resist the urge to just coat the rot with "black gunk."

Bungalows were simple. If there is evidence of leader heads or fancy downspout strapping, then those can be put back. If not, stick with plain downspouts and strapping. And try to keep the downspouts in inconspicuous locations as much as possible—off the front façade and away from important decorative details.

Copper gutters were usually too expensive for a bungalow, even at early-twentieth-century prices, but the builder of this Memphis bungalow (or possibly a subsequent owner) decided to go with copper gutters, which is certainly the longest-lasting material you can use. Copper weathers to a lovely green color, as it has here on the gutters, leader head, and downspout. A swagged plaster decoration in the porch gable does give it somewhat the look of a classical pediment, but the concrete planters and sturdy block columns, not to mention the slotted gable vent, would be unlikely on a Greek Revival home.

COMPROMISE SOLUTION

Replacing wood gutters with aluminum or copper will cut down on maintenance, but at least match the profile of the wood gutter. Trough or box gutters can be re-lined with copper or aluminum, but they can't really be replaced with hanging gutters without ruining the integrity of the eave line. Hacking off rafter tails for gutters is not allowed, even as a compromise. If someone before you hacked them off, that's another story. It would be nice to put the exposed rafter tails back, if it's in the budget. On the other hand, if there are no gutters at all, notching existing rafter tails to install gutters is okay, but they should be the half-round style. Decorative gutter brackets are available for attaching gutters to rafter tails that end at the roof edge.

Regardless of what kind of gutters there are, they still have to be cleaned. The various gutter guards, helmets, screens, etc., usually make things worse.

Metal gutters traditionally were made of copper, lead-coated copper, galvanized iron or steel, tin-plate or terne-plate, and, occasionally, lead. In the twentieth century, aluminum came into use. Metal gutters formerly were assembled from short sections, joined by riveting or soldering. Naturally this lead to leaks at these joints. The invention of a small truck-mounted machine that could bend continuous lengths of gutter from a coil of metal led to the currently popular "seamless" gutters. They're not really seamless—they still have to have end caps or mitered returns, which can leak, and they're only seamless until they have to turn a corner. Nonetheless, it's still an improvement. Galvanized steel was the most popular metal for many years, but it can rust (and usually does), so painted aluminum is now the most popular metal for gutters. Whatever metal is used, it should all be the same metal for gutters, hangers, downspouts, and fasteners. Differing metals lead to galvanic corrosion, where metal molecules from one metal go wandering off to join with molecules from the differing metals. You do not want diversity in your metal gene pool.

You can also buy vinyl gutters. Don't.

TAKE ME TO YOUR LEADER

Gutters are slightly sloped so that the water will drain to a *drop outlet* (hole) leading to the downspout or *leader* (because it leads the water down? Who knows?), which is attached to the wall of the house with straps. Straps could be fairly plain or a little bit fancy. Because of the wide overhangs found on bungalows, an elbow or two is required to get from the drop outlet to the downspout, and at least one more elbow is required at the bottom to get the water into an underground drainage system or at least onto a splashblock. Sometimes the top of the downspout has a *leader box* or *leader head,* which may be decorative as well as functional and may have more than one outlet dropping into it. Sometimes this box is called a *scupper,* even though technically a scupper is a metal-lined hole that pierces a parapet wall to allow water to escape. Half-round gutters traditionally have round downspouts, although round downspouts may be used on other styles as well. Bungalows typically had round or rectangular (2- by 3-inch or 3- by 4-inch) downspouts. Rectangular downspouts were flat, not ridged like modern ones are. Downspouts typically run down the outside wall, but sometimes they may be run in stupid places like inside the wall or through the middle of a porch column. This is all well and good until the downspout starts to leak—then you're in trouble. Frank Lloyd Wright didn't believe in downspouts—he thought a column of water pouring out of a drop outlet looked cool. It does, but it's still not a good idea.

Many bungalows have had their decorative rafter tails amputated to allow the installation of inappropriate gutters. Others have had their box or trough gutters repaired with the dreaded "black gunk," or had their rotted wooden gutters replaced with inappropriate K-style aluminum, or worse, vinyl.

ALL ABOUT EAVES

The edge of the roof is where bungalows really begin to differ from other house styles. Exposed rafter tails, purlins (horizontal roof beams), brackets, knee braces, and other structural details define the edge of the roof. Wide overhangs, from 1 foot to as much as 4 feet wide, are one of the defining features

Paired brackets with more "pegged thru-tenons" add interest to the two jerkinhead gables of a Milwaukee bungalow. Simple corbel blocks below hold up a small molding on the enclosed porch. All of it would be a lot more interesting if the entire house wasn't painted white.

The gable of a Memphis bungalow has more decorative beam ends than could possibly be necessary to actually hold up the roof, even if they were really holding the roof up, which is doubtful. A round vent helps ventilate the attic, and below the stucco, a few rows of the multicolored brick used to build this bungalow are visible.

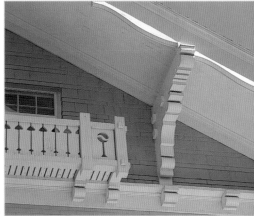

A shaped fascia board, a row of corbels, a really complex knee brace, and a small balcony with a pierced railing are only a few of the things going on in the gable of a Denver home. Close examination of the fascia board shows it is actually two boards sandwiched together. None of these elements were meant to be painted white.

The exposed eaves around a second-floor porch on this Vancouver bungalow retain the original 1- by 4-inch tongue-and-groove boards.

LEFT: The West Adams district of Los Angeles is home to this bungalow that, unfortunately, has been encased in stucco (see how the stucco is level with the trim around the gable vent?). Nonetheless, the home's many brackets, pyramid-shaped blocks, interesting porch columns, and pierced window box sitting on zigzag brackets remain, although one has to wonder exactly how anything could be planted or maintained in a window box that isn't under an actual window. The unfortunate belief that covering a wood-sided house with stucco or siding will make it "no maintenance" is all too prevalent—all it really does is rot the siding underneath and ruin the house.

BELOW: Nothing says Prairie style like a really wide overhang, and the eaves on this Memphis bungalow measure a good 5 feet wide. This home was designed by architect Victor Dunkerley, who had worked in Frank Lloyd Wright's office during the first decade of the twentieth century. Dunkerley worked in Memphis from 1911 to 1915, then returned to Chicago. The built-in box gutters are picked out in cream paint at the edge of the beadboard lining the underside of the eaves.

The open eaves of a Vancouver bungalow reveal the skip-sheathing on which the wooden roof shingles are laid.

ABOVE: These rafters in Vancouver, British Columbia, have had their ends rounded and notched.

RIGHT: Flared or "kicked" eaves are taken to extremes on this Japanese-influenced apartment building in Milwaukee, Wisconsin. The lighter horizontal lines near the roof edge are the built-in gutters. The inclusion of random stonework accents in the brickwork and the diagonal orientation of the porch pillars make for an interesting yet difficult to classify piece of architecture.

EAVES AND RAFTER ENDS

OBSESSIVE RESTORATION

Rafter tails and anything else not protected by the roof overhang are prone to rot. The solution will depend somewhat on whether the rafters, brackets, etc., are actually part of the structure or not. Often the visible rafter tails are larger than the actual rafters (which are usually two-by-fours) and extend only to the outside wall of the house. On the other hand, the rafter tails may be the ends of the real rafters. One solution is to replace only the rotted ends, attaching the new ends to the existing rafters underneath the roof overhang using a scarf (diagonal) joint or some other kind of joint. (This method can also be used to replace rafter ends hacked off by some previous owner.) The problem with this is that the old wood may be somewhat weathered and ridged and the new wood will be perfectly smooth, making the join somewhat obvious. And the philosophical question is whether to make it really obvious with a complicated scarf joint so that it's obvious the ends were replaced, or try to make it inconspicuous. Another option is the use of epoxy consolidants—these come in both liquid and putty-like forms. The liquid form soaks into the wood and consolidates the rotted wood fibers. The putty form is used to fill holes and build up missing parts of the wood. The hardened epoxy can be worked with regular woodworking tools and can also be molded to replicate missing carvings on corbels or other woodwork. If the wood is to be painted, this is a good solution. If the wood is not painted and was not meant to be painted, it's more problematic, since the putty doesn't look much like wood. It can be faux-painted to look more like wood, but this won't bear close inspection, so it may depend on how visible the wood happens to be. As a last resort, replacing the wood all the way back to the wall of the house will solve the problem.

Often exterior woodwork rots because the wood it's made from isn't from a particularly rot-resistant species. For instance, on the West Coast, Douglas fir is the most popular wood for the structural components of a house. But it rots a lot faster than redwood or cedar when exposed to the weather, so Douglas fir rafter tails are often rotted. It is probably worthwhile to replace the exposed wood with something less prone to rotting, even if that isn't the most obsessive thing to do. Practicality does enter into it, at least occasionally.

Often the bead board or other wood underneath the eaves is replaced with plywood, usually during a re-roofing job. Plywood is not an acceptable finish for the exposed eaves of a bungalow. Or worse, someone has put up that dreadful aluminum or vinyl soffit—rip it down immediately! Unfortunately, replacing the plywood with beadboard will involve either removing several courses of roofing or painstakingly fitting the new boards between the existing rafters. Feel free to curse the roofers and/or the previous owner while doing so. Aluminum and vinyl soffit should just be banned. Period.

Sometimes decorative woodwork has been removed entirely in a misguided attempt to "modernize." Often "ghosts" of what was removed are left as an outline in the paint, or it may be possible to tell from other clues like nail holes, notches, etc. Often in bungalow neighborhoods, a whole series of houses was built by the same builder, so woodwork still existing on neighboring houses may offer a clue as to what was removed. Old photographs are also useful in this regard.

COMPROMISE SOLUTION

Most kinds of millwork that are made in wood can also be made in fiberglass, polyurethane, or other plastics. They have to be painted and have to have a faux finish to look like wood, but they weigh less, and they don't rot. These kinds of fakes generally can't be used for anything structural, but they work for decorative purposes.

Sometimes rafter tails or other exposed woodwork will be wrapped with metal in an attempt to keep them from rotting. Usually this just traps the moisture underneath, accelerating the process.

In lieu of bead board, there is a grooved paneling product that resembles bead board and comes in 4- by 8-foot sheets. Up close it's not very convincing because the grooves aren't deep enough, but 10 feet off the ground it looks acceptable.

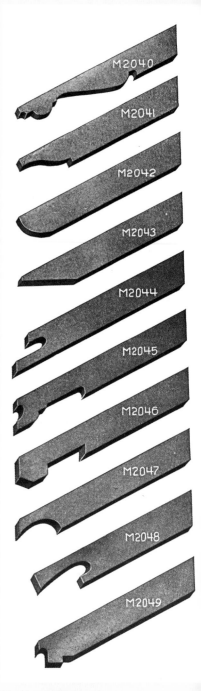

The Morgan Woodwork Organization of Chicago produced house plans as well as selling house parts, and this page in their 1921 catalog shows the various pre-fabricated rafter tails that they offered.

of bungalows. They can also block the hot summer sun from the windows while allowing the lower winter sun to stream in.

Rafter tails, which may be the ends of the real rafters (the wooden pieces that support the roof) but often are not, commonly extend beyond the edge of the roof and are often cut into decorative shapes. Rafters may also be cut or notched to accept gutters, depending on the gutter style. Brackets, knee braces, or corbels, often triangular in shape, decorate gable ends, dormers, and other areas. While generally brackets and corbels are assembled from lumber, sometimes corbels may have decorative carving or other ornament. (And sometimes corbels are called *modillions,* although a modillion tends to be more horizontal than a corbel.) Brackets, knee braces, or corbels may be doubled up or otherwise grouped. The exposed ends of purlins are also often cut or carved in decorative shapes (as with rafters, these are often false). Any of these may or may not extend beyond the edge of the roof. The underside of the roof overhang may be lined with tongue-and-groove 1- by 4-inch lumber (sometimes called beadboard, matchboard, or car siding), or sometimes the underside of the roof sheathing. With a wood shingle, tile, or slate roof, the overhang may show the battens or skip-sheathing and the underside of the roofing. Prairie-style bungalows may have boxed-in eaves with a flat fascia (sometimes called bargeboard or verge board, although usually that term is applied to fascia boards on gable ends) and the underside may be wood or stucco, sometimes with a decorative design formed with small strips of wood. Gable ends and dormers also have fascia boards, which may have decorative cutouts as well or be pierced (or appear to be pierced) by the ends of knee braces or brackets. Bargeboards may also have decorative applied trim, such as scroll-sawn cutouts or wooden "nailhead" trim. Or they may be cutout themselves.

The shapes, sizes, and combinations of rafter tails, brackets, corbels, and knee braces were limited only by the imagination of bungalow designers and builders, and these people had pretty wild imaginations.

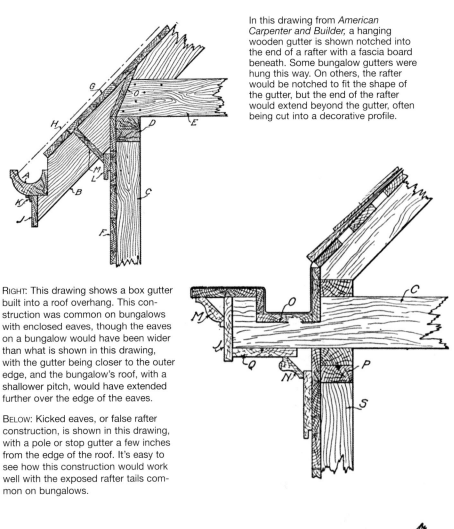

In this drawing from *American Carpenter and Builder,* a hanging wooden gutter is shown notched into the end of a rafter with a fascia board beneath. Some bungalow gutters were hung this way. On others, the rafter would be notched to fit the shape of the gutter, but the end of the rafter would extend beyond the gutter, often being cut into a decorative profile.

RIGHT: This drawing shows a box gutter built into a roof overhang. This construction was common on bungalows with enclosed eaves, though the eaves on a bungalow would have been wider than what is shown in this drawing, with the gutter being closer to the outer edge, and the bungalow's roof, with a shallower pitch, would have extended further over the edge of the eaves.

BELOW: Kicked eaves, or false rafter construction, is shown in this drawing, with a pole or stop gutter a few inches from the edge of the roof. It's easy to see how this construction would work well with the exposed rafter tails common on bungalows.

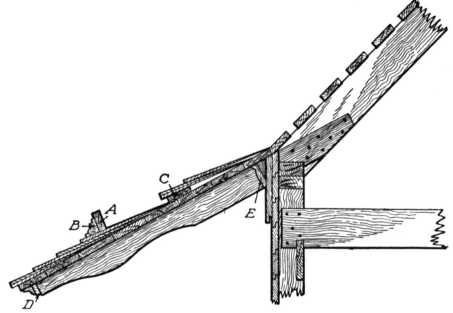

SQUAB THE DECK

"but it's not against any religion
To want to dispose of a pigeon."
— Tom Lehrer, from the song
"Poisoning Pigeons in the Park"

No discussion of bungalows would be complete without mentioning pigeons. Pigeons just love bungalows—they love to sit on the brackets, nest under the eaves, and leave pigeon poop all over the sides of the house. This would be merely annoying, except that it accelerates the deterioration of the exterior. Pigeons aren't that smart, but boy, are they persistent. As one expert said, "The pigeons will exploit every crack and crevice, and will certainly find every flaw of your well-planned exclusion effort." Since they can also find their way back from thousands of miles away, catching them and relocating them doesn't really help, either.

About the best you can do is discourage them. First of all, DON'T FEED THEM. DON'T LET OTHER PEOPLE FEED THEM. Get rid of your bird feeder—the other birds are not going to starve.

There are numerous products on the market to discourage pigeons. One not to waste your money on is an inflatable owl or hawk—pigeons aren't scared of these. Pigeons aren't scared of anything—they used to sit on a bracket two feet from the open window where one of my cats would be sitting, just going, "Come on, I dare you!" You'll just come outside one day and a pigeon will be sitting right on the owl's head. Shiny mylar tape is in this "waste of money" category, as well as various

Towers aren't that common on bungalows, but this Milwaukee home is one of three in a row where all have towers of varying shapes; this particular one is octagonal. Unfortunately, the front door has been replaced with a cheap home-center special.

TURRET SYNDROME

Found only occasionally on bungalows are such things as cupolas, belvederes, turrets, or towers. A *cupola* is a small structure that projects from the roof, is usually round, and is often used for ventilation. It is usually placed on top of a ridge. A *belvedere* is also a cupola, except it's square and has windows in it. A *turret* may be round or square and is kind of like a tower, except that it starts somewhere above the ground, often on a corner of the building. A *tower* is a turret that goes all the way to the ground.

Similar to a belvedere but larger is the upstairs room found on airplane bungalows, often called a *pop-top, pop-up,* or *cockpit.*

Unfortunately, the twin beams, corbels, and other structures of this Memphis bungalow provide numerous perching and nesting places for pigeons.

RIGHT: A home in Los Angeles, designed by E. W. Stillwell, is kind of bungalow on the left and Queen Anne on the right. Certainly the brackets in the left-hand gable, the tripartite window in the center, and even the concrete block foundation and porch railing are well within bungalow parameters. Personally, I enjoy this sort of architectural cognitive dissonance.

BELOW: A nicely proportioned pop-top on this airplane bungalow from the *Women's Weekly* 1923 supplement, "The Home," is almost enough to divert one from the overabundance of notching: notched rafters, notched beams, notched corbels, notched window box, etc. It does have an interesting porch railing, if one isn't distracted by the elaborate pillars. The magazine admitted as much in the caption, "A Design of Extreme Novelty but Great Attraction." And what's up with the neoclassical urn in the foreground?

ultrasonic devices. You can also buy gunk called tanglefoot or hotfoot—sort of a sticky caulk. The problem with this is it only works when it gets a nice layer of dirt on it. By the way, the pigeons can get stuck in it or ingest it and die. Now maybe you are thinking, "Yes! Die, pigeon, die!" until you realize that now you have dead pigeons decorating your knee braces.

Here are some of the things that DO work, at least for a while. Spring wire coils spread out along the surface will keep birds from landing. Slinky-type toys work well for this and are inexpensive. Netting can prevent them from nesting in overlapping roof sections, open porches, and such. Stainless steel or plastic needle strips serve the same purpose as wire coils, although pigeons have learned to drop twigs and debris on them, rendering them useless. And they cost way more than a Slinky. You can also buy various kinds of electrified track, which gives the pigeons a slight shock when they land on it.

Another method that shouldn't be used is to box in the knee braces with plywood—yes, it works, but it makes the house ugly. Don't do it with chicken wire either. Shooting at them doesn't work too well, either—unless you're a really good shot, you'll probably end up breaking a window or something. And surprisingly, it STILL won't discourage the pigeons. Ditto for throwing rocks at them (tried it) or dousing them with the hose. One has to grudgingly admire their persistence.

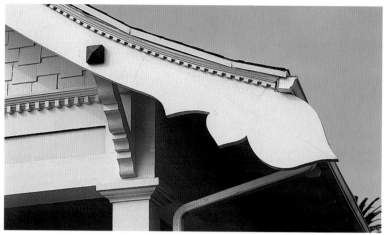

Dentil molding, a zigzag shingle pattern, a fancy bracket coming through a rather cartoonish fascia board, and a sturdy square column below are par for the course on the average West Adams district bungalow in Los Angeles.

Fancy rafter tails, dentil molding, round holes in the shaped fascia, a rather horizontal bracket, and three tapered wood columns provide an intricate interplay of light and shadow on the front of this West Adams bungalow.

ABOVE: Sculpted corbels support a flat roofed "skirt" on a gabled dormer that repeats a similar treatment on the wide eaves of the house below. The eaves are lined with tongue-and-groove beadboard, which is common in boxed-in eaves like these as well as on open eaves with exposed rafters, where beadboard is used as sheathing from the roof edge up to the outside wall of the house.

Thick corbels and notched rafters blend with limestone columns on a Memphis, Tennessee, front porch. Squares and skinny rectangles pattern the front windows and, this being a warm climate, the front porch has a ceiling fan.

ABOVE: A Pasadena, California, bungalow court is home to this small bump-out that sits on five oversize corbels. On either side, classic two-light casement windows open to the breeze.

LEFT: A bracket composed of six stepped four-by-four timbers contrasts with the unpainted stucco in the gable of a bungalow in British Columbia. Again, a color other than white would have been preferable.

RIGHT: The woodcarving tradition of Milwaukee's German emigrants shows up in this bracket carved with a lion's head. Half-timbering decorates the rough brick, and the round downspout is attached with a fancy cast-iron strap.

RESOURCES

THATCH ROOFS

McGhee and Co.
www.thatching.com

Custom Roof Thatch
www.roofthatch.com
(513) 772-4974

Oz Thatch
www.ozthatch.com.au

Rustic Africa
www.rat.com.au

African Thatch
www.african-thatch.com.au

WOODEN SHINGLES & SHAKES

Cypress

Cypress Shingles & Shakes
www.cypressshakesloghomes.com
(662) 226-1685

Museum Resources
www.museum-resources.com
(800) 966-1800

Redwood

California Redwood Association
www.calredwood.org
(888) 225-7339

www.recycledredwood.com
(707) 986-7237

Amarant Wood Products
(800) 423-2205

Redwood Empire
www.redwoodemp.com

Cedar

Kedgwick Lumber Co.
www.klc.ca
(888) 867-8944

www.woodroof.com
(604) 476-1579
(also white oak)

Teal Cedar Co.
www.tealcedar.com
(888) 995-TEAL

The Cedar Guild
www.cedar-guild.com
(800) 270-2541

Fancy Shingles
www.fullmoondesigns.com
(866) 66-FANCY

British Columbia Shake and
Shingle Association
www.bcshakeshingle.com
(604) 855-5775

Cedar Shake and Shingle Bureau
www.cedarbureau.org
(604) 820-7700

FAUX WOODEN SHINGLES & SHAKES

Re-Con Building Products
www.re-con.com

EcoStar, Inc.
www.ecostarinc.com
(800) 211-7170

ASPHALT SHINGLES

Malarkey Roofing Company
www.malarkey-rfg.com
(800) 545-1191

IKO
www.iko.com
(800) 433-2811

Emko
www.emkobp.com
(800) 567-2726

Certainteed
www.certainteed.com
(800) 233-8990

Tamko
www.tamko.com
(800) 641-4691

Elk
www.elcor.com

GAF
www.gaf.com
(973) 628-3000

Georgia-Pacific
www.gp.com
(800) 284-5347

Owens-Corning
www.owenscorning.com
(800) GET-PINK

CONCRETE SHINGLES

Eagle Roofing Co.
www.eagleroofing.com
(909) 355-7000

Unicrete Products
www.unicrete.com
(800) 570-4733

Columbia Concrete Products
www.columbiarooftile.com
(877) 388-8453

Superior Roof Tile
www.superiorrooftile.com
(866) 629-TILE

Westile Roofing Products
www.westile.com
(800) 562-8500

Vande Hey Raleigh
www.vhr-roof-tile.com
(800) 236-8453

Comacast Corp.
www.comacastcorp.com
(800) 273-1034

Hanson Roof Tile
www.hansonrooftile.com
(800) 411-TILE

Monier
www.monierlifetile.com
(949) 756-1605

CLAY ROOFING TILES

Ludowici
www.ludowici.com
(800) 917-8998

The Tile Man, Inc.
www.thetileman.com
(919) 853-6923

MCA Tile
www.mca-tile.com
(800) 736-6221

Builder's Imports
www.buildersimports.com
(888) 826-8453

Gladding McBean
www.paccoast.com
(800) 776-1133

Custom Tile Roofing, Inc.
www.customtileroofing.com
(303) 761-3831
(author of *Historic and Obsolete Roofing Tile*)

Northern Roof Tiles
www.northernrooftiles.com
(888) 678-6866

Tile Roofs
www.tileroofs.com
(888) 708-TILE

ASBESTOS-CEMENT ROOFING

Custom Tile Roofing, Inc.
www.customtileroofing.com
(303) 761-3831
(salvaged asbestos-cement shingles for repairs)

METAL ROOFING

Follansbee Steel
www.follansbeeroofing.com
(800) 624-6906

Accel Roofing, Inc.
www.accelroofing.com
(800) 468-1441

Peterson Aluminum Co.
www.pac-clad.com
(800) 722-7150

Everlast Roofing
www.everlastroofing.com
(888) 339-0059

Conklin Metal Industries
www.metalshingle.com
(800) 282-7386

Zappone Manufacturing
www.zappone.com
(800) 285-2677

Copper Sales, Inc.
www.unaclad.com
(800) 426-7737

SLATE ROOFING

New England Slate Company
www.neslate.com
(888) NES-LATE

Rising and Nelson Slate
www.risingandnelson.com
(518) 642-3333

Greenstone Slate
www.greenstoneslate.com
(800) 619-4333

Echeguren Slate
www.echeguren.com
(415) 206-9343

Jenkins Slate
www.jenkinsslate.com
(814) 786-9085
(author of *The Slate Roof Bible*)

Slate and Copper Sales, Inc.
www.slateandcopper.com
(814) 455-7430

MISCELLANEOUS

BV Enterprise (software for designing a patterned roof)
www.sosele.com/co/bventerprise
(562) 693-2192

SKYLIGHTS

Solar Innovations
www.solarinnovations.com
(800) 618-0669

Velux
www.velux.com
(800) 88-VELUX

Bristolite Skylights
www.bristolite.com
(800) 854-8618

Creative Structures
www.creativeconservatories.com
(800) 873-3966

Glass House Conservatories
www.glasshouseusa.com
(800) 222-3065

Roto Frank of America
www.roto-roofwindows.com
(800) 243-0893

Albert Wagner and Son, Inc.
www.albertwagnerandson.com
(773) 935-1414

CHIMNEYS

Ahrens Chimney Technique
www.ahrenschimney.com
(800) 843-4417

Guardian Chimney Liner
www.guardianinc.com
(800) 545-6607

Supaflu Chimney Restoration
www.supaflu.com
(800) 788-7636

Buckley Rumford Company
www.rumford.com
(360) 385-9974

Superior Clay Corporation
www.superiorclay.com
(800) 848-6166

Northern Roof Tiles
www.northernrooftiles.com
(888) 678-6866

Protech Systems, Inc.
www.protechinfo.com
(800) 766-3473

Golden Flue
www.chimneys.com
(800) 446-5354

Heat-Fab
www.heat-fab.com
(800) 772-0739

Homesaver Chimney Liners
www.homesaver.com
(866) 466-3728

Solid/Flue Chimney Systems
www.solidflue.com
(800) 444-3583

The Chimney Pot Shoppe
www.chimneypot.net
(724) 345-3601

Gladding McBean
www.paccoast.com
(800) 776-1133

Slate and Copper Sales, Inc.
www.slateandcopper.com
(814) 455-7430

METAL GUTTERS

Old World Distributors, Inc.
www.oldworlddistributors.com
(269) 353-0726

The Bungalow
Gutter Bracket Company
www.bungalowgutterbracket.com
(859) 335-1555

Classic Gutters, LLC
www.classicgutters.com
(269) 382-2700

Hurricane Architectural Metals
www.hurricanarchitectural
metals.com
(239) 643-6847

The Rain Gutter Store
www.raingutterstore.com
(800) 330-4337

John F. Graf Heating
and Sheet Metal
www.gaudeteforge.com
(414) 445-1190

AB Raingutters
www.abraingutters.com
(714) 577-8369

Copper Craft
www.coppercraft.com
(800) 486- 2723

Vintage Copper
www.vintagecopper.com
(877) 220-5355

CSC Sheet Metal
www.cscsheetmetal.com

Gutterworks
www.gutterworks.com
(888) 376-6871

Slate and Copper Sales, Inc.
www.slateandcopper.com
(814) 455-7430

Park City Rain Gutter
www.pcraingutter.com
(435) 649-2805

Rutland Gutter Supply
www.rutlandroofing.com
(407) 859-1119

Dynamic Metal Rendering
www.dmrgutters.com

Rain Trade Corporation
www.guttersupply.com
(888) 909-RAIN

WOODEN GUTTERS

Blue Ox Millworks
www.blueoxmill.com
(800) 248-4259

Mad River Woodworks
www.madriverwoodworks.com
(707) 668-5671

WOODEN EAVES

Ryan Wholesale, Inc.
www.ryanwholesale.com
(800) 799-3237

Hull Historical Millwork
www.hullhistorical.com
(817) 332-1495

McCoy Millwork
www.mccoymillwork.com
(888) 236- 0995

Windsor One
www.windsorone.com
(707) 838-7101

A Crown Specialty Moldings
www.crownspecialty
moldings.com
(608) 751-2040

Windfall Lumber
www.windfalllumber.com
(360) 352-2250

San Francisco Victoriana
www.sfvictoriana.com
(415) 648-0313

NON-WOODEN GUTTERS

Amvic, Inc.
www.amvicsystem.com
(877) 470-9991

Burton Mouldings
www.burton-mouldings.com
(888) 323-8926

Architectural Ornament
www.architectural-ornament.com
(800) 567-3554

Fypon, Ltd.
www.fypon.com
(800) 955-5748

Hennis Enterprises
www.hennisenterprises.com
(888) 643-2879

Melton Classics, Inc.
www.meltonclassics.com
(800) 963-3060

Profile Mouldings, Ltd.
www.profilemouldings.com
(888) 882-0641

ANTI-PIGEON DEVICES

Nixalite
www.nixalite.com
(888) 624-1189

Bird-X
www.birdx.com
(800) 662-5021

Bird Guard
www.birdguard.com
(800) 331-2973

Pigeon Control Advisory Services
www.picasusa.org
(715) 747-2626

CHAPTER FOUR

THE ENVELOPE PLEASE

"In early days, when people were content to live natural lives, and before the ruthless destruction of forests had reached its present stage, houses were built as they should be (substantial, well put together, and lasting). Conditions of today, however, preclude such construction."

— *Frank D. Graham, in* Audel's Carpenters and Builder's Guide #3, 1923

SIDE SHOW

Mr. Graham might have written those same words today, though in fact he was lamenting the demise of timber framing, which used seriously big pieces of wood held together by mortise-and-tenon joints and pegs, and its replacement with balloon and platform framing, which utilized smaller and lighter pieces of wood. And he'd barely seen the beginning of "ruthless destruction of forests."

STUD SERVICE

Balloon framing was adopted in the nineteenth century and involves continuous wall studs (upright framing members) that go from foundation to roof. In platform framing (sometimes called Western framing), the walls begin and end on each floor: after the first-floor walls are built, the floor of the next level is built on top, then the walls for that floor are built. This is the type of wood framing mostly used in bungalows and typically used today, because it is easier to build

and uses shorter pieces of wood. The wall studs were covered first with *sheathing,* 1- by 6-inch boards laid horizontally or diagonally to stiffen the frame. The sheathing was covered with building paper (asphalt-saturated felt), then some kind of siding was applied.

And I may have to hit the next person that says to me (usually in the context of why bungalows are not worth saving) that they were "cheaply and badly built." Compared to tract home building practices in the last fifty years, bungalows are incredibly well built, even the smallest of them utilizing old-growth lumber where the two-by-fours were actually two-by-four inches, not one-and-a-half by three-and-a-half. The old-growth lumber alone makes them worth saving, not to mention their other charms.

Obviously a bungalow has to have walls, otherwise it would be a gazebo. Different building materials were used for walls, often depending on the region of the country, locally available materials, and the skill set of the local workers. Often the prevalent building construction method had much to do with local immigrant groups and what was

OPPOSITE: Several different varieties of concrete block make up the façade of a Denver home. Rough-faced ashlar blocks are used for the pillars, while more regular blocks with chamfered (diagonally cut) edges are used for the walls and porch foundation. Above the porch roof (note that there is no way to actually get up there except for a ladder) a row of stepped corbel blocks form a decorative band around the building.

customary in their home country. So if there were a lot of people who knew how to do masonry, it's more likely there will be a lot of masonry. In areas where wood was plentiful, wood frame construction was common, although it was also pervasive thanks to kit houses. In areas with plentiful clay deposits and brick kilns nearby, brick walls were popular. Other structural wall materials included stone, concrete, concrete block, hollow clay tile, and logs.

The usual practice for a wood-framed bungalow would be two-by-four walls with wood sheathing on the outside, covered with some kind of siding, and either plaster or wood-paneled walls on the inside. Occasionally there would be no studs; instead the outside walls would consist of vertical boards side by side, the seams between them covered with smaller boards. This is known as *board-and-batten* construction, although board-and-batten was also used over sheathing. Often this sort of construction was used for vacation bungalows that would only be used in the summer, or for outbuildings. This doesn't present a problem unless you want to live there year-round or want to run electrical wiring, then it becomes a challenge.

Walls weren't always straight, either. I am refraining from making the obvious joke here. Some of them were *battered* (slanted and wider at the bottom). Sometimes the upper walls overhung the lower ones. Sometimes they were curved.

LEFT: The magazine *American Homes and Gardens* featured this interesting bungalow in a 1907 issue. It was built at Deal, New Jersey, a town on the Jersey shore. According to the article, it was designed by William G. Massarene and built from the refuse left after the construction of sixteen other cottages and was said to "imitate a Mexican hut." The lower floor is covered with vertical logs which still retain their bark, applied over sheathing and building paper, and the upper floor is sided with shingles. "Funky" doesn't even begin to cover it as a description of the architecture. The town of Deal as a whole was probably a lot funkier in 1907, but since then, starting in the 1920s, it became quite the coastal getaway for the wealthy, and now is home to numerous impressive houses on large lots.

BELOW: A bungalow pictured in the December 1915 *American Carpenter and Builder* sits on a high stone foundation, which, according to the copy, allowed for the installation of a heating plant in the basement, something necessary if it was to be built in a colder climate than the bungalow's original warm climate origins. The chimney is also stone, and massive corbels hold up the cross beam of the front porch.

LOG OFF

Log walls were used on some bungalows. Traditionally the ends of the logs were notched and the spaces in between filled with *chinking,* although in some kinds of log buildings the logs are squared-off, or scribed, so they fit together and eliminate the need for chinking. Originally clay or mud was used for chinking, later replaced by mortar, and in current practice, replaced with various acrylic-based compounds. The logs in a log wall could be either horizontal or vertical, and sometimes combinations of both were used. Logs were popular enough that it was also possible to purchase log siding, made from logs cut in half lengthwise, which could be attached to a regular wood-frame building.

Log building is an art unto itself, as is the restoration of log buildings, and would require a whole book of its own (and indeed, there are many books available on the subject).

THICK AS A BRICK

Brick is also a common bungalow wall material. Commonly two or three *wythes* wide (a wythe is a layer one brick thick),

the inner wythes were constructed of softer brick since it would not be exposed to the weather, while the outer layer used harder bricks. On some bungalows, the front façade featured more expensive *face brick,* while the sides and back used *common brick,* which was less expensive. An expensive bungalow would use face brick on all sides. Brick or stone construction was often mandated in cities where there had been huge fires, like Chicago. Unfortunately, it was also used in cities where earthquakes are common, like San Francisco. Since the only thing holding a brick wall together is gravity and mortar, a brick building will collapse in an earthquake as if it were made out of stacked Pez candies.

Bricks were traditionally made from clay. The clay was formed in wooden molds, allowed to dry, then removed from the molds and baked in wood-fired kilns. Brick kilns were built like tunnels, with the fire at one end. The bricks closest to the fire were burnt, partially vitrifying (turning into glass), and became bent and misshapen. Up until the time of the Arts and Crafts Movement, these bricks were just thrown away (kind of like you always have to throw out the first pancake), so there ended up being a big pile of them out behind the brickyard. They were called *clinker bricks* because of the

The log walls of this Milwaukee bungalow include an interesting (and apparently structural) log canopy over a set of arched windows, which mirror the shape of the roofline above. On the left, one of the original wooden windows has unfortunately been replaced with an inappropriate metal window, and the white trim is a jarring contrast with the dark logs.

sound they made when they landed on the pile. Because they were considered useless, they were cheap or free. Bungalow designers adopted them partly for that reason, but also because they had interesting shapes and colors, ranging from red to purple and brown. And a whole wall or column built out of them had a wonderful texture. Of course, once clinker bricks became popular, then brick manufacturers went to great lengths to produce them on purpose.

The bricks that were a little further from the fire also got quite hard, as the outside surfaces of those also vitrified, and these were used primarily as face brick or for pavers. The bricks furthest away from the fire were softer and used for side walls or for layers of the wall that were not exposed to the elements.

Many bricks today are made from concrete, which doesn't look the same at all, but clay bricks are still widely available.

BRICKS AND MORTAR

OBSESSIVE RESTORATION

The mortar commonly gives out before the bricks, *as it's supposed to,* leading to a need for *re-pointing* (removing part of the old mortar and replacing it with new). Old mortar was softer than modern portland cement–based mortars, the idea being that if there was movement in the wall it would be taken up by cracking the mortar rather than the more valuable bricks. Thus, it's important that soft lime-based mortar be used for re-pointing, otherwise the bricks can be damaged. The color of the mortar and the style of the joints should also be matched. For instance, clinker bricks, because of their unevenness, usually had deeply set joints and dark mortar.

Chipped glaze on glazed bricks will have to be touched up with paint, unless you are prepared to remove the brick entirely from the wall, figure out the components in the glaze (no small task), then reglaze it and put it back in the wall. Even I am not that obsessive.

Often bricks have been painted, either because people are morons, or because they actually had a good excuse like needing to cover a repair or addition built with bricks that didn't match. Getting paint off bricks, while it can be done, is a huge pain in the neck. Removing paint from smooth bricks isn't too bad, but getting it off rough or wire-cut bricks is very difficult.

COMPROMISE SOLUTION

You still have to use soft mortar—hard mortar *will* destroy the bricks. I guess the compromise is that if you remove mortar from *all* the joints, you can re-point with a different color.

BOND, JAMES BOND

Brick sizes are standardized and have been for centuries, at 4 by 4 by 8 inches. (Except for *Roman brick,* a favorite of Frank Lloyd Wright, which measures 4 by 2 by 12 inches.) Even clinker bricks started out being that size before they warped and swelled from the fire. There are many colors and textures of brick and many ways of laying them, called *bond.* Familiar to most people is *running bond,* where the joints in each row are staggered by half a brick. *Flemish bond* features one brick turned on end every other brick. *English bond* was played by Sean Connery. Use of multicolored brick in patterns was called *tapestry brick.* Brick could also be laid unevenly and randomly, known as *eccentric brickwork.* In bungalows, brickwork was sometimes combined with river rocks to form what is generally referred to as *peanut brittle* because of its lumpy appearance. This was a particularly common practice in southern California. Occasionally some use was made of *glazed bricks,* which are just what they sound like—bricks that have been fired, then glazed and fired like pottery.

An inset of diagonally laid, terra-cotta-colored textured brick is set into a field of lighter colored spotted bricks under a window on a Chicago bungalow.

Red bricks on a Denver bungalow were scratched by hand in random patterns before being fired, making each brick different and giving an interesting texture to the wall.

Another wall in Denver is built of misshapen clinker bricks laid up in a random pattern often known as "eccentric brickwork."

These bricks have been wire cut with vertical lines, then textured on top of the lines. Cities that had seen devastating fires, like Denver, where these are located, and Chicago, often rebuilt with brick. Additionally, Denver was home to numerous Italian emigrants, many of whom were skilled masons.

Another interesting texture decorates the face of these bricks in Chicago, which range in color from gold to burgundy to green.

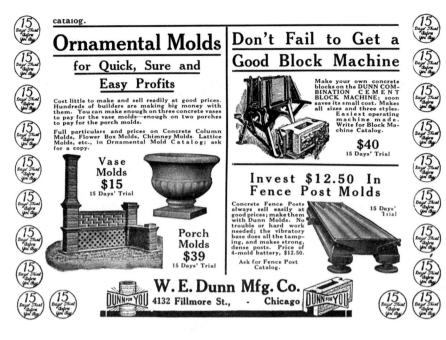

ABOVE: The W. E. Dunn Manufacturing Company showed the many items that could be made with their concrete block machine in their ad in the June 1915 *American Carpenter and Builder*. Besides the basic blocks, special porch molds, fence post molds, and vase molds were available on a fifteen day free trial. The porch and vase molds must have been popular, because thousands of bungalows and other house styles have porch railings and planters that look exactly like these.

BELOW: The Hobbs Concrete Machinery Company also had a free trial, but their claim was that theirs was the only machine that produced "natural" broken ashlar. Interestingly enough, this claim is still being made by the producers of "cultured stone"—only theirs is made with molds "taken from actual stones."

Make No Mistake!

If You Want the BEST You Must Buy the HOBBS

It is the one Block Machine that produces a **natural** rock face because of the Hobbs Composition Face Plates—the only Block Machine which makes **real** Broken Ashlar (see picture).

We ship on trial and absolutely guarantee these advantages—also the following:

The wettest block because of the oval cores and drawing device.

The greatest speed due to the simple design, the quick changes and the **automatic dividing plates.**

"Greater capacity"
"Wetter mixture"
"Wider range"
"Much finer, stronger block"

Every claim proved by free trial

Adjustable to over 2,000 sizes and adjustments simple as A, B, C.

The best made and finished piece of concrete machinery you ever saw.

Make no mistake! Positively no other Block Machine can produce such results or make you money like the Hobbs.

Send today for a Hobbs catalogue and get started and get started right.

Hobbs Concrete Machinery Co.
724 Peter Smith Bldg. :: DETROIT, MICH.

STONE FACE

Stone walls, while less common than wood or brick, did make an appearance in some bungalows. Irregular walls of fieldstone, river rock, or rubble stone had the natural look prized by bungalow designers, and a wall of *split-face ashlar* (rectangular-cut stone with an irregular face), though a bit more formal, still fit the parameters.

MUDSLINGING

In some areas, primarily the southwestern United States, adobe bricks were used as a wall material. Traditionally composed of straw and mud (clay), adobe bricks were made by hand in wooden molds, then dried in the sun. Adobe bricks are larger than regular bricks, measuring 4 by 10 by 16 inches. Because adobe bricks are not fired, they are not very impervious to water, so as a rule, adobe buildings are plastered or stuccoed on the exterior. They are customarily built in places where it doesn't rain much. Still, in the southwestern U.S., adobe is so much a part of the architecture that one can actually purchase FAKE adobe siding, made of portland cement and vermiculite and cast in molds taken from actual adobe bricks.

CONCRETE EVIDENCE

During the first decades of the twentieth century, advances in concrete manufacturing and the development of concrete block-forming machines resulted in widespread use of ornamental concrete block in residential buildings. Concrete and concrete block were touted as fireproof and were much less expensive than stone or brick. Henry Chapman Mercer, a major proponent of the Arts and Crafts Movement and founder of the Moravian Pottery and Tile Works, built his home, Fonthill, out of concrete. The Lanterman House in La Cañada-Flintridge, California, is a 1911 bungalow constructed of reinforced concrete. Concrete block machines could be acquired through mail-order catalogs and were easily operated by one person, allowing a homeowner to produce building materials for his own house, though it was more likely that the machines were used by contractors than by homeowners. Unlike the utilitarian concrete blocks of today, these machines produced blocks that resembled rough stone, cobblestone, ashlar, or brick. The stone face block was so popular that it came to be the standard mold that came with the block-making machine. The blocks could be beveled or tooled on the edges, and molds for capitals, porch columns, corner blocks, and curved blocks were also available. Initially the block sizes were different depending on the machine, but by the 1920s, the size had been standardized to 8 by 8 by 16 inches. Concrete block was especially popular for foundations and porches. It was also popular for garages, especially in jurisdictions where wood-frame garages were not allowed because of the fear of fire.

Concrete blocks were heavy, so various materials were tried as aggregate to make them lighter in weight. One of the first of these was cinder block, patented in 1917, and now pretty much the generic name for concrete blocks. By the 1930s, the ornamental faces had been abandoned for the plain blocks that bore us today.

HOLLOW, MY NAME IS...

Hollow clay tile was also advertised as fireproof, decay-proof, and long-lasting. An ad for the Dickey Mastertile Company in 1922 boasted, "A Dickey Mastertile home will last for generations without weakening and practically without care. Upkeep and repair bills are practically unknown, and resurfacing and exterior painting are unnecessary." This may have been a slight exaggeration, given that hollow tile buildings were usually covered with stucco.

SYMPATHY FOR THE BEVEL

(All together now—woo, woo!)

Some wall materials formed both the wall and the finished surface of the wall (like brick, stone, and logs), but wood-frame buildings needed some kind of siding.

Wood siding or *weatherboarding* could involve either boards or shingles, as well as weirder things like half-logs or bark. The most common siding types are *bevel siding* (boards sawn with one edge thicker than the other), *drop siding* (a patterned upper edge with a lapped or grooved lower edge), and *vertical siding* (square edge boards applied with

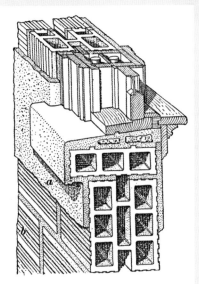

The 1918 Cyclopedia of *Architecture, Carpentry, and Building* contained this drawing showing wall and window construction using hollow clay tile. The ridges in the blocks help the stucco to adhere more firmly.

The National Fireproofing Company touted their tile as fireproof, damp-proof, and sound-proof, which was probably true. Their claim that it was "the safest from every standpoint of investment as well as occupancy" turned out not to be true, at least in earthquake-prone areas. Hollow clay tile has a tendency to break into shards during an earthquake, which tends to cause the building to collapse.

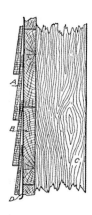

Methods of laying clapboard siding (on the left) and bevel siding (on the right) are shown in a drawing in *American Carpenter and Builder*. The clapboards leave a slight gap behind, while the bevel siding has a rabbet (notch) that fits snugly over the board below.

A shingled bungalow shown in *American Carpenter and Builder* in 1915 uses shingles which are all the same width, laid in a pattern of alternating wide and narrow exposures, which gives a horizontal striped effect. A half-inch space is left between each shingle.

battens over the joints, or tongue-and-groove boards, which could also be applied horizontally). Then it gets more complicated: bevel siding may also have a patterned upper edge and a lapped lower edge, drop siding may be beveled, and any of them may have extra grooves, beads (a decorative groove) or other molded features, and drop siding may also be tongue-and-groove. Add to that the regional nomenclature (Dutch lap, German lap, shiplap, V-rustic, novelty siding, channel siding, bungalow siding, log siding, Anzac bevel, Dolly Varden, clapboard, cottage siding, car siding, etc.) and the confusion is complete. Wood siding was usually smooth-sawn. The kinds of wood that were commonly used for siding included redwood, cedar, fir, pine, cypress, and other softwoods.

Shingles, on the other hand, are not very complex. There are only shingles and shakes (thicker than shingles), and shakes usually weren't used on walls. It's true that the ends of the shingles can be cut into fancy patterns, but most fancy patterns in shingles are the result of how they are applied. Sidewall shingles may be as long as three feet but usually not wider than twelve inches, to prevent cupping. Shingles could be applied in many different patterns. Each row of shingles is called a *course*. Common patterns on bungalows included *double-coursing* (each row of shingles is two shingles thick,

which gives a deeper shadow line), alternating wide and narrow shingle exposures, or dropping the butt of every other shingle down an inch or two for a crenellated look. On top of that, there were all kinds of original designs made up by individual shinglers. *Fancy butt* shingles, with the butt ends cut into shapes like hexagon, diamond, octagon, diagonal, half-cove, arrow, round, and fish scale, were occasionally added as accents but not to the extent they might be found on Victorian houses. Shingles were usually plain but sometimes might have decorative grooves cut into them.

BARKING UP THE WRONG TREE

For a really rustic look, tree bark could be applied to walls in much the same way as shingles, and the lumber mill would usually give it to you for free. The bark might also be left on logs used in log building.

PLASTER THAN A SPEEDING BULLET

Historically, stucco referred to interior ornamental plasterwork, but since the nineteenth century, the term has been used in the U.S. to include exterior plastering, also called *render* or *rendering*. Before the mid-nineteenth century,

Bevel siding in a pattern of varying exposures was used on the Gould House in Ventura, California, designed by architect Henry Greene after his brother and partner, Charles, had left Pasadena for Carmel.

stucco consisted of hydrated lime, sand, and water, with animal hair or straw as a binder. With the introduction of portland cement, lime was gradually phased out except in the finish coat. Most stucco found on bungalows is the portland cement variety, which was more prevalent after 1900, but lime-based stucco was still being used then—much depended on the individual plasterer. Modern stucco uses gypsum (calcium sulfate) instead of lime because it shrinks less and hardens faster. Stucco mixes were dependent on local materials and customs, and might contain mud or clay, brick dust, marble dust, or mineral pigments for color.

Stucco can be applied directly to masonry walls like brick, stone, concrete, or hollow clay tile, but a wood-frame house required some sort of lath, either wood or metal. The idea of lath is that the stucco oozes through the spaces between the lath and then hardens (called *keying*), which attaches it to the house. Building paper was applied to the sheathing, furring strips (narrow pieces of wood) were applied on top, and the lath (either wood strips or metal mesh) on top of that. Furring it out left a space for the stucco to ooze into. Stucco is applied in three coats: the first coat is called the *scratch coat,* because when it is partially dry

it is scored to provide something for the second coat, called the *brown coat,* to hold on to. The brown coat may also be scored to provide tooth for the finish coat. The first two coats are smooth, but the finish coat is where the creativity starts. Stucco is usually gray. The finish coat may be tinted with brick dust or various mineral pigments for color. Various aggregates were also added to the finish coats, such as sand, crushed granite, colored pebbles, marble, sandstone, quartz, or gravel. But the real art of stucco is in the texture of the finish coat. There are probably as many textures as there are plasterers, and even two plasterers doing the same texture would come up with different results. Some of the more common stucco textures include *smooth-troweled; stippled,* in which a smooth-troweled finish is stippled using a broom; *sand-floated,* involving a smooth-troweled surface which has sand sprinkled on it while it is still wet, then the surface is gone over with a wood float in a circular motion; *sand-sprayed,* where the surface is dashed with a creamy mixture of portland cement and sand using a whisk broom; and *spatter-dash,* in which fairly wet stucco is spattered on the wall using a whisk broom or fiber brush. A very bumpy version of this texture is also known as *harling, rough-cast,* or *wet-dash.* Sometimes small pebbles or crushed stone were mixed in with the stucco. *Pebble-dash* or *dry-dash,* which is accomplished by having one plasterer throw dry pebbles or stones (about $1/8$ to $1/4$ inch diameter) at a coat of wet stucco applied by another plasterer. The stones are thrown with a scoop and have to have enough velocity to stick to the plaster. Sometimes the surface is then smoothed with a wooden float to embed the stones a little further. *Shell-stone* is a variation in which seashells are used instead of stones. Other textures could be made using various tools including brooms, rags, burlap bags, and such. Then there are textures that were made up by individual plasterers and are unlike the stan-

Pebble-dash stucco enhances the front gable of a Denver bungalow, accompanied by half-timbering, simple square corbel blocks, and twin two-by-six ridge beams.

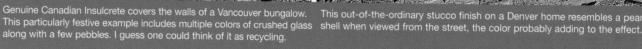

Genuine Canadian Insulcrete covers the walls of a Vancouver bungalow. This particularly festive example includes multiple colors of crushed glass along with a few pebbles. I guess one could think of it as recycling.

This out-of-the-ordinary stucco finish on a Denver home resembles a peanut shell when viewed from the street, the color probably adding to the effect.

dard textures. Unfortunately, the artistry involved in the finish coat makes it difficult to match textures when patching or repairing stucco. Pebble dash is particularly difficult to match, since matching pebbles have to be procured. This is not an excuse to paint over stucco that hasn't previously been painted.

Stucco can be made to take any shape depending on the structure underneath, and bungalow builders used that to their advantage. There is no end to the imaginative shapes that builders could make using stucco. It could be made to mimic stonework or brick; it could be molded for decorative accents. It could be formed into simple or elaborate arches, sometimes with stucco "keystones." Stucco could make even a small bungalow look substantial. It was and is an inexpensive and long-lasting siding.

Often stucco was not painted, being left in its natural color or with a tinted finish coat. But later bungalows, especially those from the 1910s and '20s, had painted stucco. And of course, many bungalows that started out unpainted didn't stay that way.

Contrary to popular belief, stucco is not waterproof. The idea is that any moisture that gets behind the stucco will be stopped by the building felt. It's important to give the water a place to get out, so modern stucco is installed with a *weep screed* at the bottom of the wall, and the stucco stops a few inches above the ground. Old stucco was usually run right down to the ground and often didn't have a way for the water to get out. This can sometimes lead to rotting and decay of the wood studs and sheathing behind the stucco. The rot isn't obvious, as it might be

with wood siding, because it's hidden by the stucco. I've seen a few houses where the walls were mostly being held up by the stucco itself, the framing having rotted away.

LET US SPRAY

Related to stucco, though not seen often on bungalows, is a spray-on cementitious product called *shotcrete* or *gunite*. It was more often used for swimming pools. Another cement-based siding product is *Insulcrete*. When I first saw this product in Canada, it looked like a variant of pebble-dash with some kind of shiny pebbles in it. But no, it was explained to me in the sort of horrified tones that preservationists usually reserve for aluminum siding, Insulcrete was retrofitted onto numerous Canadian homes with the encouragement of the government. The shiny pebbles were, in fact, crushed beer bottles. There were two basic colors: gray with green beer bottles and pinkish with brown beer bottles. I guess you have to admire the recycling aspect.

Another kind of stucco was not a cementitious product at all—it was made from *magnesite* (magnesium carbonate, asbestos, sand, and sometimes wood fiber mixed with magnesium chloride solution instead of water). This allowed it to be applied even during freezing weather. It was applied in two coats instead of the usual three. A similar mixture was used for flooring and decking. One product was even called San-A-Bestos (a combination of sanitary and asbestos). Other well-known brands included Kellastone, Elastica, Kragstone, Magnesite, and Rocbond. Except for the asbestos, this substance wouldn't really be a problem. Given that asbestos *is* a problem, you might want to get your stucco tested for asbestos before you cut any holes in it (say, to install insulation or repair rot in the sheathing behind it). Contractors are unlikely to take asbestos into consideration, because most of them don't realize that asbestos was ever used in stucco—it was before their time, and most contractors who aren't specifically restoration contractors are unaware of magnesite stucco.

FOAM AT THE MOUTH

But real stucco wasn't good enough for some people. EIFS, which stands for Exterior Insulation and Finishing System, was introduced shortly after World War II in Europe. Manufacturers sort of had an excuse—they were looking for ways to rebuild quickly after the war, and EIFS was used for commercial buildings, which were generally framed with either steel or concrete. EIFS consists of expanded polystyrene foam (EPS) covered with spray-on acrylic stucco. It began to be used on residential buildings in the 1980s, but it hadn't occurred to anyone that attaching a water-impervious cladding to a wood-frame building was going to result in rot and mold when water vapor began to condense behind the foam. Naturally, that was what happened; lawsuits followed and are continuing.

Random rough-faced stonework with concave mortar joints makes up the porch foundation of a bungalow in Memphis, Tennessee.

SAN-A-BESTOS STUCCO

Gives Your Buildings a Pleasing Distinctive Effect

San-A-Bestos Stucco has an individuality all of its own. It lends itself to the most artistic and pleasing finishes—finishes that are permanent, soiling of course with time, but that can be cleaned so as to look like new again.

San-A-Bestos possesses great tensile strength and is not affected by climatic conditions. It possesses flexibility that gives with settling or other disturbances, making cracking improbable. It is fire-proof and damp-proof. Give your customers better and more permanent finished buildings, it costs no more and helps you.

Responsible, Local Men Wanted

We also manufacture San-A-Bestos Composition Flooring, at a low cost. Flooring material the equal of tile, terrazzo or marble. Our catalogue of San-A-Bestos Building Products is sent Free to all Builders who write for it.

FRANKLIN R. MULLER COMPANY
Waukegan, Illinois

San-A-Bestos stucco is shown on a bungalow in a 1915 advertisement by the Franklin Muller Company. The advantage of magnesite stucco was that it could be applied even in below freezing weather. They were hedging a little in the ad, saying cracking was "improbable."

Most EIFS was used for new construction, but not all of it. I watched in horror as the new owners of an Oakland house—the one used as a model of a *brown shingle* (the local term for a two-story shingled house of the Arts and Crafts era) in the book *Rehab Right*—covered it with EIFS, complete with fake quoins (cornerstones). I did laugh when someone backed into their EIFS-covered garage and put a big dent in it.

Manufacturers of EIFS say they've fixed the water problems now. They haven't. Not to mention that you can pull off EIFS with your bare hands. I guess that's good if you need to remove it as I hope someone will someday from the poor Oakland house. (Of course they threw out the windows, too, and ruined the inside, but at least the next owners will have a picture to go by.)

BRICK-A-BRAC

Brick could also be used as a facing on a wood-framed or concrete block house, as this was cheaper than building the walls entirely with brick. The *brick veneer* was separated from the wood sheathing in a frame house by a layer of building paper and attached to the sheathing every so often with metal ties. This is still done today, often with thin slices of brick, facetiously known as *lick-a-brick*. Brick facing is definitely a better idea in earthquake country. You are *not*, I repeat, *not*, allowed to use commercially-made "used" brick for this purpose.

VENEER REAL DISEASE

Stone was also used as facing in much the same way as brick. Sometimes it would go only part way up the wall in a random manner, making the bungalow look like it had grown out of the ground, or it could be applied to the entire wall to make the house look as if it was actually built of stone. So much for honesty of structure.

BAD FORM

American ingenuity being what it is, of course someone would invent a substitute for stone siding, commonly known by the trade names Permastone and Formstone. Permastone was first produced in 1929, followed by Formstone in 1937. There were other competitors as well. The products were produced on-site by local dealers and contractors, using proprietary molds and mixes (portland cement, aggregates, mineral colors, and additives) provided by the manufacturers. One exception was Rostone, which was produced in modular panels off-site using a process whereby pressurized shale, lime, and water were combined and put into molds and then subjected to heat, starting a chemical reaction that caused the mixture to harden.

Permastone and Formstone were applied directly to the building in a three-coat process similar to stucco. For Permastone, once the second (brown) coat had been applied, the finish coat was immediately applied, using molds to simulate natural-stone. Formstone was a little more labor-intensive: once the brown and finish coats were applied, waxed paper was applied to the wall, then textured rollers were run over the wall, possibly more than one size or texture. Then the wax paper was removed, and mortar "joints" were cut with a special tool. The resulting groove was either left empty or later pointed with mortar. The surface could be further treated with mica, pigments, stone dust, or mineral chips embedded in the surface. Formstone was marketed as a product to refurbish or modernize existing buildings, whereas Permastone was advertised both for retrofitting and for new construction. Baltimore, Maryland, home to a large number of buildings made of extremely soft local brick, is not only the place where Formstone was invented, it is also the Formstone capital of the world.

As with other fake sidings, these were promoted as "maintenance free" and "long lasting," and with suggestions that applying it would "make your home the neighborhood showplace." Not.

A favored look for simulated masonry was multicolored sandstone, rarely found in real stone buildings. Film director John Waters, a Baltimore native, calls Formstone "the polyester of brick."

Unlike some of the other faux sidings, at least faux stone is kind of amusing. It's been around long enough to be considered historic in its own right. Faux stone is still around. It's gotten a little more realistic with improvements in technology, and now it's called *cultured stone*. It's very popular on "Craftsman" tract houses these days—you know, the ones where they think putting three knee braces in the gable and a couple of fake stone piers on the front porch makes it Craftsman. Geez, people, get some real rocks! Rocks are still plentiful, last I heard.

CEMENT THE DEAL

Another kind of fake siding was asbestos-cement shingles. One of the first supposedly "no-maintenance" sidings, asbestos shingles were often installed over wood siding. Concerns about fire were another reason for their use—after the big 1923 fire in Berkeley, California, hundreds of houses were retrofitted with asbestos shingles. Asbestos shingles were usually embossed with a grooved pattern imitating weathered shingles. The bottom edges were sometimes cut in a wavy pattern. They were installed with an 8- or 10-inch exposure and were all the same 12-inch width, so they didn't really resemble wood shingles very much.

Asbestos-cement clapboards were also manufactured but were not as popular as the shingles. Asbestos siding was sold by "blue suede shoe boys," similar to the more famous "tin men" who sold aluminum siding by means of the exaggerated claims and deceptive sales practices that are still widely used today to sell substitute siding materials.

Asbestos has been replaced by wood fiber in the new generation of cement sidings. Some of these look pretty decent when painted, but the jury is still out on their longevity, because they haven't been around long enough.

Asbestos siding can be removed (carefully, so as not to break it and release fibers) and sent to special landfills. It might be better to hire an abatement company than to do it yourself, although in many jurisdictions owners are allowed to do it themselves. If you do it yourself, get instructions from the local hazardous waste collection agency about the proper way to do it. Mostly this involves getting it wet, so the fibers don't float into the air. Wear a respirator that is rated for asbestos, not just a nuisance dust mask (those are pretty much useless even for nuisance dust). Don't be cavalier about the whole thing—even if you are wearing a respirator, people passing by are not.

WHITE (TRASH) SIDEWALLS

But the most low-rent siding around was asphalt shingles. I'm sure that someone reasoned that if they held up on the roof, you could put them on the side walls, or maybe someone just had some extras laying around. At first they were used in the gable ends of the house. Manufacturers started marketing hexagonal and rectangular asphalt shingles for siding purposes in 1929. In 1931, both Johns-Manville and Certainteed offered a strip shingle with a 2 1/2-inch exposure and a 9-inch tab in an imitation brick pattern complete with mortar. But it became popular enough that manufacturers started to produce specialty shingles for use as siding and even experimented with bonding the asphalt product to fiberboard, so that they could hype the insulation value. Usually asphalt siding was made to resemble bricks, but the fiberboard product was sometimes made to resemble stone. Like the other fake products, asphalt siding was often layered on top of wood siding. It's so trashy that I actually have a certain fondness for it.

ALUMINUM WAGE

Until vinyl siding came along, possibly no kind of fake siding was hated more by preservationists than aluminum siding. *The Old House Journal* even coined the term "alumicide" to describe the act of covering a historic structure with aluminum siding.

Aluminum itself is innocent enough. One of the most abundant metallic elements on Earth, it occurs naturally as alum but isn't found in a natural metallic state. It wasn't until 1886 that a process was discovered that could produce metallic aluminum in large quantities. Anodizing, an electrochemical coating process developed in the early 1920s, allowed color to be applied to aluminum and also made it resistant to corrosion.

Aluminum could be cast, extruded, or made into sheets. It was also alloyed with other metals. It was prized for its pale, silver color and light weight, and buildings of the Art Deco or Moderne period made particularly good use of its qualities.

Clapboard siding units of embossed steel or iron had been patented in 1903, and embossed steel siding in stone and brick patterns was offered by Sears in the 1920s. These tended to warp, until an Indiana machinist by the name of Frank Hoess created a interlocking joint in which a flap on the top of one panel joined with a U-shaped flange on the bottom of the previous panel. He patented the idea in 1939.

Initially aluminum siding was offered unpainted—it would weather to a silvery-gray color, or it could be painted. In 1948, Jerome Kaufman of the Alside Corporation invented a baked-on enamel process of electrostatic spray painting followed by infrared baking. The success of prepainted siding caused other manufacturers to follow suit.

Large companies like Reynolds Aluminum and Kaiser Aluminum stopped producing siding in the 1950s and instead concentrated on providing sheet stock to smaller fabricators. By the mid-1950s, increasing competition between small producers brought about shady sales practices and scams. Since the postwar housing crisis had abated, aluminum siding companies turned their sights towards existing houses and remodeling. By 1961, three million homes had aluminum siding.

As a rule, aluminum siding was embossed, usually in a really fake-looking wood pattern featuring large whorls and exaggerated grain, although stippled, pebbled, and even basketweave textures were available. Fake clapboard is almost the be-all and end-all of aluminum siding profiles, most often with

A shingle pattern using different width shingles with an even exposure, though still with a half-inch space in between, was utilized by Charles and Henry Greene on the 1906 Bolton House in Pasadena. Here it surrounds a narrow art-glass window designed by Charles.

an 8-inch or longer "exposure" rarely found on real clapboards. Imitations of various kinds of drop siding were also produced.

Take it off—aluminum is worth quite a bit at the recycling center.

VINYL CONFLICT

In 1926, Waldo Semon, a chemist at B. F. Goodrich, concocted a new kind of plastic called *polyvinyl chloride*. Although it didn't catch on immediately because of the Great Depression, by the time of World War II it had begun to be used as waterproofing and to replace rubber in some applications. The use of vinyl for siding didn't begin until the 1960s. Initially vinyl siding was quite flimsy and would break down after exposure to ultraviolet light. It would also become brittle in cold weather and would shatter on impact. New additives lessened these problems, though it didn't solve them, and vinyl began to surpass aluminum siding in popularity in the 1980s. As of 2002, over four billion square feet of vinyl siding had been

FAKE SIDING

OBSESSIVE RESTORATION

The biggest problem with any kind of fake siding applied to a historic building is that invariably the historic fabric of the building will be destroyed to apply it, or moisture trapped behind the new siding will cause the real siding behind it to decompose. Often siding was applied because of peeling paint, without dealing with the moisture problem that led to the peeling paint. After the siding is applied, the moisture is still there, but now it's trapped. Furring strips are nailed to wood siding, architectural details are hacked off or covered up, and masonry may be gouged or scored for the application of cement-based fake sidings. Until the fake siding is removed, there's no way of knowing how bad the damage might be. Remove it anyway. Then deal with the damage, whether that means replacing some of the siding, repairing it, rebuilding the details, or re-pointing the masonry.

COMPROMISE SOLUTION

Fiber-cement siding has improved in looks in recent years. It doesn't rot, but you still have to paint it.

installed in the United States. Yup, four billion square feet of really toxic siding, busily off-gassing vinyl chloride into the atmosphere, producing dioxins and hydrogen chloride when it burns, and polluting the groundwater when taken to the landfill.

Like aluminum, vinyl comes in fake clapboard and other wood siding patterns, with the same lovely fake wood grain embossed into the surface. (Haven't these people EVER figured out that most painted wood is SMOOTH?) You can even get, yes, fake vinyl log siding! But don't. Many of the same companies that produced aluminum siding jumped over to vinyl when it became more popular.

VENEER OF CIVILIZATION

The ancient Egyptians had already figured out that if thin pieces of wood veneer were glued in layers with the grain on each layer running perpendicular to the next, the result was something much stronger than the individual layers. But it wasn't until the Industrial Revolution that mass marketing of plywood began. The invention of a rotary cutting machine in 1890 allowed the veneers necessary to be mass-produced. Prototype plywood panels, made one at a time using animal glue, debuted in Portland, Oregon, in 1905. For many years, plywood veneers came from old-growth trees, making for really excellent plywood. As old-growth trees dwindled, plywood veneer began to be cut from

second-growth, faster-growing trees, leading to more knots and defects. In response to this, OSB (oriented strand board), which utilizes wood scraps, was developed in the 1970s and has taken much of the market share in sheathing, underlayment, and roof decking where plywood was traditionally used.

Eventually some idiot at a wood products company thought, "Hey, we could make some cheap siding out of this stuff and sell it to an unsuspecting public." So grooved plywood siding came to be. Usually referred to by the generic name "T-1-11," although that refers to only one of the grooved patterns available, the siding is a 4- by 8-foot sheet with a rough-sawn veneer layer interrupted by spaced grooves. Plywood is a useful product for many applications. Siding isn't one of them. There really is NO style of architecture that plywood siding is appropriate for—even a nasty house from the 1970s would be better with some other kind of siding.

Plywood siding has replaced asphalt shingles as the low-rent siding of choice. Personally, I think asphalt shingles are more attractive. The good news about plywood siding is it works fine as sheathing, so often it can just be covered up with something better.

Another product invented in the early twentieth century was hardboard, invented by William H. Mason in 1924, and often called masonite after the inventor. Hardboard consists of small bundles of wood fiber bound together with resins and wax, then compressed under high heat and pressure. The most familiar use of hardboard is the ubiquitous perforated variety, pegboard.

Hardboard siding was first introduced in 1963. Siding made from OSB was introduced in the 1980s. Shortly after, reports that both kinds of siding were prone to warp, buckle, swell, or rot when exposed to moisture began to appear. Lawsuits followed in the 1990s and continue today.

And there's a problem with fake siding that no one ever mentions: vermin can take up residence behind it! Depending on how much room is behind the siding, the vermin can range from mice to termites to cockroaches; as well as the usual toxic mold, fungus, and such. This isn't just icky (though it is)—it can also make you and your family ill.

HOUSE BLEND

While many bungalows had only one kind of siding, different kinds of siding could be combined on one house, and the combinations were limited only by the imagination of the architect or builder. Shingles on the bottom, stucco on the top, or vice versa; clapboard on the bottom, shingles on the top, or the opposite; three different patterns of drop siding, three different patterns of shingling, brick and stucco, stone and stucco, clapboards and stucco, bevel siding and brick, board and batten with shingles—you get the idea. Or the

Logs below and shingles above constitute the siding on Gustav Stickley's home at Craftsman Farms in New Jersey. The diamond-pane windows were originally painted white, but that doesn't mean you should do that on your house. Stickley wasn't right about everything, you know.

A 1915 bungalow featured in *American Carpenter and Builder* has a foundation of brick, then 10-inch clapboards up to windowsill level, with shingles above that. The window to the left of the front door opens into a small den with a window seat that is in a nook off the living room. The copy mentions that the window allows you to sit there with a good book and "if people come to see you whom you don't want to see, you can remain in hiding and they will think that nobody is home!" We think that people used to be more sociable than we are now, but even back then they valued their privacy.

PAINT REMOVAL

Paint removal is probably the most tedious of all restoration tasks, but it is often necessary. This will not be a primer on paint-stripping, just an overview. The choice of method boils down to hand-scraping, heat, or chemicals.

Hand-scraping can be used on siding that is smooth—obviously it won't work all that well on masonry. Scraping works well on peeling paint, and somewhat less well on paint that's holding on for dear life. Different shapes of scrapers are available to use on molding and such. Scraping produces lead dust, so keep everything wet and wear a respirator. *Do not use belt sanders or orbital sanders for paint removal; or those flappy wire wheels that fit on the drill.*

Heat methods include heat guns, heat plates, or infrared heaters. *Do not use blowtorches!* Even with heat guns or plates, there is danger of setting the house on fire, so make sure you have a fire extinguisher on hand. Heat methods cause the layers of paint to bubble up and release their hold on the substrate, at which point they can be scraped off. The upside of using heat is that it removes many layers at once. And once the layers cool off, they harden again so you don't end up with toxic goop like you do with chemical strippers (though it is still lead paint and suitable precautions should be taken). A high enough temperature can vaporize lead, but even at lower temperatures the fumes are toxic, so wear a respirator. Heat will take off most of the paint, but a chemical stripper will probably be required to get the last bits of paint off. Heat really only works on wood siding—masonry siding just absorbs the heat and the paint doesn't come off well.

Chemical methods involve (usually) toxic chemicals, and even the strippers advertised as non-toxic (like those based on citrus) are still strong chemicals, so wear chemical-resistant gloves. The really toxic chemicals, like methylene chloride, work faster than the citrus-based strippers, but they are poisonous. All the residue should be taken to your local hazardous waste collection point, not put in the regular trash. Basically you slap on the stripper in a thick coat, wait for the paint to bubble up, then either scrape if off (for wood siding) or scrub it off (for masonry). It will probably require several applications to strip off all the paint.

There are some proprietary products on the market, including *Peel-Away* and *Remov-All*. Peel-Away uses a method where you apply the stripper, then cover it with a special material and leave it on for a certain period of time before removing it. The paint and stripper ostensibly sticks to the material, so that when you peel it off, the paint comes with it. According to my friend Adam Janeiro, the trick with Peel-Away is to make several test patches,

A low brick bungalow with an unexpected Palladian-windowed dormer has unfortunately been painted green. It's not a bad color, but given that the original brick is fairly textured, it would be nearly impossible to strip the paint off, leaving a succession of owners stuck with painting it periodically. This bungalow is located in Memphis, and it's likely that the brick was originally some shade of red, as the majority of brick tends to be.

because there is a certain ideal amount of time (anywhere from twelve to twenty-four hours) to leave it on for maximum "peelage."

Remov-All is a product that breaks the bond between the paint and the substrate at the molecular level, supposedly causing the paint to just peel off in big sheets. It's supposedly non-toxic. It also costs about four times as much as regular paint stripper, which might be worth it if it really works.

house might have one kind of siding on the front and a different kind on the sides and back. Sometimes that was because the front siding cost more, as in the face brick on the front of some bungalows, but sometimes there was no cost difference, it was just what the builder wanted to do. If there was more than one kind of siding, the walls would often be divided in thirds, so there might be one kind of siding from the ground to the first-floor level, and a second kind from there up, with maybe a third kind in the gable ends. Or the division might be two-thirds/one-third instead, with the larger portion at the bottom.

STAIN ALIVE

As befitted the natural look aspired to by most bungalow designers, wood siding was usually stained rather than painted—this was especially true of shingles. Stain protected the wood from the elements somewhat and could also be used to add color. There were (and are) transparent, semi-transparent, and opaque stains. Transparent stains allow the grain of the wood to show through, while semi-transparent stains contain some pigment but still allow the grain to show somewhat. Opaque stains have more pigment and cover the grain but are still thinner than paint. Stains soak into the wood rather than forming a film on top as paint does, so repeated applications of stain do not build up the way paint layers do. Historic stains contained creosote as a wood preservative, which was usually combined with linseed oil, turpentine, and pigments.

While shingles were generally not painted, sometimes other kinds of wood siding were, commonly using flat rather than glossy paint. Earth tones like brown, green, ochre, rust, brick red, or gold were favored. Paints were often mixed on-site by the painter, using pigments, linseed oil, and white or red lead. Ready-mixed paints began to be

available around 1860, but many painters continued to mix their own well into the 1920s.

In 1985 yet another horrifying invention was introduced—liquid vinyl siding. Oh yes, encase the entire house in a toxic film—there's a good idea.

Stucco was often left unpainted, although the finish coat could be tinted using pigments that were not affected by the lime. The pebble-dash varieties were not painted, since that would kind of be pointless. (Of course, later owners would paint it, apparently being unclear on the concept.) Some stucco was painted from day one, generally on bungalows built later (1920s and beyond) when the Arts and Crafts Movement was on the wane and there was less emphasis on the natural. Painted stucco bungalows

Stained with Cabot's Shingle Stains.
Hollingsworth & Bragdon, Arch'ts, Cranford, N. J.

Cost Much Less Than Paint
Wear Longer—More Artistic

"Your stains have proved most satisfactory. I have five lakeside cottages finished with them. My one painted cottage *costs me almost as much as all the rest* to keep fresh looking. My cottages are considered quite artistic."   *Joseph H. Scranton, Washington, N. J.*

Cabot's Creosote Stains

have *proved* their artistic effects and wearing and wood preserving qualities in every climate for thirty years. You are *sure* of them. Don't take substitutes made of kerosene and crude colors.

You can get Cabot's Stains everywhere.
Send for samples and name of nearest agent.

SAMUEL CABOT, Inc., Mfg. Chemists, Boston, Mass.

Cabot's Stucco Stains—for Cement Houses.

Another bungalow in New Jersey, this one designed by Hollingsworth and Bragdon, is shown in a 1918 advertisement for Cabot's creosote stains, used on its shingle siding. It's a classic side gable bungalow, with catslide roofs on front and back, a shed dormer, and large tapered wood porch columns. Cabot's is still in business and still makes similar colors of stain, though no longer with creosote.

Vertical redwood board-and-batten siding was used on this southern California bungalow. The vine-covered porch was originally open but was enclosed not long after the house was built.

LEAD ASTRAY

As with asbestos, lead is a useful product that makes for strong, long-lasting paint. Unfortunately, lead is also toxic and virtually indestructible (which is good in paint but bad in humans). At high levels, it can cause brain swelling, convulsions, coma, and even death. At low levels, it is associated with anemia and damage to the brain, nervous system, and kidneys, as well as causing vomiting, digestive problems, and bizarre behavior. It also poses a hazard to developing fetuses, and can affect the reproductive systems of both men and women. Because lead accumulates in bones and tissue, problems may persist over a long period of time. It is especially toxic to infants and toddlers, whose developing brains are particularly susceptible and who are more likely to eat flaking paint chips. The effects of long-term exposure in children are permanent. It's not good for adults either.

The lead companies had evidence of lead toxicity as early as the nineteenth century. By the 1920s, concerns about lead poisoning among professional painters caused one company to issue a paint in which the lead was replaced with zinc, though they continued to produce lead paint as well. Lead companies not only covered up the data, they continued to promote lead for painting children's rooms and toys, and as an additive for gasoline. Lead was not banned from paint in the U.S. until 1978, and was not phased out of gasoline until 1996. For comparison, lead paint was banned in France in 1917. Approximately six million tons of lead paint was applied to housing in the U.S. prior to the ban. There are approximately 10 million metric tons of lead in the environment—in the air, water, and soil.

Lead paint in good condition is not a hazard. It is when the paint peels, chips, cracks, or is sanded or otherwise abraded that it becomes a problem. Most hardware stores sell a simple lead test swab that turns pink in the presence of lead, although it's not always capable of detecting small amounts of lead. Your local city or county will happily provide you with lots of information concerning lead paint and what to do about it. Or not to do about it.

SANDBLASTING

Sandblasting (which includes blasting with glass beads, walnut shells, water-blasting, etc.) should NEVER, EVER be used for paint removal. Sandblasting brick removes the hard outer surface of brick, making it susceptible to water infiltration. It also damages the mortar joints. It abrades the softer spring wood on wood siding, leaving a fuzzy, uneven surface that will weather more quickly than intact wood. And it just removes stucco entirely. Even pressure-washing, which many paint contractors use as part of the prep work, can damage the wood. Even metal, unless it is heavy ironwork (sandblasting originated as a way to prepare heavy ironwork for painting), will be pitted and damaged by abrasive cleaning.

THAT DON'T NEED TO BE PAINTED! Paint is hard to remove, especially from brick, stone, or shingles, so don't paint them in the first place!

GABLE TV

Gable ends were frequently subject to decorative treatments such as *half-timbering,* originally a construction method involving timber-framed walls in which the spaces between the timbers are plastered or filled with stone or brick. On bungalows, in spite of the reverence for honesty of materials and structure within the Arts and Crafts Movement, half-timbering was invariably fake, merely wood embedded in stucco or masonry. Gable ends were also a prime location for decorative shingle, brick, or stonework patterns, interestingly shaped windows, inset porches, and decorative vents. They also provided an opportunity for creativity in the form of brackets, beam ends, moldings, *outriggers* (which are sort of like knee braces except they stick out farther), window boxes, balconies, railings, boards with decorative cutouts, and anything else that either the builder or the designer could think up.

VENT ELATION

Unlike most homes today, bungalows didn't employ soffit vents or ridge vents; rather, bungalow attics were traditionally vented through gable vents or dormers. Gable vents were often decorative, filled with different kinds of latticework or louvers. A window might be part of the system as well, flanked by vents, while allowing light into the attic. The vent frequently filled most of the peak of the gable, especially in warmer climates. Wire screening was installed behind the latticework to keep out insects, birds, and small dogs. As a rule, there would be a vent at both ends of the house, though not always.

were by and large done in fairly light colors.

Brick and stone were not painted, except by idiots. (Or sometimes to disguise the fact that repairs had been made, windows filled in, or additions put on with brick that didn't match, or it turned out that the local brick was too soft and didn't hold up well—this is about the ONLY excuse for painting brick.) Asbestos shingles were typically painted.

And this can't be said enough: DON'T PAINT THINGS

The openwork timbers of a New Jersey bunga-low's porch gable rest on curious triangular con-structions that top square pillars of local stone.

Highly textured, gold-painted stucco accents the porch gable and shed dormer of a Milwaukee bungalow. The colors of the trim and window sash harmonize with the textured bricks of the bay window on the right. The cutouts in the porch fascia are highlighted with an accent color.

Rough-cast stucco, half-timbering, dentil molding, and an inset porch adorn the gable of a bungalow in Vancouver, British Columbia. Half-timbering is common on Vancouver bungalows, as well as diamond-pane windows, owing to the British influence.

Bead board covered by rounded frames, two windows (unfortu-nately painted over) with a shelf beneath held up by stepped cor-bels, curved and notched knee braces, and notched corbels are the features of another Californian West Adams gable.

Sometimes the attic wasn't vented at all. These vents are not always adequate by modern standards. Rather than adding soffit vents in the eaves, which can be obtrusive, it may be better to install a ventilating fan in the roof. These may be electric, or there are solar-powered models available. There is some argument as to whether the primary purpose of attic ventilation is to remove heat in the summer, to remove moist air in the winter, or both.

WELL-PADDED

Fuel used to be cheap, so the majority of bungalows were built without insulation in the walls or the attic. Some kinds of siding provided a certain amount of insulating value by themselves—for instance, wood shingles have an R-value of about 1, as does wood siding. (R-value is basically a material's resistance to heat transfer from one side to the other.) Three-and-a-half inches of fiberglass measures R-11. Stucco, on the other hand, has an R-value of .20, only slightly above air at R-.17. Log walls are

A diagonal vent in the peak, two windows with a diamond-muntin pattern, and an up-and-down shingle pattern are the main features in the gable of a West Adams district bungalow in Los Angeles.

The entire gable of a Memphis bungalow has vertical cutouts that allow it to serve as an attic vent. Note the transoms above the tripartite window below.

1900

The gables tended to be the place where bungalow designers went a little crazy, as on this gable in Los Angeles' West Adams district. Tapered pilasters (half-columns applied to a wall) flank a window and two vents, a plethora of corbels, stucco and shingles, dentil molding, and a scalloped shelf. The pilasters are, of course, a completely different shape from the bulging columns below.

A different gable in the same West Adams neighborhood has the same diamond-pattern window, but now flanked by a sunrise effect with curved lattice vents and half-timbering, stucco and bevel siding, different corbels, more bevel siding beneath the corbels, and paired tapered columns below.

quite energy efficient, because though rated only R-10, logs have *thermal mass:* the ability to absorb, store, and slowly release heat over time as temperatures go down. Hollow clay tile was hyped for its insulating properties, though it has an R-value of about .54, not much better than asphalt shingles at .44. The thick walls of adobe are not R-rated, so to speak, but they have thermal mass as logs do. Bricks rate at .20 per inch, so a 4-inch-thick wall would equal 1, about the same as wood shingles. Different ways of constructing brick walls cause variations, and masonry of any kind has thermal mass as well. Various kinds of insulation were available at the time, and there were a few builders who took advantage of them. The really low-tech insulation method was to use layers of newspaper, which is always good for providing a clue as to when the house was built or remodeled. Cellulose insulation, which today is primarily made from recycled newspapers, was used at the time as loose-fill insulation, as it still is. Mineral wool or rock wool, an inorganic fibrous material made by steam blasting furnace slag or molten glass, was often employed, generally as loose fill, but it was also put between layers of kraft paper and stapled between studs. One of the most interesting kinds of insulation was made by Cabot, and featured eel grass *(zostera marina),* an aquatic plant, which was layered between two sheets of kraft paper. Fiberboard, first made in 1921 from a by-product of sugar cane but now generally made from wood scrap, was also utilized. Although glass fibers had been experimented with for years, and a glass fiber dress was shown at the 1893 World Columbian Exhibition in Chicago, fiberglass insulation wasn't invented until 1938 by Russell Games Slayter at Owens-Corning. It was marketed as a substitute for asbestos, which was in short supply because of World War II.

JEKYLL AND (FORMALDE) HYDE

Fiberglass (as well as rock and mineral wool) has been identified as a possible human carcinogen. Various studies have been done, but so far results are inconclusive. Like vinyl, fiberglass is hard to avoid, there being about a gazillion square feet of fiberglass insulation installed worldwide. Fiberglass utilizes formaldehyde (also a possible human carcinogen) as a binder, which can off-gas into living space. Some companies have started to offer formaldehyde-free insulation, as well as insulation encapsulated in plastic, which theoretically keeps the fibers from escaping, unless of course you have to cut into it to fit it into a cavity . . . . There seems to be agreement that, as with asbestos, it's often best to leave existing fiberglass alone, or encapsulate it somehow.

New forms of insulation continue to be tried: products that foam, cellulose that's blown in wet, insulation made from recycled soda bottles (or pop, if that's your local vernacular), cotton, wool, hemp, reflective barriers with bubble wrap in between, and even radiant barrier chips (basically little pieces of foil used as loose fill in the attic—I don't know if they work, but they sure look festive!). There are also numerous kinds of rigid insulation boards, from fiberboard to expanded polystyrene to various kinds of closed-cell foam, with and without foil radiant barriers attached.

There is little agreement on what kinds of insulation are best, since every kind tends to have some drawbacks. There isn't even agreement on whether insulation is a good idea. But probably the biggest drawback to retrofitting insulation into bungalows is knob-and-tube wiring. This kind of wiring, which is perfectly fine as long as the insulation on the wires is intact, was designed to have airspace around it. Surrounding it with insulation can cause heat to build up in the wires, which can cause short circuits and even fires. Not often, but it happens. So first you have to replace the electrical wiring. Or you can take your chances.

Modern houses that are insulated and weatherstripped and double-glazed within an inch of their lives have been made so tight that they actually require mechanical air

Cabot's quilt was sold both as insulation and for sound-proofing and fire-proofing. Given that it had two layers of kraft paper, the fire-proofing use might have been a bit questionable.

exchangers in order to get fresh air into the house. So essentially making a house that tight you may lower your energy bill, but you'll also be trapping all the off-gassing volatile organic compounds from rugs, vinyl tile, and such, as well as setting yourself up for toxic mold and radon poisoning.

OPPOSITE: Bevel siding and shingles combine on the gables of this bungalow. Twin brackets in the gable peaks are flanked by single brackets on either side.

VAPOR OR PLASTIC?

In new construction, a vapor barrier is placed on the inside of the wall, which keeps warm, moist air inside the house from migrating into the wall cavity and condensing in the insulation, which can cause rot and mold. Generally another barrier, called *housewrap*, is installed on the outside of the wall to prevent air infiltration from the outside. There are those who believe that this is what has led to the current epidemic of toxic mold. Bungalows, on the other hand, generally leak like a sieve, and that's not all bad. The main thing about water vapor or water is not so much that it gets IN the building but that it has a way to get OUT. An empty wall cavity allows that to happen pretty easily.

If wall insulation is to be added to walls that don't have it, it's a bit problematic to install a vapor barrier without removing the interior wall covering. Vapor-barrier paint will solve part of the problem, and shellac on woodwork makes a decent vapor barrier for those parts, but moisture will still try to sneak through cracks and electrical outlets. About the best one can do is to try to get water vapor out of the house by other means, like fans in the kitchen and baths. You have to USE the fans, though.

Obviously if the interior of the wall is down to the framing, it's much easier to install a vapor barrier (usually plastic sheeting or radiant barrier foil stapled on top of the studs), not that anyone should take the wall down just for this purpose.

Insulation can be blown into existing walls by drilling 2-inch holes in each stud bay from either the outside or the inside. On the outside, this is fairly easy if the siding is shingles, as individual shingles sacrificed to the process can be replaced fairly easily. (Obviously, a good time to insulate is during reshingling. It's a good time to do a lot of things—run wiring, plumbing, etc.—while the walls are accessible.) Wood siding will have to be patched, and the patches are hard to disguise. Stucco presents a similar problem. Masonry walls have enough thermal mass that they shouldn't be insulated. Insulation may cause water problems when moist air gets into the cavity between two wythes—normally it condenses there and runs down to the bottom, where weep holes have been provided (hopefully) for it to escape. Insulation interferes with this. If inside walls are plaster, it's better to insulate from the inside, since plaster is much easier to patch. In rooms with wood paneling, it may have to be removed for the purpose, which is annoying.

Many different sources will tell you that most of the

This gable sports a vent in the peak, an oriel window, shingle siding, and notched knee braces.

heat is escaping through cracks around doors and windows, electrical outlets, and so on, and that you should caulk all these cracks and weatherstrip the windows and doors, which is time-consuming and a huge pain in the ass. I'm not saying you shouldn't do that. I can only relate this from personal experience: I owned one bungalow that had insulated walls (blown-in cellulose) as well as an insulated attic. The double-hung windows were neither weatherstripped nor caulked, and they rattled every time it was windy. (Here in California, almost no one has storm windows.) In spite of that, that house had the lowest heating bill of any bungalow I've ever owned. Another thing: a cold wall actually sucks heat out of your body, making you feel cold regardless of the indoor temperature. So I guess I'm coming down on the side of insulation.

OPPOSITE: Cutout fascia boards and vertical half-timbering add interest to the porch gable of a Memphis home. Although Arts and Crafts in style, it is not a bungalow, being two full stories tall.

RESOURCES

LOGS

Michigan Prestain
www.michiganprestain.com
(800) 641-9663

Little Cedar Log Homes
www.littlecedarloghomes.com
(800) 388-6072

Wholesale Log Homes
www.wholesaleloghomes.com
(919) 732-9286

BRICKS

Gavin Historical Bricks
www.historicalbricks.com
(319) 354-5251

Chicago Antique Brick, Inc.
www.chicagoantiquebrick.com
(800) 828-1208

Boral Bricks
www.boralbricks.com
(800) 526-7255

Boren Brick
www.borenbrick.com
(800) 277-5000

Cunningham Brick
www.cunninghambrick.com
(336) 248-8541

Richtex Brick
www.richtex.com

Pine Hall Brick
www.pinehallbrick.com
(800) 334-8689

Custom Brick Company
www.custombrick.com
(800) 543-1866

Elgin-Butler Brick Company
www.elginbutler.com
(512) 385-3356

Endicott Clay Products, Inc.
www.endicott.com
(402) 729-3323

Hebron Brick Company
www.hebronbrick.com
(800) 292-2980

Watsontown Brick Company
www.watsontownbrick.com
(800) 538-2040

Acme Brick Company
www.acmebrick.com
(800) 792-1234

Belden Brick Company
www.beldenbrick.com
(330) 456-0031

Castaic Brick, Inc.
www.castaicbrick.com
(800) CASTAIC

Kansas Brick and Tile
www.kansasbrick.com
(800) 999-0480

Redland Brick
www.redlandbrick.com
(800) 366-2742

Old Mississippi Brick Company
www.oldmississippibrick.com
(662) 252-3395

McNear Brick and Block
www.mcnear.com
(415) 454-6811

BRICK MATCHING

Stone Art, Inc.
www.brickmatching.com
(423) 357-1464

Brick Imaging
www.brickimaging.com
(877) 419-3292

Color Match Masonry
www.brickstain.com
(410) 444-5373

Nawkaw Corporation
www.nawkaw.com
(630) 681-1400

MISCELLANEOUS BRICK

The International Brick Collectors
Association
1743 Lindenhall Drive
Loveland, Ohio 45140

ADOBE BRICK VENEER

Grand River Supply
www.grandriversupply.com
(877) 477-8775

CONCRETE BLOCKS

Vintage Block
www.vintageblock.com
(360) 681-2880

HOLLOW TILE

D'Hanis Brick and Tile Company
www.dhanisbricktile.com

WOOD SIDING

Buckley Lumber
www.cypresssiding.com
(877) 274-5685

Wood, Steel, and Glas, Inc.
www.whitecedar.com
(203) 245-1781

Haida Forest Products
www.haidaforest.com
(604) 437-3434

Liberty Cedar
www.libertycedar.com
(800) 882-3327

Barnes Lumber Manufacturing
www.barneslumber.com
(800) 441-2340

Granville Manufacturing Company
www.woodsiding.com
(802) 767-4747

Ward Clapboard Mill
www.wardclapboardmill.com
(802) 496-3581

RECLAIMED WOOD

TerraMai
www.terramai.com
(800) 220-9062

AntiQuus
www.antiquuswood.com
(800) 852-9224

Bear Creek Lumber
www.bearcreeklumber.com
(800) 597-7191

Duluth Timber Company
www.duluthtimber.com
(218) 727-2145

Big Timberworks
www.bigtimberworks.com
(406) 763-4639

SHINGLE SIDING
(see roofing also)

Shakertown
www.shakertown.com
(800) 426-8970

Cedar Valley
www.cedar-valley.com
(800) 521-9523

STUCCO

La Habra Stucco
www.lahabrastucco.com
(714) 778-2266

Cementics, Inc.
(Milestone hybridized portland cement)
www.cementics.com
(206) 719-8290

The Stucco News
www.stucconews.com

SHOTCRETE

American Shotcrete Association
www.shotcrete.org
(248) 848-3780

BRICK VENEER

Coronado Stone Products
www.coronado.com
(800) 847-8663

Chicago Antique Brick, Inc.
www.chicagoantiquebrick.com
(800) 828-1208

Brick Veneer, Inc.
www.thin-brick-veneer.com
(319) 631-3984

MISCELLANEOUS CEMENT PRODUCTS

GAF
(replacement shingles to match
old asbestos siding)
www.gaf.com
(973) 628-3000

Nichiha Fiber Cement
www.n-usa.com
(866) 424-4421

James Hardie Building Products
www.jameshardie.com
(888) JHARDIE

CHEMICAL PAINT REMOVAL

Franmar Chemical (Soy-Gel)
www.soysolvents.com
(800) 538-5069

Back To Nature Products (Ready-Strip)
www.ready-strip.com
(800) 211-5175

Dumond Chemicals (Peel-Away)
www.dumondchemicals.com
(212) 869-6350

Napier Environmental Technologies
(Remov-All)
www.removall.com
(800) 663-9274

Soyclean
www.soyclean.biz
(888) 606-9559

W.M. Barr and Company (Citristrip)
www.citristrip.com
(800) 235-3546

American Building Restoration Products
www.abrp.com
(800) 346-7532

K and E Chemical Company
www.klenztone.com
(800) 331-1696

INFARED PAINT REMOVAL

Paint Peeler
www.paintpeeler.com
(800) 613-1557

Viking Sales, Inc.
www.silentpaintremover.com
(585) 924-8070

MECHANICAL PAINT REMOVAL

Preservation Resource Group
(Pro-Prep scrapers)
www.prginc.com
(800) 774-7891

American International Tool, Inc.
(Paint Shaver)
www.paintshaver.com
(800) 932-5872

GABLE DESIGN

Residential Copper
www.residentialcopper.com
(866) 467-1777

The Whitfield Group, Inc.
www.whitfieldvents.com
(903) 291-9663

Kimball Design
www.kimballdesigns.com
(870) 326-4326

European Attic
www.europeanattic.com
(800) 632-9408

Vintage Copper
www.vintagecopper.com
(877) 220-5355

The Copper Mill
www.thecoppermill.com
(918) 272-5820

RADIANT BARRIER INSULATION

Reflectech
www.reflectech.com
(601) 799-6998

U-B-Kool
www.u-b-kool.com
(619) 275-6919

Innovative Insulation Inc.
www.radiantbarrier.com
(800) 825-0123

Smart Foils
www.smartfoils.com
(800) 492-6333

Horizon Energy Systems
(radiant barrier chips)
www.savenrg.com
(602) 789-1699

CELLULOSE INSULATION

Igloo Cellulose
www.cellulose.com
(800) 363-7876

GreenFiber
www.greenstone.com
(800) 228-0024

International Cellulose Corporation
www.celbar.com
(800) 444-1252

OTHER INSULATION

Woolbloc Insulation
www.woolbloc.com

Atlas Roofing Corporation
www.atlasroofing.com

Bonded Logic, Inc.
www.bondedlogic.com
(480) 812-9114

Garrison Specialty Chemicals
www.soyfoam.com

Air Krete
www.airkrete.com
(315) 834-6609

CHAPTER FIVE

GRAND ··· OPENINGS

PANE THRESHOLD

There may be no more important feature of a bungalow than its windows. More than just openings for light and air, windows are the face the house presents to the street. Different architectural styles have distinctive windows—for example, the tall, hooded windows of an Italianate Victorian or the leaded glass casements of a Tudor Revival.

Bungalows, although sharing window styles with some other early-twentieth-century houses, have a window style all their own. The windows do not exist in isolation—their proportions, pattern, materials, and placement are one of the most important elements of a bungalow's design.

Early settlers in North America didn't have glass windows—merely openings that could be covered with shutters, maybe covered with a thin piece of oiled paper or a sheet of isinglass (mica flakes bonded with shellac, or sturgeon bladders—it's a long story). When glass did arrive, it was expensive, came in small pieces, and was even taxed. To cope with the small pieces, window sashes (the wooden frames that hold the glass) were divided into *lights,* divided by small wooden bars called *muntins.* Wooden windows were made by hand, using molding planes and other tools. The joinery was complex, which also made windows expensive. The sash

frames used *mortise-and-tenon* joinery: a *tenon* is a rectangular tab on one piece of wood that fits into the *mortise,* a rectangular slot in another piece of wood—kinda like insert Tab A into Slot B . . . . In a window, the tenon was usually glued, although it might be held with a peg. The *muntins,* which had a molded profile, were joined using *cope-and-stick* joinery (coping involves cutting one piece to match the profile of the other piece), and attached to the frame with tenons. Each *light* in the sash was cut so that it had a ledge around it, called a *rabbet,* for the glass to sit on. The glass was kept in the frame with small nails, and either a small piece of molding or linseed oil putty (composed of linseed oil and chalk, although sometimes white lead or asbestos fibers were added) was also used to hold the glass in place. Somewhat later the small nails were replaced by tiny triangular pieces of sheet metal, called *glaziers points.* Wooden windows are still made this way, although now much of the process is done by machine.

By the nineteenth century, mechanization and steam-powered woodworking equipment had made it easier to manufacture windows in large quantities, putting them within reach of more people. Improvements in the manufacturing of glass had resulted in larger pieces of glass being available, so window styles changed in response.

A pair of six-over-one, double-hung windows is flanked by two of the tiniest windows on the planet, each with its own shelf supported by a long corbel. The windowsill of the larger window is supported by square corbel blocks that match the knee braces in the gable of this shingled Berkeley, California, bungalow.

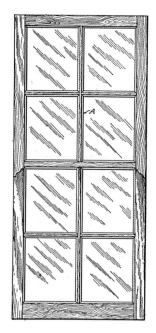

Another drawing shows two, one-over-one double hungs (no lugs on the upper sash on these) with transom windows above. The larger piece separating the two windows is the mullion. The dividing piece above is also a mullion.

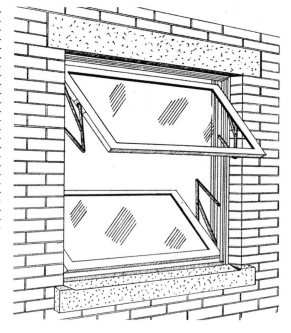

This illustration shows an austral window, where the upper sash opens outward like an awning window, and the lower sash opens inward like a hopper window. When closed, this window resembles a double-hung window but provides far more ventilation when open. For some reason, austral windows are not common in the U.S.

A drawing from the 1915 *American Carpenter and Builder* shows a four-over-four double-hung window with muntins. Notice that the upper sash of this window has decorative "lugs" at the lower ends of the stiles (vertical side pieces). The function of lugs is unclear—possibly to cushion the glass somewhat should the sash hit the windowsill while being lowered.

Nineteenth-century and early-twentieth-century glass was made by the *cylinder* method—a large cylinder of glass was blown, then cut down one side and flattened out. Because the outside diameter of the cylinder was slightly larger than the inside, when the glass was flattened, the extra glass on the outside would form tiny ridges or ripples in the glass, and there would also be air bubbles from the blowing. This is the type of glass found in most bungalows.

In 1905, a process of vertically drawing a consistent-width sheet of glass from a tank was perfected, known as *drawn glass*. Commercial production using this method began in 1914. Various improvements were made in the process, and by 1928 the method still in use was perfected. Modern window glass is made by this process and lacks the subtle ripples and imperfections of the old cylinder glass.

Cylinder glass is still available, though it's expensive. Another option is to buy old window sashes (or even just glass) at the salvage yard. (Make sure it's wavy, though—not all of it is. Take some glass cleaner and paper towels with you—the glass will invariably be dirty and it's hard to tell whether it's wavy or not under all the dirt.)

There were and are various styles of windows. *Fixed* windows are not movable and are simply for letting in light. *Casement* windows are hinged on the side and open either in or out like doors. *Double-hung* windows have two sashes that slide up and down in channels, balanced by counter-weights. (Frank Lloyd Wright hated double-hungs—he called them "guillotine windows.") There are also *single-hung* windows with only one sliding sash and *triple-hung* windows. There are no windows that are hung like a horse.

Other kinds of windows include *sliding* (sashes slide in horizontal tracks); *awning* windows, which are hinged at the top and open upward; *hopper* windows, which are hinged at the bottom and open downward; *austral* windows, in which one sash opens like an awning and the other opens like a hopper; *pivoting* windows, in which the whole sash tilts on two pins set into the frame; and *bi-fold* windows, where two sashes are hinged together on one side, with pins that run in a track top and bottom so they can be folded, accordion-style, to the sides of the window. There are also *pocket* windows, which slide into a pocket in the wall. *Louvered* or *jalousie* windows are a later invention and don't belong on a bungalow. And no, I don't care if you live in Florida.

Most windows were square or rectangular, but windows with curved tops, oval and round windows (also known as *oculus, roundel,* or the particularly charming *oeil-de-boeuf,* or bullseye, though I prefer the literal translation, "eye of beef"), diamond shapes, and other variations also existed.

With rare exceptions, bungalow window frames were made of wood. With the advent of power machinery for making sash, it was possible to make sash with elaborate muntin patterns, so they did. On double-hung windows, the muntins were confined to the top sash, the lower sash being plain. Probably the most popular pattern was a nine-light design that could be described as a variation on Tic-Tac-Toe. But if a pattern could be thought up, it was made. Geometric patterns were the most common, but patterns involving curved elements appeared on many bungalows. On some bungalows, only the front windows had muntins, and the side and back windows were plain. On others, all the windows had muntins. If the designer or builder was going hog wild, the muntin patterns might vary on different sets of windows.

The upper sash of a double-hung window may or may not have *lugs,* an extension of the sides of the sash frame below the bottom rail, usually cut into an *ogee* (S-shape) but occasionally into an even fancier shape. The presence or lack of lugs is entirely regional—in some places they're traditional, some places they aren't.

Just a warning here—many bungalows were built with very plain, one-light sashes. Don't succumb to the temptation to fancy up the windows into something they were never meant to be. Embrace the plainness—it's very Zen. One-light sashes are easier to clean too. By the same token, people with complex muntin patterns on their sashes should not replace them with windows that have snap-out muntin grilles just to make them easier to clean.

Bungalow windows might also have leaded glass or *art glass* (stained glass). Art glass was offered in geometric patterns as well as more realistic designs of flora and fauna, scenery, and such. *Obscure glass* such as etched, glue-chip (in which the surface of the glass is chipped by the action of a particular kind of hide glue, giving the effect of ice crystals), sandblasted, and *patterned glass,* made by squeezing semi-molten glass between two rollers, one of which has a pattern on it, were also offered. There were and are many varieties of patterned glass, including hammered (*so* Arts and Crafts), cathedral, Flemish, reeded, seeded, and my personal favorite, chinchilla. Yup, looks like fur. Each manufacturer had their own patterns, so one company's "Rain" may be another's "Niagara."

On the front façade, the windows were often arranged as a tripartite featuring a large fixed window flanked by two operable windows (sometimes known as a *Chicago window,* after its common use in early-twentieth-century Chicago office buildings). *Ribbon windows,* a series of casement windows in a row, were favored by the architects of the Prairie School style but also found their way onto bungalows. On the sides and back, windows might be positioned haphazardly according to the function of the rooms inside, or arranged more aesthetically. A chimney on an outside wall was commonly flanked by high windows, frequently featuring art glass. Bay or bow windows were much used, particularly on front façades. Other walls were more likely to have oriel windows that were rectangular, trapezoidal, curved, or V-shaped.

Chicago bungalow windows were greatly influenced by the art glass of Frank Lloyd Wright and other architects of the Prairie School style. (Most Chicago bungalows were built in the 1920s, after the heyday of the Prairie School.) The geometric designs favored by Wright and others filtered down to bungalows, such as these gold-accented windows in an abstracted wheat pattern.

SCAM, SCAM, SCAM, SCAM, SCAM, SCAM, LOVELY SCAM!

"Or Lobster Thermidor Crevette with a mornay sauce served in a Provencale manner with shallots and aubergines garnished with truffle pate, brandy and with a fried egg on top and scam."
— With many apologies to Monty Python

Just in case the heading didn't make it clear, this section is going to be a little harsh. Okay, a lot harsh.

Wood windows are one of the most vulnerable of historic building elements—millions are being dumped in landfills every year. And that is an absolute travesty. The multibillion-dollar window replacement industry would like you to believe that historic windows are drafty, not energy-efficient, don't work well, and require constant maintenance. Almost every day the newspaper is filled with ads for replacement windows with headlines like, "Are your windows costing you money?" or "Whole house window replacement—only $2,995!" Probably your local public utility will give you a rebate for ripping out your original windows to put in vinyl replacements. Often the local building code demands insulating windows in new construction or remodeling. Go back to the earlier sentence and consider the phrase "multibillion-dollar"—with that much money at stake, do you think these companies have your best interests at heart? THEY ARE LYING, and when they aren't lying outright, they are conveniently failing to mention numerous pertinent facts. Here's a list from one Internet replacement window Web site (which shall remain nameless):

Signs that will let you know your windows should be replaced:

- *There is condensation or frost buildup.*
- *Drafts—if air is coming through a closed window.*
- *Window needs support to stay open.*
- *Candles do not stay lit near a closed window.*
- *If windows show signs of deterioration.*

The sample window shown in this advertisement for the American Sash Trimmer doesn't even begin to cover the variations in muntin patterns that were possible.

Here's another site: "Don't bother to fix a window that has cracked glass, rotted or otherwise damaged wood, locks that don't work, missing putty, or poorly fitting sashes." And another: "Homeowners with windows over twenty-five years old should consider replacing them . . . . A home is an ideal candidate for a window replacement if its windows are sealed or painted shut . . ."

Okay, I am gasping in disbelief, but let's take these one at a time. If there's condensation on the inside, there's too much moisture in your house. If there's frost on the outside, it's winter. Get a storm window. If you have a storm window on the outside and there's still frost on the inside window, the storm window leaks. Weatherstrip it.

If there are drafts, it means air is getting in through the exterior trim or around the edges of the window. Caulk will fix the first problem, and weatherstripping and a storm window will fix the second one.

Window needs support to stay open: replace the freaking sash cords! If you don't want to replace the sash cords, use sash chain—it's noisy, though. (And don't feel bad if you're propping the window open with a stick—it's a perfectly functional way to keep it open, and I did that for years before I learned how to replace sash cords.)

Window shows signs of deterioration: missing putty should be replaced; rot or open joints, which are almost always at the bottom of the lower sash, can be repaired with epoxy consolidants or even just wood putty...ditto for deteriorating sills, frames, or trim. If the glass is cracked, replace it! If the putty is missing—put on some more putty! Because on a single-glazed window, you can.

Locks don't work—ARE THESE PEOPLE KIDDING? (It wasn't even a window company site.) Geez, get a new lock—it's not exactly brain surgery.

If the window is painted shut, a putty knife, a hammer, and a little elbow grease (what a weird phrase) will fix that easily.

Any one of these things will not cost as much as a replacement window, even if you pay someone else to do it.

Not all claims by replacement window companies are outright lies, more like obfuscation (which means "con-

The porch gable of a bungalow in Eagle Rock, California, features an oeil-de-boeuf, or oculus window—basically round. This gable has unusual wavy trim.

The upper sash of a window in Vancouver has lugs that are more decorative than the usual ogee pattern. The majority of original windows in Vancouver don't have lugs at all.

fuse"—I like to use a two-dollar word occasionally).

OBFUSCATION #1. *Replacement windows will significantly reduce heating costs.* Only twenty percent of the heating loss (or cooling gain) in a building is through the windows. The other eighty percent is lost through roofs, walls, floors, and chimneys, with most of it going out the roof. And most of the cold air is sucked in through the floor from the basement or crawl space. Reducing the heat loss through the windows by fifty percent (double-glazing) will only result in a ten percent reduction in the overall heat loss. The average cost to replace ten windows with double-glazed units is approximately $9,500 for vinyl and $16,000 for aluminum-clad wood. And that's only ten windows—the smallest bungalow I ever owned had twenty windows. Misleading the public about actual costs is one of the sleazy tactics employed. But let's say some mythical person, obviously not me, decides to replace their twenty windows with vinyl. They pay $19,000 for them. Let's also say that their utility bill averages a ridiculous $200 a month (actually my average combined gas and electric bill here at the 3,800-square-foot bunga-mansion). A ten percent reduction on their heating bill amounts to $20 a month, or $240 a year. At that rate it would take just over 79 years to recoup the $19,000 investment. At a more realistic heating bill average of $100 per month, the payback time would be 158 years. But wait—according to the Environmental Protection Agency, 40 percent of the average household energy budget goes to heating and cooling. So at $200 per month, only $80 goes to heating and cooling. Saving 10 percent on that would only be $8 a month, putting the payback time at 197.9 years. For the same amount of money (or less!) that replacement windows would cost, you could insulate the attic and the walls and install a damper on the chimney and get an 80% reduction

in heat loss. And probably vacation in Tahiti on the money you'd have left.

Or you could spend that money on storm windows. A recent study conducted at the Oak Ridge National Laboratory using actual wooden windows (removed from a house that was being demolished) showed that the addition of storm windows reduced air leakage by a considerable amount. They used a double-hung window with loose sashes, no weatherstripping, gaps between the sashes and frame, missing caulk, cracked glass, and dry rot in the frame. The second window was a double-hung dual pane with loose sashes and no weatherstripping. For storm windows, they used non-thermally broken aluminum storms with operable sashes and no weatherstripping. Interestingly enough, the addition of storm windows to both windows reduced the energy flow of the first window substantially compared to the dual pane window. Using a measurement which took into account both air infiltration and conduction through the glass, without storms, and with a wind speed of 7 mph, the single-glazed window lost about 565 BTUs per hour, while the dual-glazed window lost 644. With the storms added, the single-glazed window lost 131 BTUs per hour, while the dual-pane window lost 256. Then they removed the storm and weatherized the first window, which involved squaring up the frame so the sashes fit more tightly, replaced rot in the frame, reglazed the panes, caulked cracks in the frame, installed a sweep at the bottom of the lower sash, and installed a new window lock to improve closure—then ran the tests again. At 7 mph, heat loss for the weatherized window was 256, compared with 131 for the unweatherized window with a storm. By comparison, the dual-pane window WITH A STORM also had a heat loss of 256. They didn't compare weatherstripping PLUS a storm window, but clearly, a storm window gives you more bang for the buck (about a seventy-five percent reduction in heat transmission) and weatherstripping alone gives the same reduction as a double-glazed window. The test used a lousy storm window—a high-quality storm window would work better.

Another study done in New England in 1997 showed that vinyl jamb liners saved about 80 cents a year in heating costs, weatherstripping saved $1.70, and storm windows saved $2.50.

In the book *Burglars on the Job,* authors Richard Wright and Scott Decker, after interviewing hundreds of burglars, concluded that burglars avoid houses with storm windows, believing that the sound caused by two separate panes of glass breaking is more likely to alert the neighbors.

John Myers, who wrote the "Preservation Brief" on historic wood windows for the National Park Service, had this to say about energy-efficient windows: *"Energy conservation is no excuse for the wholesale destruction of historic windows* (italics mine), which can be made thermally efficient by historically and aesthetically acceptable means."

OBFUSCATION #2. *Maintenance-free exterior—no painting or staining required.* No painting or staining POSSIBLE, in the case of vinyl. What if you get tired of the color? And you know how funky that cheap resin outdoor furniture looks after a couple of years? That's what the vinyl or vinyl-clad window will look like. And you know how plastic has static electricity that attracts dirt? As for aluminum, even an anodized coating doesn't last long, at which point you have to paint it. If it's not anodized, then it corrodes and turns white.

OUTRIGHT LIE #3. *Extremely durable and long-lasting.* A vinyl window has a life expectancy of approximately twenty years, aluminum about ten to twenty years, a new wood window from twenty to fifty years. An original wood window that is consistently maintained and kept painted can last as long as 200 years, if not longer . . . . Part of the reason that an old wood window lasts longer than a new one is that old windows are made of old-growth timber, which grew very slowly and is extremely close-grained and dense, whereas new wood windows are made from second-

A beveled-glass oriel window is sheltered under the porch roof of a Berkeley, California, home designed by architect and builder Leola Hall. Julia Morgan gets all the credit for being one of the first female architects in Berkeley, but Leola Hall was also a builder at a time when that was a rare job for a woman—as, frankly, it still is.

A flared oriel window decorates the corner of a shingled Berkeley home, designed and built by Leola Hall. Locally, these types of houses are called "brownshingles," and Berkeley has hundreds of them.

growth wood, much of it from fast-growing trees harvested from tree farms, where the growth rings are much further apart. The softer sapwood resulting from fast growth is far less durable.

And let's talk for a moment about "springs, strings, and plastic things," as David Liberty, a window restorer in Boston, calls them. Windows used to be simple: in a double-hung window, two weights are attached to sash cord or chain that runs through pulleys and totals exactly the weight of the window sash so that the window slides up and down effortlessly; in a casement window, there are hinges on the side (or occasionally, the bottom) so it opens like a door; ditto for awning or hopper windows; pivoting windows turn on metal pins, and all of this hardware is made of metal. It is eminently repairable, and most of it is fairly standardized. But after World War II, these simple and eminently repairable systems were replaced by spring balances, crank-out casements, and other "springs, strings, and plastic things." In the words of an engineer looking at modern replacement windows, "too many things to go wrong."

A spring-loaded suspension system has a serious flaw. When the window is closed, the springs are fully extended. How long it takes for the springs to lose all of their tension depends on the quality of the metal and the weight of the sash, but they will lose their tension, and then the top sash won't stay up and the bottom sash won't GO up. A crank-out casement has gears, and eventually the teeth fail. And that's not even mentioning the fact that a double-glazed sash weighs twice as much as a single-glazed sash, making it even more likely to strain the springs and plastic things. And the strings and plastic things are all proprietary, which means if you want to replace one of them you have to make sure you're getting the *right* little plastic doohickey out of the 300 plastic doohickeys you'll have to choose from. And not all of the doohickeys will be available at your local hardware store.

What happens if the glass breaks? In a single-glazed window, the glass is easily replaced using items available at any hardware store, costing maybe twenty bucks, depending on the size of the replacement glass. In a double-glazed

The art-glass windows with an arched transom on this Chicago bungalow have a rose pattern reminiscent of the designs of Scottish architect and designer Charles Rennie MacIntosh. The windows on the sides of the bay have a different arched transom, but all the transoms have a leaded sunburst pattern.

OUTRIGHT LIE #4. *Economical. For whom?* Let's say you went for the $2,995 ten-window special—that's $299.50 per window. Yeah, that keeps their economy going. For that price you could easily pay someone to repair, reglaze, and weatherstrip all ten windows, or you could buy ten custom storm windows instead.

OUTRIGHT LIE #5. *Tilt sashes are easier to clean.* Well, it sure looks that way when the salesperson demonstrates it on that little tiny sample window. Now try to imagine tilting in and holding a sash that weighs fifty pounds and is longer than your arm, a sash that is only held up by two small plastic clips. Do you think you can hold up fifty pounds with one hand while washing the window with the other? And how long do you think the plastic clips will last?

OUTRIGHT LIE #6. *Your home will be more attractive and easier to sell.* Could I just repeat the first rule of real estate here? Location, location, location. Not replacement windows, replacement windows, replacement windows. New windows aren't going to fool anyone into thinking the house is new—people who want a new house usually buy a new

A Los Angeles bungalow has this set of three slightly arched casement windows with horizontal muntins that echo the curve of the arch. The two side windows have an extra vertical muntin dividing them into uneven lights, but the set of windows is symmetrical. The area underneath the window is recessed, giving it the look of being a bay, yet it is actually in the same plane as the upper walls. Shingles shouldn't be painted, especially not white.

ABOVE: A large fixed window on a West Adams bungalow has a typical division into one-third/two-thirds, with the top third divided into twenty-two separate lights. The side casings are curved and flare at the bottom.

window, the glass is all specially sealed units, which have to be ordered from the manufacturer (assuming the manufacturer is still in business), and which cost $85 to $100 apiece (or more—depends on size), and that's if you can even order replacement glazing units—sometimes you have to buy a whole new sash, or even a whole new window. And then you have to pay someone to install the new glazing, because it's not really a do-it-yourself thing.

But here's the thing they're really hiding: the average life span of a double-glazing unit is TEN YEARS OR LESS. The seal around the glazing can fail within ten years, causing the glass panes to fog. And the plastic and neoprene seals used to hold the panes in new windows degrade in ultraviolet light. Imagine trying to find a replacement/gasket after the window company has gone out of business.

house. All they do is destroy the historic integrity of the house. There is, in fact, a direct correlation between historic integrity and market value. Second, in a historic building, windows make up a large part of the façade. The pattern of the sash, the window framing, and the other architectural detail surrounding the window was carefully designed as an integral component of the building, and replacing the windows destroys this. Even a replacement sash that replicates the muntin pattern and trim will not look the same, because it will not have the wavy glass and muntin profile of a single-glazed window, and no matter how much they try to disguise the necessary spacer, a double-glazed window just doesn't look the same. As for easier to sell, that depends more on what the real estate market is like.

OBFUSCATION #7. *No swelling or shrinking due to humidity and moisture.* No, only swelling or shrinking due to temperature fluctuation! Vinyl expands and shrinks at twice the rate of wood, and it expands at seven times the rate of glass—how long do you think it will be before the sealant that holds the glass in fails? Once vinyl starts to distort, it doesn't resume its original shape, as anyone with a warped vinyl record can attest. Aluminum cladding won't swell much, but the wood underneath will.

OBFUSCATION #8. *Insulates against noise.* Sure, until you open it. Actually, a single-glazed window has an STC (sound transmission class) rating between 20 and 27, depending on how thick the glass is and how airtight the window is. In a dual-pane window, the STC rating is governed somewhat by the distance between the two panes—the larger the distance, the better the rating. (This suggests a storm window might be better than double-glazing,

Two window illustrations from the Morgan Woodworking Organization's 1921 Building with Assurance catalog show a double hung with three vertical muntins in the upper sash and another with two. The window on the left has an angled casing at the top.

Three different sets of Morgan casements with different muntin patterns and surrounding trim was offered in their 1921 catalog.

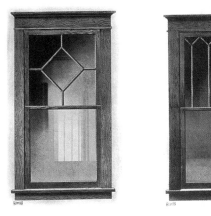

These two Morgan windows have small crown moldings on the top casing and two completely different muntin patterns in the top sash.

being further away.) For each doubling of the airspace between the panes, the STC increases by about three. If the panes are close together, the rating may actually be lower than for a single pane, because the airspace acts like a spring and transfers vibration from one pane to the other. Triple glazing provides the same noise reduction as double glazing, unless the spacing between panes is quite large. On average, dual-pane windows have an STC rating of 28–35. A single layer of $1/4$-inch laminated glass (which has a layer of plastic in the middle) has an STC rating of 33, which suggests that it might be better to replace the glass in a single-glazed window with laminated glass if noise is an issue, instead of wasting the money on new windows.

OUTRIGHT LIE #9. *New windows won't be drafty like the old ones.* Yes, they will, and here's why: convection. Warm air in the house contacts the cold window glass and then cools, which draws more warm air towards the glass, setting up convection currents in the

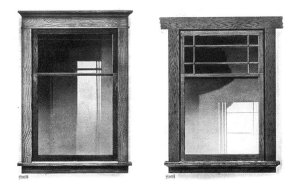

These Morgan windows have smaller upper sashes, also a common bungalow variety. The Morgan sashes don't have lugs.

WINDOW REPAIR

OBSESSIVE RESTORATION

Original wooden windows are eminently repairable. Repairing windows tends to be time-consuming and tedious, but it's not brain surgery. The National Park Service has a good Preservation Brief on restoring wood windows, or you can purchase Terry Meany's fine book, *Working Windows,* or see the condensed instructions on page 113. Few windows are so far gone that they can't be repaired, though if you don't do it yourself, it may be difficult to find someone locally who will. If a sash is truly beyond repair, a millwork shop can make a new custom sash. If there's no one local, there are national companies that do this as well, although I would urge you to deal locally, if possible. Look in the *Yellow Pages* under Windows—Wood, after first thumbing through page after page of window replacement companies. (We are apparently lucky here in the Oakland-Berkeley area, as there are six or seven custom window shops. The average cost here for a one-light single-pane sash is about $100.)

COMPROMISE SOLUTION

If you still have the original windows—see Obsessive Restoration. I refuse to compromise on this. On the other hand, if some previous owner has already removed the original windows and replaced them with some dreadful vinyl or awful aluminum or something, you have my permission to replace them—with wood.

An art-glass window on a Memphis bungalow has a head casing that wraps partially around the sides, and the apron below the sill has short "legs." Notice how the cream-colored trim still draws attention to the window while harmonizing better with the khaki color of the drop siding.

room. The air won't be coming from outside, but you will still feel a draft.

OUTRIGHT LIE #10. *New technology is better.* One Web site made this claim: Glass was invented over 4,000 years ago, so single-pane glass is 4,000-year-old technology. Dual-pane glass is a 25-year-old technology, and dual-pane with Low-E and argon gas is today's technology. Their argument is that today's technology is best. I would argue that 4,000-year-old technology has a track record, and their technology already has a high failure rate. Also, and I can't say this enough, if no one buys into their B.S. by keeping their old windows, these companies WON'T MAKE ANY MONEY. (Cue sound of violins.)

OUTRIGHT LIE #11. *Snap-in muntin grilles look just like real divided-light windows.* Not real but an amazing simulation! What's amazing is that they get away with it. Even the so-called "true divided-light" windows don't look like actual divided-light windows. Even worse, they also make grilles which are sandwiched in between the glass, or the really cheapo alternative—a grid of white tape applied directly to the glass. The snap-in grilles and the grilles between the glass are supposed to make the window easier to clean. That may be true, but who said everything was supposed to be easy? And it's not like window cleaning isn't still tedious, whether there is one pane or several.

Then there's the fact that replacement windows that are installed are often smaller than the existing windows. Often the window trim is removed entirely, and the old opening filled in to the size of the replacement window, leaving the new window embedded in a perfectly flat wall without any trim around it. Interesting window shapes (arched, etc.) are made rectangular to fit the standardized replacements.

SCORN ON THE COB

Think I've been harsh up to now? Just wait. I reserve my highest scorn for the dreadful sliding aluminum window. A window that is not appropriate for ANY building style, in my book. A window that has destroyed the historic integrity of more buildings than any other window. A window that is cheap, ugly, not very functional, easily removed from its track (making it not very secure), having no insulation value at all—what's to like? Just because this is the only kind of window sold at most home improvement centers doesn't mean anyone should buy them. The aluminum extrusion companies even have a national initiative called KAW—Keep Aluminum Windows. Do you sense their desperation? Well, at least aluminum windows aren't toxic, but that's about the only good thing I can say about them. Rip them out—that aluminum is worth money at the recycling center.

FIXING WINDOWS

The most common window type in older houses, regardless of the style of the house, is the double-hung window. A double-hung window has two *sashes* (a sash is the wooden frame that holds the glass) that move up and down in channels. *Sash cords* in channels on the side of the sash run through pulleys at the top of the window and are connected to *sash weights* in pockets inside the wall, which counterbalance the weight of the sash so it doesn't crash down on your fingers. The channels are formed by the *parting bead* or *strip,* a thin piece of wood that sits in a slot in the *jamb* (the side of the window frame) and separates the two sashes, and the *stop,* a piece nailed to the jamb on the interior side, at right angles to the *casing* (the interior trim around the window). The most common problems with these windows are broken sash cords, windows being painted shut, cracked or broken glass, or rot and fungus damage in the wood.

Here are the tools and supplies you will need to fix a double-hung window:

- stiff-bladed putty knife (a 5-in-1 tool, available at paint stores, works well)
- hammer
- flat pry bar
- utility knife
- slotted screwdriver
- sash cord ($1/4$- or $5/16$-inch diameter) or sash chain
- 4d and 8d finishing nails
- WD-40 or other lubricant
- optional but handy: locking pliers

If the window is only painted shut, it's an easy fix. Slide the putty knife in between the sash and the stop to break the paint film. You may have to hammer it in. Work your way around the sash—you may also need to break the film between the sash and the stool (the inside windowsill) and between the upper and lower sash at the top. If you're lucky, it was only painted shut on the inside, and you will now be able to open it. It also helps to lubricate the channels the sash slides in—anything from paraffin to soap to WD-40 will do the trick. (And by the way, when you're painting, do not paint the sash channels—eventually the paint buildup will keep the sash from sliding.) If the window is also painted shut on the outside, you will need to go outside and repeat the process. If it's a second-floor window, see directions about how to remove a sash.

If the sash cords are broken, you will have to remove the sashes. Using the putty knife, pry off one or both of the interior stops. This will allow the lower sash to be removed. Pull the sash cord out of the channels (the knot may be attached with a finishing nail—pry it out with the screwdriver). If only one cord is broken, allow the other one to ride up—the knot will prevent it going through the pulley. To remove the top sash, carefully pull out the parting bead on one side, starting at the bottom (locking pliers work well for this). When you get about halfway up, lower the top sash to the bottom of the window, and pull the rest of the parting bead out from the top. If you're lucky, it won't break, but if it does, go down to the lumberyard and get another piece. Then the top sash can be removed.

There are two ways to get to the sash weights. Some windows have a removable pocket cut into the jamb (usually held with a screw) for access to the weight pocket. These are generally more trouble than they're worth. The other way to access the weights is by prying off the inside casings—do this carefully to avoid damaging the surrounding plaster. Remove the nails from the stops and the casings by pulling them through from the back—removing them from the front will cause visible damage.

With the side casings removed, the weight pockets should be exposed. It's best to replace all the cords, even the ones that aren't broken. Remove the weights and cut the old sash cords off them. Cut the new sash cord to length, a little bit longer than the existing cord. (It frays, so wrap a piece of tape around the end first.) Tie a knot close to one end—the knot will fit into a hole drilled in the side of the sash. Run the other end through the pulley and down into the weight pocket. Start with the upper sash. Once the cords are through the pulleys, put the knots into the holes on the side of the sash, press the cord into the channels, then fit the sash into the window and push it up to the top (a helper is useful here). Tie the other end of the cord to the weight, using a double or triple knot. Make sure that the weight hangs just above the sill—it should not touch. Once both weights are attached, run the sash up and down a few times to make sure it slides smoothly—it should go all the way down without the weight hitting the pulley. This is a good time to squirt a little lubricant on the pulleys. Then, with the sash pushed down to the sill, reinsert the parting bead into the slot—it's a bit tricky because it has to slide between the jamb and a piece of triangular molding on the sash. Once the upper sash is in, the lower sash is replaced in the same way.

Once the sashes are in, first nail the casings back in place using finishing nails, then nail the stops, making sure they don't cause the sash to bind as it goes up and down. (If the woodwork has a natural finish, you may want

More!

FIXING WINDOWS *Continued!*

to substitute small brass wood screws for the nails, making the stops easier to remove in the future.)

A very common window problem is cracked, broken, or missing glass. A glass company will charge $80 to $100 to replace broken glass, so you can save quite a bit by learning to do it yourself. The first thing to do is remove the old glass and glazing compound (putty) that holds the glass in the sash. It is easier to do this if you can remove the sash from the window frame and lay it flat, but that isn't always possible.

The glass rests against a lip cut into the frame of the sash (called a rabbet). A thin bead of glazing compound cushions the glass where it rests against this lip. The pane of glass is held in by glazing points. In older windows these are small diamond- or triangular-shaped pieces of flat metal. One of the points is pushed into the wood of the sash frame; the rest of it lays flat against the glass. Depending on the size of the pane, there may be anywhere from one to five of these on each of the four sides. Then glazing compound is applied over the points and tooled to a smooth angled surface, allowing water to run off and keeping moisture out of the sash frame. The glazing putty remains flexible (for many years, anyway), allowing for movement and expansion and contraction of the sash parts.

The battered side casings continue beyond the head (top) casing around a leaded-glass window in the dormer of a Victoria bungalow. Those fascia boards look sharp enough to hurt somebody. Again, white trim is a little too harsh with the dark green shingles.

Eventually, however, it becomes hard as a rock. There is no particularly easy way to remove it. If you are lucky, it will crack and fall out in big chunks, but a much more likely scenario is that you will have to chisel it out tiny piece by tiny piece. One of the best tools to use for this purpose is a 5-in-1 painter's tool, along with a hammer. It needs to be done quite carefully, so as not to break the glass or notch the sash. A chisel can also be used, but even more care is required with this method. You can also use a heat gun to soften the putty, although this will crack the glass unless you shield it from the heat (a piece of cardboard wrapped in aluminum foil works well for this purpose)—it will also remove paint from the sash. Be sure to have a fire extinguisher or a spray bottle of water on hand—I once set a sash on fire! For those with more patience, a coat of paint remover will soften the putty, given an hour or two. There is also a tool called the Putty Chaser, more or less like a router bit that fits into a drill— *it does not work*. Don't waste your money.

If money is no object, you can buy a product called Steam Stripper. It's basically a large steam chamber. You put the entire sash inside and leave it for an hour or so. The steam softens the paint and the glazing so that it can be easily scraped off. If you have a whole lot of windows to restore it might be a worthwhile investment.

Once the putty is removed, pull out the glazing points with needle-nose pliers and then remove the glass. It's a good idea to wear gloves for this. If the glass is old and wavy and the chunks are fairly large, you might want to save it in case you ever need to reglaze a smaller or multi-light window. Clean any remaining putty off the sash, so the rabbet is smooth to receive the new glass. Then coat the rabbet with a mixture of boiled linseed oil and turpentine (if you have lots of time to wait, like until tomorrow), or primer (such as Kilz or 1-2-3) if you are in a hurry. The purpose of the primer is to prevent the linseed oil in the putty from leaching out into the wood.

The next step is to measure for the glass. Measure the rabbet from edge to edge. The glass needs to be $1/16$ inch smaller on each side than the sash; in other words, subtract $1/8$ inch from each measurement. Sashes are not standardized, so you may end up with weird measurements like 27 $13/16$ by 22 $5/8$ inches. Obey the old carpenters' adage: "Think three times, measure twice, cut once." Except I'd measure three times, at a couple of different points, because the sash may not be square. Use the smallest measurement, because you can't trim $1/16$ inch off a piece of cut glass. At this point you can either go to the hardware store or glass company and have a new piece of glass cut, or you can cut it yourself.

To cut glass, you will need a glass cutter, which will be locked up in a case at your local hardware store, since young people have taken to using them to score graffiti onto shop and bus windows. Once convinced that you are a responsible homeowner, they will let you purchase one. Lay the glass on a padded surface, such as a piece of carpeting or several layers of newspaper. Score the glass with the glass cutter, using a straightedge. Move the glass to the edge of the table or workbench so the smaller part is hanging off the edge. Wearing gloves, carefully bend that part downward—the glass should break along the scored line. (If it doesn't, you'll have to start over with a new piece.) Old glass tends to be brittle and is more difficult to cut. Make sure it is clean before cutting it. It helps to lubricate the cutter with a little 3-in-1 oil first. Some hardware stores and glass companies will cut old glass for you, usually charging a dollar or two for the cut, which is cheaper than buying a new piece of glass.

Once the glass is cut, test—fit it into the sash. If it's too big, don't try to force it in—it will crack. The smallest amount that can be shaved off is $1/8$ inch—if that will make the glass too small, it's probably better to start with a new piece. Prepare the sash to receive it by laying down a thin bead of putty on the narrow lip of the rabbet to cushion the glass. There are two kinds of putty available—traditional linseed oil putty (DAP 33) and acrylic putty. I personally don't like acrylic putty—it doesn't tool well. I prefer time-tested materials; linseed oil putty has been used for hundreds of years. There is no easy way to lay down this first coat of putty. If the sash is laying flat, you can roll it into a thin snake and lay it in the groove, but if the sash is still upright in the frame, you'll just have to slap it on bit by bit with the putty knife. It should be about $1/16$ inch thick once you squish it into the rabbet. Lay the glass into the rabbet and gently press it down around the edges to flatten the

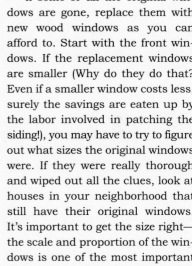

This home, part of a Pasadena bungalow court, has two sets of casements that are accented with an extra trim board on each side. The small blocks on the trim look to be pegs anchoring the horizontal board that connects the two vertical ones, though it's likely they are really just nailed on.

putty. Then, using the putty knife, carefully push the glazing points into the sash to secure the glass. Use at least one glazing point per side, more for a large window (one every 12 inches or so). Make sure they are flat against the glass.

Now for the part that requires some skill. Roll the putty into a rope about $1/2$ inch thick and press it along the edge of the sash on top of the glass and the glazing points. I recommend doing one side at a time. Then, holding the putty knife at a 45-degree angle, and using quite a bit of pressure, tool the putty into a 45-degree wedge from one corner to the next. The excess putty should fall away in a ribbon. The angled part of the wedge should be flat, and you should not be able to see the edge of the putty on the inside of the sash. In an ideal world, this would only take one pass. In reality, it will take several—there will be low spots to be filled in, it won't be smooth, or the angle will be wrong. Just keep working with it until it's even. Dipping the putty knife in paint thinner will help. The putty should be mitered in the corners. Give the putty about a week to cure, then prime and paint.

Repairing leaded or art glass windows may be more complex than most homeowners would care to tackle—much depends on the degree of damage and the complexity of the design. Some windows might be within the capabilities of a homeowner with previous stained-glass experience, or you could always take a few classes in stained glass before you tackle the repair. Art glass that is extremely complex or valuable for some reason (like your house was designed by a famous architect or the glass is by Louis Comfort Tiffany) should be dealt with by experienced restoration professionals.

If some or all the original windows are gone, replace them with new wood windows as you can afford to. Start with the front windows. If the replacement windows are smaller (Why do they do that? Even if a smaller window costs less, surely the savings are eaten up by the labor involved in patching the siding!), you may have to try to figure out what sizes the original windows were. If they were really thorough and wiped out all the clues, look at houses in your neighborhood that still have their original windows. It's important to get the size right—the scale and proportion of the windows is one of the most important aspects of a bungalow, and one of the reasons most new "bungalows" just don't look right. Other houses may provide clues about muntin patterns, as well. If there really aren't any clues available, the modified Tic-Tac-Toe pattern is a classic. There are only one or two national companies who make a historically accurate window without all that argon/low-E, double-glazed, aluminum-clad nonsense, so you might be better off dealing with a local millwork or sash shop if there is one. Otherwise there are millwork shops that ship nationally (although you'll need to be really sure of the measurements). If you live near the Canadian border, the exchange rate for American dollars can make Canadian-made windows a good buy. If you're Canadian, it unfortunately doesn't work the other way around. (And before anybody starts writing me about "buy American" and all that, let me say this: saving money isn't always politically correct, but it's up to each person to decide what they can or cannot do with a clean conscience. I am talking about Canada here—I didn't suggest exploitation of sash makers in third world countries.)

BAR HOPPING

The only thing I detest as much as sliding aluminum windows is burglar bars. I have ripped them off several of the houses I've owned (and the suckers are hard to get off too). I don't care how bad the neighborhood is, I refuse to live my life behind bars—that's for criminals. Get an alarm, put in laminated glass, work on cleaning up your neighborhood, get a big dog, put in a fence that can't be climbed, plant thorny plants under all the windows, do whatever you have to do, but get rid of the burglar bars. (See "Erik's Bungalow Manifesto" in Chapter 2.) Okay, at the very least take them off the front. But don't complain to me about how dangerous your neighborhood is—I live in Oakland, for God's sake! I've had two break-ins this last year, but I'm still not putting up bars. Actually the thing I hate most about them is that we live in a country and a society where they're necessary.

BLOCK PARTY

Hollow glass blocks were first patented in France in 1886. Glass blocks were not widely used in America until after 1935, when Owens-Illinois introduced Insulux. The late 1930s and early 1940s were really the heyday of glass block. Bungalows built that late might have it. Glass block was often used for basement windows and for windows over bathtubs, because it was mostly impervious to water, had some insulation value, and provided privacy. It was also retrofitted into the same locations for the same reasons.

STEEL AWAY

Steel windows were only found occasionally in bungalows, but there were a few. Steel windows were available as early as 1860, but did not come into widespread use until after 1890, when technology borrowed from the steel-rolling industry made possible the mass production of rolled steel windows on a scale that made them competitive with wooden windows. In addition, devastating fires in several cities, including the earthquake and subsequent fire in San Francisco in 1906, led to the enactment of strict fire codes for multistory commercial and industrial buildings.

Rolled steel sections $1/8$ inch thick and 1 to $1\ 1/2$ inches wide were used for both sash and frame. The strength of the frame allowed for larger windows and expansive amounts of glass. The windows soon became popular for more than just industrial or commercial use because they were standardized and reasonably priced. Although many different window styles, including double-hung, pivoting, awning, and hopper windows, were used in industrial or commercial buildings, steel windows in residences were almost invariably casements, adapted from the English wrought-iron casements with leaded glass. For this reason, they were popular for cottage-style homes in various period revival styles like Tudor, Normandy, and such.

If steel windows are not maintained, they can rust. If this goes on too long, parts can rust away. Steel windows are easily repaired—you can do it yourself or send them away. They can also be made energy-efficient by the addition of storm windows.

THE PERFECT STORM

Actually, there's probably no such thing. There are only different options, and what will work best is dependent on the types of windows, aesthetic considerations, and various other factors. There are both interior and exterior storms available. Some types of windows, like outward-opening casements, awning, or hopper windows, require interior storm windows, although a storm can be attached directly to the outside of the casement sash. These same types of windows require exterior storms if they open inward. Fixed, single-hung, double-hung, or triple-hung windows may have either interior or exterior storm windows. Some types of windows, such as pivoting or austral windows, need interior storm windows that can be easily removed to operate the window if need be.

Exterior storm sashes were traditionally made of wood. They hung from special hardware (which is still available) attached to the trim at the top of the window, and were kept closed at the bottom with a low-tech hook-and-eye system.

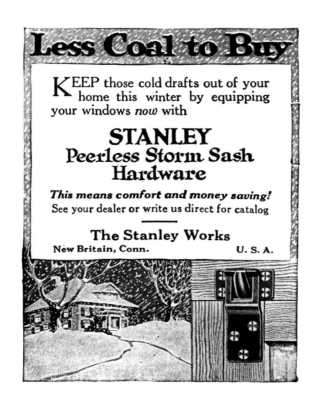

The Stanley Works (still in business) advertisement showed a driving snowstorm and the headline "Less Coal to Buy." They were right, of course, because storm windows do save energy.

A LOW-TECH INEXPENSIVE INTERIOR STORM

(Summarized from an article at
HammerZone.com by Bruce W. Maki)

Supplies needed:

- heat-shrink film
- double-sided tape
- 1- by 2-inch lumber
- wood glue/brads
- paint or varnish
- scraps of polyethylene plastic
- scraps of plastic strapping
- staple gun

Build a frame about $1/8$ inch shorter and narrower than the window opening (between the jambs and the sill, not the stops; unless you want it to go between the stops). Also, the pulleys of a double-hung window will either require a recess in the frame to allow for the pulleys, or the frame will need to go on the room side of the stops, so measure there instead. The joints can be mitered and joined with glue and small nails, or if you want to get fancy, joined with biscuits or dowels or even the very Arts and Crafts mortise and tenon. If you don't want to get fancy, you can simply join the corners with L-shaped metal angles, available at any hardware store. A large window will need a crosspiece in the middle. The frame can either be primed and painted with semi-gloss paint or stained—if stained, it will need a coat of varnish or shellac, because the double-sided tape requires a non-porous surface.

Once the frame is ready, apply the double-face tape to the frame, attach the film, and shrink it with a hair dryer. If you want to go hog-wild and make a "double-glazed" window, do the same on the back, although there will be more distortion from two layers. For a gasket, cut 2-inch strips of 4 or 6 mil polyethylene, fold in half, and staple to the back of the frame so it extends about $3/4$ inch past the edge of the wood (that way it will fold over the narrow dimension of the wood when the frame is pushed into the opening). Just overlap the strips at the corners. Make a handle from plastic strapping and staple it to the side of the window, this makes the window easier to remove. Put a label on the back so you know which window it's for, and label the top as well, because it might not fit upside down.

Push it into the window opening slowly to allow air to escape (one of the stops may have to be removed for

this). Replace the stop. If the storm is going on the room side of the stop, it may need some sort of retaining mechanism to keep it from blowing out on a windy day.

These windows are pretty fragile, so maybe they aren't for you if you have children and rambunctious dogs. In the off-season, they have to be stored somewhere so they won't get damaged. On the other hand, even if they do, you can just go out and buy another ten bucks worth of window film.

These can be made as fancy or as funky as you wish—wood to match your woodwork and fancy brass handles are an option, or at the other end of the spectrum, cheap polyethylene instead of shrink-wrap (harder to see through, but it does the trick), which would be just the thing to go with the asphalt siding. Bubble wrap works too.

Exterior storm windows have the advantage of protecting the existing window from weathering, and from damage by vandalism, burglars, or those annoying flying bricks mentioned previously. This may be particularly important if the windows are ornate or valuable (such as art glass). On the other hand, an exterior storm detracts from the beauty of your windows by covering them. The single sheet of glass in a storm window destroys the sense of depth that comes from the different ways each pane in a multi-light window reflects the light. It also makes the plane of the window flat and even with the trim, rather than being recessed as the actual sash is, and glare off the storm window makes it difficult to see the real window underneath.

Exterior storm windows are available with wood or aluminum frames. Wood storms have to be painted and maintained just like the wood windows of the house, although having exterior storms will cut down on maintenance of the main windows, since they will be more protected from the weather. Aluminum-framed storms are available both as single units that are similar to wood storms or as the dreaded triple tracks, which you're just not allowed to have. No, not even under "Compromise Solution." Anodizing has allowed aluminum storms to be offered in more colors, so it's possible to get something closer to the color of the real sash. They can even be painted, but at that point you might as well just get wood. Aluminum is less expensive than wood. If you have aluminum storm windows that are not anodized and you can't afford to replace them, at least paint them a color that matches the window sash, so they won't be so silvery.

The hardware at the top allowed them to be propped open at the bottom for ventilation, if necessary. Storm sash for larger windows commonly had a crossbar in the middle for reinforcement, and some storm sash had muntins to match the window underneath. In the summer, storm windows were taken down and stored, replaced by wooden screens that hung from the same hardware. They were numbered using a set of dies—a blow from a hammer would indent the number in the wood. This is because even windows that appear to be the same size are not quite. The ritual of putting up the storm windows in the fall and taking them down in the spring is a long-standing tradition. Admittedly, wooden storm windows are heavy, and putting them on the second floor involves ladder climbing and possible danger. This led to the invention of the aluminum triple-track storm window, second only to the aluminum slider in ugliness and stupidity. A triple-track storm has two glass sashes and one screen sash, the idea being that the two glass sashes will be utilized in the winter, while in the summer one glass sash can be slid out of the way, and the screen used instead. That way the storms could be permanently installed. And thus, a house could be ugly all year round. They were also promoted as "no maintenance." As already discussed, there is no such thing.

A much better solution, assuming ladder climbing is not your thing, is *interior storm windows.* These can be installed from inside, and the ladder can stay in the garage. A tightly-sealed interior storm actually insulates slightly better than an exterior storm, because exterior storms have to have weep holes at the bottom to let moisture escape. (Interestingly enough, experiments at Monticello have shown that a loose exterior window that allows air infiltration is better than a well-sealed window at preventing condensation between an interior storm and the outside window. Just one more reason to give up caulking.) Interior storms can be wood-framed or aluminum, but often they are simply pieces of glass or Plexiglas. Various methods are utilized for attaching them: a magnetic strip around the edges that sticks to steel channels or strips installed inside or outside the frame; spring-loaded sides for pressure fitting and a U-channel at the top; a magnetic flexible bellows, like that found on refrigerator doors; pressure fitting using gaskets or weatherstripping; various kinds of clips or channels; the ever-popular hook-and-loop tape combined with an inner gasket that provides the seal; even using foam pipe insulation around the edges. Less expensive options involve plastic film—either heat-shrinkable or not. One method involves attaching U-channels to the window frame, stretching the film tightly across and securing it with a spline, similar to the way aluminum screens are made. Another method uses double-stick tape applied to the window and heat-shrink polyolefin film, which is then heated with a hair dryer to shrink and tighten it—this is a one-season-only solution, although it is possible to use heat-shrink film with a rigid frame made of wood.

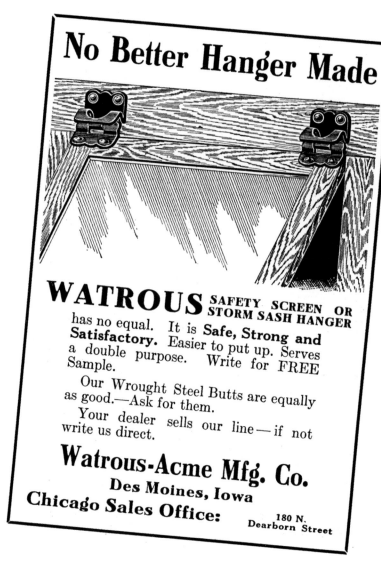

IN SPACE, NO ONE CAN HEAR YOU SCREEN

Screens are pretty much the same as storms, except they have an opposite purpose, which is to let air in, and also to keep bugs out. As with storms, they can be exterior or interior, though most are exterior. Outward-opening casements, awning, or hopper windows require indoor screens, which are usually hinged on the side so that they open inward in the same way that the casement opens outward. This allows them to be opened so that the window can be opened or closed. Another screening mechanism is the roll screen, invented by Pella in 1925. (It was patented as Rolscreen. The company name was changed to Pella when the company moved to Pella, Iowa.) This is a screen that unrolls like a window shade and rides down two metal channels attached

OPPOSITE: Do you think Wile E. Coyote ever ordered from the Watrous-Acme Manufacturing Company? Their hangers were "Safe, Strong, and Satisfactory." With a capital "S"—what more could you ask? The reference to "Wrought Steel Butts" refers to hinges.

ABOVE: Black iron and even galvanized steel screens had to be painted yearly. As you can imagine, this eventually filled the pores in the screen, not to mention being time-consuming, so bronze or copper screening was a longer-lasting alternative. Although the bungalow lifestyle was much less formal than its Victorian predecessor, it was still far more formal than we are today, when I doubt any man would be wearing a tie while painting or putting up screens.

RIGHT: Here's a lovely domestic porch scene—father reads the paper while mother and daughter relax in the hammock. "Artistic" was a key word during the bungalow era, and Vudor's Porch Shades were "artistically stained in soft, pleasing colors to harmonize (harmonizing was big too) with color-schemes of house and environment." It was also noted that they "should not be confused with the flimsy, carelessly made bamboo or imported screens which do not last and always look cheap."

AWNINGS

OBSESSIVE RESTORATION

Because fabric awnings have continued to be popular for commercial buildings, almost any town will have at least one awning company. Painted canvas is still available, though the awning company will probably try to talk you out of it. It will have to be replaced about every five years or so, depending on the climate and whether it is left out all year or taken down seasonally—it might be good to point out to them the extra work this will provide them. Steel is still available as a frame, either painted or powder-coated.

COMPROMISE SOLUTION

Okay, I've made my feelings about vinyl quite clear. Acrylic or polyester fabric will be fine, and it really doesn't look half bad. Depending on climate, it will last maybe slightly longer than cotton canvas, though it is less prone to mildew. Aluminum frames will be fine, and aluminum can also be painted or powder-coated. There are do-it-yourself awning kits available both by mail-order or through local suppliers. But I draw the line at motorized awnings unless you are old or disabled. Get up out of the chair and crank the thing by hand.

This 1925 Lewis Homes bungalow has a striped awning (retracted in the photo) over the front of its porch. The proud owners have posed with their bungalow for the photo. It must have been at least a little while after they built it, since the flower box is overflowing with blooms and the foundation plantings have become established.

to the sides of the window. Several other companies now make versions of these, and if you're really lazy, motorized versions are available too.

Wooden screens had wire screening stapled to one side and covered with half-round molding, *screen molding,* or some other kind of small molding that was tacked on with small nails or brads. The screening (or wire cloth) was made of bronze or copper, galvanized steel, black iron, and later, stainless steel or aluminum. The iron screening had to be painted periodically. Naturally, this tended to clog up the holes. All these kinds of screening are still available (except iron), with the addition of vinyl-coated fiberglass. Like the storm windows, screens were numbered using dies to indicate which screen went on which window. Aluminum-framed screens use a flexible spline to hold the screening in a channel. There are also new systems involving hook-and-loop tape and magnets, similar to the systems used for interior storms. And of course, there are the wood-and-metal sliding adjustable screens available at every hardware store and home center—good in a pinch, but not that efficient, since bugs can still creep in around the edges. Some bungalows even had decorative screens with "muntins."

It's not that hard to make wooden screens—the only difficulty is that the bottom rail has to be angled to match the angle of the windowsill, which requires a table saw. The hardware for hanging them is still available at any well-stocked hardware store or by mail-order. Yes, they have to be painted, and priming and painting the screen molding is tedious, but they look so much better than aluminum-framed screens that it's worth it. Wooden screens can also go on the inside, although they need to be operable somehow so that the window can be opened easily.

BLANK CANVAS

Canvas awnings over some of the windows were featured on many bungalows. Awnings kept the summer sun off the windows, keeping the house cooler in the days before air-conditioning, and made it possibile to leave the windows open even if it rained. In the winter, the awnings were either taken down, rolled up, or retracted, depending on the style of the awning. Awnings were traditionally made of painted canvas in colors like green, blue, red, brown, and tan, or striped (green and white, blue and white, etc., or multicolored stripes on a background of red, green, blue, or brown). The awning valance might be straight or could be cut into decorative shapes, or possibly even have an appliquéd border with fringe. Awning types included *standard* (plain or with sides), *casement* or *box* (stuck out farther from the wall), *concave, circular* (for arched windows), *oval* (for bow windows), *accordion,* and *Venetian* (like standard only with spears—particularly popular on period revival homes). Canvas awnings fell into disfavor after World War II and were replaced by aluminum awnings. Even these fell into

disfavor with the popularity of air-conditioning. Awnings continued to be used on stores and commercial buildings, as they still are. Canvas has for the most part been replaced by acrylic, polyester, or vinylized fabric, which lasts longer and is less prone to fading. Most of these fabrics come in traditional (or at least traditional-looking) stripes in addition to solid colors.

Some awnings are fixed in place, while other awnings used different mechanisms to retract or roll up—either rope-and-pulley systems or various kinds of cranking mechanisms. Frames used to be made of steel, which can corrode, but nowadays the frames are aluminum tubing. These days you can also get motorized awnings (these are usually larger and are used for porches or decks).

SHUTTER TO THINK

Although shutters were not common on bungalows, they were found on a few due to the influence of Swiss chalets. Shutters were typically louvered or paneled, or a combination of both. Sometimes they had cutout designs of trees or sailboats, or merely geometric designs. Shutters require a special kind of hinge, plus hardware to keep them open, called *shutter dogs,* because shutters are supposed to be operable. Therefore, they must be of a size that would allow them to cover the window when closed—no foot-wide shutters on either side of a huge picture window. And must I even say that shutters must be made of wood? Not plastic, not vinyl, not fiberglass—wood.

MORE DOOR

You could crawl in the window, but a door is so much more convenient. Front doors on bungalows ranged from the very plain to the very fancy, and there wasn't always a correlation between the elaborateness of the house and the fanciness of the door. The front door was usually wider than other exterior doors, which were commonly 30 or 32 inches, but that could mean a width anywhere from 36 to 60 inches. Some doors also had *sidelights,* essentially narrow windows on one or both sides of the door. In general, sidelights were fixed, but if you wanted to get really fancy, they could be operable for ventilation. If you wanted to get even more elaborate, and this was especially true if the main door was really big, the sidelights could actually be narrow doors that could be used in lieu of the main door. There might also be a transom—a window above the door, which might be fixed or operable. The door itself could be solid or have one or more windows.

There were different ways of constructing doors. The most common was *frame-and-panel.* In a frame-and-panel door, a frame of stiles (vertical members) and rails (horizontal members) surround one or more wood panels. The panels sit in channels in the edges of the frame but are not glued, which allows for movement as the wood expands and contracts seasonally. The edges of the frame around the panels could be cut square or have a molded profile. Another type of construction was *board-and-batten,* where vertical boards, usually tongue and groove, were held together by Z-shaped or X-shaped battens (boards) applied to the surface. This was one of the earliest forms of door construction. Of course, in another triumph for faux structure over real structure, a frame-and-panel door could be made to look like a board-and-batten door by using tongue-and-groove boards for the panel and applying thin boards on top to look like battens. Although *flush* or *slab* doors are thought of as a later (post–World War II) invention, they were often used on front doors for bungalows, frequently with a decorative veneer. *Dutch doors,* which are split horizontally, allowing the top and bottom halves to be opened separately, were a less frequently used door type. Doors weren't always rectangular, either—arch-top or round-top doors were also used.

On top of the basic door, whatever its construction, all sorts of decorative things could happen. Interestingly shaped panels or windows were common. Window glass might be beveled, leaded, etched, or have art glass. Windows could be operable for ventilation or for talking to someone outside the door without opening it (this is often called a *speakeasy*); applied moldings, blocks, or carvings added more decoration. A slab door might be covered in an exotic veneer and/or have inlay work or *marquetry.* Decorative butterfly-shaped keys might be used to join the boards of a slab door. Hardware of brass or bronze might be simple or intricate.

Doors were made of almost any wood imaginable, both in softwoods like pine and fir and hardwoods like oak and birch. A veneered door allowed the inside to be a wood that matched the interior paneling, while the outside was a different wood that possibly held up better to the weather, or maybe just looked different. Bungalow doors were not usually painted, because of the Arts and Crafts reverence for wood. Instead they were varnished.

GONE DOOR

The front door was meant to impress. The other doors were meant to function. These included the back or side doors; French doors (a door with glazed panels extending the full length, usually paired but not always); cellar or basement doors; doors for milk, ice, coal, or package delivery; doors to the compartment that held the gas and electric meters; and hatches leading to the crawl space (if there was no basement).

Back or side doors tended to be much more utilitarian than the front door. They were generally frame-and-panel, with varying numbers of panels. A typical back or side door would have a high window for light and panel(s) below, although eight- or ten-light doors weren't unheard of either. Sometimes the door would be solid with no window. These doors could be varnished but were more likely to be painted than the front door.

In keeping with the blurring of indoor and outdoor spaces so prized by Arts and Crafts designers, bungalows often had wraparound porches, or porches on the side or back, that were accessed through French doors, either single or double. Although French doors traditionally had rectangular glazing, on bungalows the French doors often echoed the muntin pattern of the windows, though not always.

Depending on the slope of the lot and how it was built, a bungalow might have a *walk-out* or *daylight* basement. These would have doors similar to those on the side or back, though these were more likely to be solid. Depending on headroom, these doors might not be full height. Some basements had *bulkhead doors,* a wedge-shaped bulkhead built out from the wall with a door or doors that lifted up, leading to stairs down to the basement. These are vulnerable to weather damage if not kept up, which they usually aren't. They are often replaced with metal doors. Bungalows in areas where basements aren't common would have small hatch doors leading to the crawl space under the house. These were customarily board-and-batten doors made of bead board. The gas and electric meters, and sometimes the fusebox, were located in a compartment near ground level with a similar door.

INSET: In 1921, Morgan offered this door with sidelights, under a roof held up by some really gigantic corbels.

OPPOSITE: A very wide door with a Japanese influence showing in the cloud-lift design of the upper cross piece welcomes visitors and residents alike into the living room of Greene and Greene's Pratt House. In many bungalows, the front door did open directly into the living room.

A square "shelf" supported by square or rectangular blocks is a very common sight on bungalow doors. The triangular windows paired with it on this door in Milwaukee, Wisconsin, are less common than square or rectangular windows, but there was wide variety in doors.

Rounded tops seemed to go with wrought-iron strap hinges, as they do on this side door surrounded by stone on a New Jersey bungalow.

BARAD-DOOR

(I'm sorry—I couldn't help it.)

Back when coal was the most common fuel for furnaces and boilers, the coal bin also had a door, or sometimes a window, usually operable from inside the basement using some sort of pulley system, which allowed the coal to be easily transferred to the coal bin from outside by means of a chute.

The kitchen often had an outside *icing door*, by which the iceman could put ice directly into the back of the icebox without coming into the house. This prevented dirt and water being tracked into the kitchen. In addition, the outer door could be left open during cold winter months to save on ice.

A similar setup was used for milk or package delivery doors. The delivery man opened the outer door to place the milk or package inside. An inner door, which could be locked, allowed the goods to be retrieved from inside the house.

Another kind of opening found on the walls of many bungalows is the vent. Vents may serve the kitchen *cooler cabinet* (a cabinet that is vented to the outside) or a wall-mounted exhaust fan. Cooler cabinet vents were characteristically wood or metal; most other vents were metal, though some now are plastic. In more recent times, vents that serve stove hoods, bathroom exhaust fans, dryers, or even furnaces may be exiting through the wall. Old furnace or water heater flues may also run up an outside wall on their way

The front door of the Bolton House in Pasadena shows the beautiful art glass and exotic woodwork common to the houses of Charles and Henry Greene.

through the roof. Sometimes cast-iron plumbing vents were also routed up an outside wall (a bad idea in cold climates).

AREA DOOR

(Only the serious Tolkien fans will get that one.)

In cold climates, storm doors were used to protect the exterior doors from weather, and, like storm windows, to provide thermal insulation. A storm door was normally pretty simple, regardless of how lavish the door underneath might be. It usually had a window, and some storm doors were made in such a way that the glass could be traded out for a screen insert in the summer.

Screen doors served to keep bugs out in the warmer months. A screen door was often more elaborate than a combination storm/screen, at least on the front door. Side and back screens were more practical. But the front screen could have fairly complex woodwork, often repeating the muntin pattern of the windows. Screen doors almost invariably were mounted on spring-loaded hinges to keep them closed. This caused them to bang shut. They're supposed to bang shut (either that, or *bang shut* is some new kind of Thai food). A simple hook-and-eye was used to keep them closed. But if there were a lot of kids running in and out this could get to be annoying; thus the pneumatic door closer that we are familiar with today was

DOOR REPAIR

COMPROMISE SOLUTION

If the original door has been removed, or too badly abused, replacement is an option. It may be less expensive to use a door from the salvage yard, although the cost savings may be eaten up in the labor required to hang it. But with new wood doors costing $1,000 and up, it may still be the less expensive choice. Also, you have to find one the right size that's in decent condition. Environmentally, it's better to reuse existing resources instead of consuming new ones. There are also numerous companies and shops manufacturing Craftsman- or bungalow-style doors. In wood doors, there is generally a choice of solid wood or engineered wood. In solid wood, the stiles and rails are solid wood, whereas engineered wood can be anything from built-up solid wood pieces, *finger-jointed* wood with veneer, MDF (medium-density fiberboard) with veneer, and probably particleboard with veneer as well (which I would avoid). I have mixed feelings about engineered wood. It does make use of scrap products and sawdust, which would otherwise be thrown away, and can utilize smaller trees instead of old-growth timber—all a good thing. But I question the longevity of some of these products—I just can't see that an MDF core door is going to hold up that well in the face of moisture. Certainly an engineered wood door will be less expensive, and might be fine for a sheltered porch. A solid wood door is certainly beautiful, and offers the opportunity for carving.

I probably need to mention that there were no sliding doors, only sliding windows, which were primarily limited to sleeping porches. I know it is possible to buy sliding doors with divided lights and all, but that doesn't mean you should. If there's no room for an in-swinging door, then get an out-swinging door. If you absolutely insist on having a slider, then get a wooden one, and put it in the back where no one can see it.

There are also fiberglass, steel, and carbon (similar to fiberglass but without the fiber reinforcement) doors. These usually have a foam core for insulation, which makes them about R-5. Big whoop. You can get the same R-value by adding a storm door. Although the manufacturers trumpet their resemblance to wood doors, the fact is, they have to be painted. So to get them to resemble wood, they require a faux finish. I've nothing against faux finishes, but it does kinda go against the whole Arts and Crafts "honesty of materials" thing. It amuses me that not a single Web site for fiberglass or steel doors dared to show them close up. The fiberglass doors also suffer from the "wood grain" embossing that plagues fake siding, although a smooth finish is available. The steel doors dent and corrode. (There are also stainless steel doors, which can be quite beautiful in their own way but don't belong on a bungalow.) Steel and smooth fiberglass doors don't look too bad when painted a solid color, and they certainly cost less than wood doors. It might be an okay choice for side and back doors, and even the front if you're on a very tight budget. Just stay away from

OBSESSIVE RESTORATION

If a bungalow was well taken care of, the front door is usually in good shape and may only require paint-stripping or a new coat of varnish (which should be some kind of varnish based on natural resins, NOT polyurethane or other synthetic varnishes. Spar varnish works well and contains UV inhibitors that protect the wood from breaking down). If the house was not well taken care of, the door may have been abused. Typically this means veneer that is separating, peeling paint, trim elements missing, hardware missing or replaced with some cheap modern substitute, glass broken or missing, and the door has usually been drilled for numerous deadbolts. In addition, the door may have sagged or the joints separated. Sometimes the door is missing altogether and has been replaced with some cheap door from a home center. (I swear, those six-panel "colonial" doors should just be banned.) Sometimes the replacement door isn't even cheap, just inappropriate. (Those replacement doors with beveled glass and brass "leading" spring immediately to mind.) In that case, a more appro-priate door from a salvage yard or a newly-built door of suitable design should be installed. If the original door has been abused, it's still best to try to save it, though it's up to you to decide when to take it off life support. Veneer can be reglued or replaced—if parts of it are missing (often at the bottom of the door). It may be easier to cover up the missing parts with a brass kickplate. Glass can be replaced, but one of the big problems with old doors is that often the glass is essentially held in by the door structure, rather than being held in with putty or molding as it would be in a window—this requires taking the door apart in order to replace the glass. Not all doors are like this—some use small molding instead, and these are obviously easier to reglaze. Missing trim elements often leave "ghosts" that provide clues as to their shape and size. A custom millwork shop can replicate these, or simple ones (like corbel blocks) can be made using commonly available power tools. Cheap hardware can be replaced—the biggest problem will be what to do about the numerous 2-inch holes drilled for deadbolts.

the six-panel "colonial" doors, and the brass "leading."

There were many houses with beautiful doors that we might have photographed for this book except for one thing—the door was covered by a repulsive and inappropriate steel or aluminum storm door. Often they had the particularly awful "wrought iron" curlicues that I guess are supposed to evoke New Orleans. Even in New Orleans, fake wrought iron would be wrong. Given that, I do realize that the choices in storm doors at the local home center are limited. There are two choices: get a real wood storm door, or do without. Doing without isn't such a radical concept—you can still double the R-value with weatherstripping and caulking (see the window section). Most bungalow doors are sheltered on a porch anyway. And although there is a solid vinyl screen door available, do not buy it.

And I've got to keep saying this: Don't fancy up a modest little bungalow by getting a teak/art glass/carved Greene and Greene–style door with sidelights and a huge surround—no matter how much you might want one. Invest in some nice Greene and Greene reproduction furniture instead. It will cost about the same anyway.

Art glass on Chicago bungalows extended to doors as well as windows, and if you paid a little extra, you could get your initial in gold.

You can try patching them with 2-inch plugs cut from the same species of wood, trying to match the grain as closely as possible, though it will still be pretty obvious. A better option might be to enlarge the hole to some geometric shape, which could almost be considered decorative, and fill that with contrasting wood like it was done on purpose. It may also be possible to find door hardware with a really large backplate that will cover the hole(s). Sometimes paint is the only option—it's much easier to hide the various patches that way. Sagging doors, or doors with joints that have opened up, can be taken apart and reglued. Of course, often the previous owner's solution to a sagging door was to plane it, sometimes severely. Sometimes the door frame has been hacked up as well. (Obviously if the door frame is out of square, both that and whatever structural problem might have caused it need to be dealt with first.) Once the structural issues have been dealt with, a piece of wood can be attached to the edge(s) where the door was planed to make it square again. (You can use screws, biscuits, dowels, mortise and tenon, whatever strikes your fancy, and glue.)

Replacement doors are available in many wood species, including oak, mahogany, fir, cedar, ash, alder, cherry, birch, and others, as well as tropical hardwoods like teak and nyatoh.

If by some unbelievable chance the original storm or screen door is still there—same deal. Fix it. If it's not there—get a new one. There are many companies and shops that manufacture wooden screen and storm doors.

invented. In at least one instance, a clever builder also put in a *pocket* screen door, which slid back into the wall when not in use. The few screen doors that did not employ spring hinges used regular hinges and a small mortise lock with a lever on one side and a small knob on the other. Screen doors used the same system as window screens— screening stapled over the opening and covered with a small molding.

All these doors were made out of wood. There were no metal "security doors." And there shouldn't be now. I don't care how dangerous your neighborhood is; I don't care if a

elements were combined gives bungalows a subtle beauty different than the more "in your face" ornament of nineteenth-century houses. Not that I'm against that sort of ornament, it's just different. Although the functional reason for much of the trim was (and is) to cover the joints between various materials, this utilitarian purpose still allowed for great creativity on the part of the designer. Other trim such as windowsills actually served a practical purpose on the house. And some trim was merely decorative, though it may have been pretending to serve a structural purpose. Trim could be made of wood, stone, or concrete.

Window and door casings made of wood ranged from flat boards to various kinds of molding, or combinations of flat boards and molding. Flat boards measuring $3/4$ to 1 inch by 4, 5, or 6 inches, relieved on the back to provide a better fit against uneven walls, were joined with butt joints (two pieces meeting at right angles) or miter (diagonal) joints. Sometimes flat boards were *battered* (wider at the bottom). The top casing might extend past the side casings by a small or a considerable amount. Some flat boards were decorated with *back-banding,* the addition of a smaller piece of molding on the edge, or the look of back-banding could be achieved by cutting the molding profile into the edge of the board (this method required a miter joint, whereas back-banding could be applied over a butt joint). Openings in brick

A close-up shows the heavy leading and clover motif on a Chicago window. The roof tile of the house next door (the bungalows were built very close together) is reflected in the window.

security door allows you to keep the doors open in the summer. Get rid of it.

CASING THE JOINT

Unlike the flat, unadorned walls and barely trimmed openings that are the unfortunate legacy of modernism, bungalow walls had a complex interplay of recessed and projecting elements, as well as decorative moldings and other kinds of trim and ornamentation. Though the molding and other ornament on bungalows was simple compared to most of the preceding nineteenth-century styles, the ways in which these simple

walls required *brickmold,* and there was also a special molding often used for stucco that allowed the stucco to be applied flush with the outer edge of the molding.

Other wood moldings included *water table* (a horizontal molding at the first-floor level that keeps water from running down the foundation wall); *cap* molding (which went on top of windows and doors); window sills and *aprons* (the trim board underneath the sill); *bed* moldings (like crown

OPPOSITE: A bungalow door in a style so universal as to be iconic (though sometimes it has eight windows) adorns the front porch of a bungalow in Seattle, Washington.

Flat casings with a top over-hang cut on the diagonal sur-round a beveled-glass door with corbels and multi-light sidelights on a bungalow in Victoria, British Columbia. A hanging black-iron porch light has matching sconces flank-ing the door, and the bead board ceiling has been left natural. Deep, rich colors are typical in this part of Canada, though the white trim con-trasts rather more than it ought to with the deep cran-berry shingles and dark green sashes; a cream color would have been more harmonious.

molding, only smaller—used where the wall meets the roof and similar places); *crown* moldings (wider than bed molding but used in the same places); and a variety of other moldings. Other woodwork included *pilasters* (shallow rectangular columns); *cornerboards* (covered the end grain of wood siding); *corbels,* decorative half-timbering (boards embedded in stucco, brick, or stonework); *quoins* (rectangular corner pieces derived from masonry architecture); *brackets* (not just for the eaves—also used to hold up flower boxes, shelves, or nothing); *beams* (usually fake but making it look like the real floor joists were protruding); decorative *blocks* (smaller than corbels); and miscellaneous moldings used to divide differing siding materials, divide walls into sections, or just put up there for the heck of it.

Projecting horizontal moldings like windowsills and water table moldings have a small groove cut in the bottom. As far as water was concerned, that groove is the Grand Canyon—it comes to a screeching halt and opts to drip off instead.

Brick bungalows could have a stone or concrete water table, or they might have a projecting *belt course* or *string course* instead. Stone or concrete lintels (the supporting beam across the top of a door or window) were used on some bungalows, while others made use of brick arches. Decorative insets of molded or carved stone, cast stone, or concrete were used on some bungalows.

Often the windowsills, whether wood or stone, were extended all the way around the house as a decorative feature mimicking the water table molding below. Often the same was done with the window and door lintels, giving a horizontal line that ran all the way around the house, tying all the various elements together.

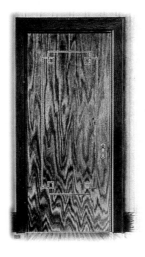

A veneered slab door could also be inlaid, like these two examples from the Morgan catalog, one with beveled glass windows.

Two other Morgan doors show a striking woodgrain effect on the left, and "butterfly keys," usually employed to join boards in a tabletop, used for decorative effect in the veneer of the Dutch door on the right (even though veneer doesn't technically need to be joined in this way).

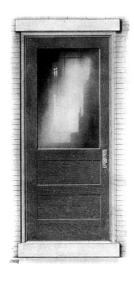

These two doors from the Morgan 1921 catalog were typical of the sorts of doors that would be used for side, back, or basement doors, as well as for side doors on garages or outbuildings.

No. 2   No. 3

OUTSIDE DOORS

A CHARACTERISTIC feature of any well designed
home is the front door. The doors furnished with
Lewis Homes combine beauty and strength. The
doors regularly furnished are manufactured from solid
white pine. If veneered oak are ordered there will be
a small extra cost.

No. 1   No. 4

No. 6   No. 7

INSIDE DOORS

THE five-panel door which is regularly furnished
with Lewis Homes combines beauty and stability
and is without question the most popular interior door
manufactured today. In all Lewis doors the wood
used is always selected for its attractive grain. The
two-panel door can be used at a small additional cost.

No. 5   No. 8

The Lewis Homes
1925 catalog had
this page showing
the various exterior
and interior doors
that were available.
Their doors were
made of white
pine, though it was
noted that
veneered oak
could be furnished
at a small additional
cost.

RESOURCES

RESTORATION GLASS

Bendheim (new cylinder glass)
www.bendheim.com

Fairview Glass (old glass)
www.fairviewglass.com
(301) 371-3364

ART GLASS

Theodore Ellison Design
www.theodoreellison.com
(510) 532-7632

Anne Ryan Miller Glass Studio
www.anneryanmiller
glassstudio.com
(812) 988-9766

Wallis Stained Glass
www.jackwallisdoors.com
(270) 489-2613

Little/Raidl Design Studios
www.sonic.net/little-raidl
(707) 632-5569

Brian McNally
BrianMcNallyglassartist@cox.net
(805) 687-7212

Lyn Hovey Studio
www.lynhoveystudio.com
(617) 261-9897

Unique Art Glass
www.uniqueartglass.net
(425) 481-6046

Sybaritic Studios
www.sybariticstudios.com
(262) 635-8267

WOOD WINDOWS

Weston Millwork Company
www.westonmillwork.com
(816) 640-5555

Smith Restoration Sash
www.smithrestorationsash.com
(401) 351-1222

Hoffmeyer's
www.hoffmeyersmill.com
(877) 644-5843

Wewoka Window Works
www.wewokawindowworks.com
(405) 257-2839

Old Fashioned Windows
and Millwork
www.oldfashionedwindows.com
(973) 589-3181

Wood Windows
www.woodwindows.com
(610) 896-3608

Re-View
www.re-view.biz
(816) 741-2876

H. Hirschmann, Ltd.
www.hhirschmannltd.com
(802) 438-4447

Grabill Windows and Doors
www.grabillwindow.com
(810) 798-2817

Jarrett, Inc.
www.jarrett-windows.com
(800) 533-5097

Aaron Wood Windows, Inc.
www.aaronwoodwindows.com
(604) 538-4618

Bear Wood Windows
www.bearwoodwindow.com
(888) 704-2709

Custom Trades international
www.customtrades.com

Sabana Windows
www.sabanawindows.com
(305) 825-1256

Horner South Florida Millwork
www.southfloridamillwork.com

Reilly WoodWorks
www.reillywoodworks.com
(631) 208-0710

Tradewood Industries
www.tradewoodindustries.com
(800) 410-0268

Woodstone
www.woodstone.com
(802) 722-9217

The Window Man
www.thewindowman.com
(902) 462-4576

Bagala Window Works
www.bagalawindowworks.com
(207) 878-6306

American Heritage
Window Rebuilders
www.vintagewindows.com
(866) 866-3973

Kronenberger and Sons
Restoration, Inc.
www.kronenbergersons.com
(800) 255-0089

Marlowe Restorations
www.marlowerestorations.com
(203) 484-9643

Hawk Retrofit, Inc.
www.hawkretrofit.org
(410) 757-0895

Restoration Works, Inc.
www.restorationworksinc.com
(815) 937-0556

Custom Window Company
www.customwindow.com
(800) 255-1920

Millwork Specialties
www.millwork-specialties.com
(800) 592-7112

Hull Historical
www.hullhistorical.com
(800) 990-1495

Caoba Doors
www.caobadoors.com
(215) 747-6577

H.I.C. Window and Door Company
www.homeideaccenter.com
(615) 371-8080

The Sash Window Workshop
www.sashwindow.com

STEEL WINDOWS

Seekircher Steel Window Repair
www.design-
site.net/seekirch.htm
(914) 725-1904

FIBERGLASS WINDOWS

Fiberglass Windows
www.fiberglasswindows.com
(617) 269-6397

The Duxton Company
www.duxtonwindows.com
(204) 339-6456

MISCELLANEOUS WINDOWS

Window Restoration Systems
www.steamstripper.com
(207) 725-0051

Window Repair.com
www.windowrepair.com
(617) 782-9410

INTERIOR STORM WINDOWS

Innerglass
www.stormwindows.com
(800) 743-6207

Window Saver Company
www.windowsaver.com
(800) 321-WARM

Soundproof Windows
www.soundproofwindows.com
(877) 800-3850

Rusco Windows and Doors
www.ruscons.com
(902) 456-5259

The Energy Doctor
www.northerntropic.com
(800) 408-5554

Thermopress Corporation
www.thermopress.com
(804) 355-9147

EXTERIOR STORM WINDOWS

Air-Tite Storm Windows
www.airtitestormwindows.com
(800) 722-4424

Allied Window
www.alliedwindow.com
(800) 445-5411

Vintage Woodworks
www.vintagewoodwork.com
(250) 386-5354

Old Fashioned
Windows and Millwork
www.oldfashionedwindows.com
(973) 589-3181

Weston Millwork Company
www.westonmillwork.com
(816) 640-5555

Re-View
www.re-view.biz
(816) 741-2876

American Heritage
Window Rebuilders
www.vintagewindows.com
(866) 866-3973

Grabill Windows and Doors
www.grabillwindow.com
(810) 798-2817

Victoriana East
www.victorianaeast.com
(856) 546-1882

WINDOW SCREENS

Euroscreen
www.eurollscreen.com

Connecticut Screen Works
www.connscreen.com
(203) 741-0859

Rollaway Disappearing Screens
www.rollaway.com
(888) 526-4111

Heirloom Screen Door Company
www.heirloomscreendoors.com
(541) 426-4811

Victoriana East
www.victorianaeast.com
(856) 546-1882

Screen Technology Group
www.wovenwire.com
(800) 440-6374

Air-Tite Storm Windows
www.airtitestormwindows.com
(800) 722-4424

Vintage Woodworks
www.vintagewoodwork.com
(250) 386-5354

Old Fashioned
Windows and Millwork
www.oldfashionedwindows.com
(973) 589-3181

Grabill Windows and Doors
www.grabillwindow.com
(810) 798-2817

Pella Corporation
Pella.com
(800) 847-3552

SHUTTERS

Withers Custom Shutters
www.withersind.com
(843) 376-0013

S.A. Shutter Mill
www.sashuttermill.com
(877) 675-7861

Ament Shutters
www.amentshutters.com
(715) 829-7686

Snugg Harbor Woodworking
www.snuggharbor.com
(800) 424-7778

Vixen Hill
www.vixenhill.com
(610) 286-0909

DOORS

Floating World Wood Design
www.perceptionofdoors.com
(828) 230-0134

Custom Glass Doors
www.customglassdoors.com
(832) 445-0686

Homestead Hardwoods
www.homesteadhardwoods.com
(419) 684-9582

Craftsman Doors.com
www.craftsmandoors.com
(866) 390-1574

Great Northwest Door Company
www.greatnwdoors.com
(800) 895-3667

Omega Too
www.omegatoo.com
(510) 843-3636

Jurs Architectural Glass
www.art-glass-doors.com
(800) 679-9772

Sheppard Door and Glass
www.beveldoor.com
(832) 644-2444

International Door and Latch
www.internationaldoor.com
(541) 686-5647

Crisp Door and Window
www.crispdoor.com
(281) 540-5551

H. Hirschmann, Ltd.
www.hhirschmannltd.com
(802) 438-4447

Doors by Decora
www.doorsbydecora.com
(800) 359-7557

Public Lumber Company
www.hardwoodint.com
(313) 891-7125

Fevreco Door Products
www.fevreco.com
(520) 844-1099

Simpson Door Company
www.simpsondoor.com
(800) 952-4057

Fine Doors, LLC
www.finedoors.com
(800) 395-3667

W.G.H. Woodworking
www.wghwoodworking.com
(520) 798-1133

Hull Historical
www.hullhistorical.com
(800) 990-1495

Northstar Woodworks
www.northstarww.com
(360) 384-0307

Caoba Doors
www.caobadoors.com
(215) 747-6577

Karona, Inc.
www.karonadoor.com
(800) 829-9233

Pinecrest, Inc.
www.pinecrestinc.com
(612) 871-7071

Alternative Timber Structures
www.alternativetimber
structures.com
(208) 456-2711

YesterYear's
Vintage Doors and Millwork
www.vintagedoors.com
(800) 787-2001

Upstate Door
www.upstatedoor.com
(800) 570-8283

Select Millwork Company
www.selectmillwork.com
(269) 349-7841

H.I.C. Window and Door
www.homeideacenter.com
(615) 371-8080

Millwork Specialties
www.millwork-specialties.com
(7180 768-7112

Madawaska Doors, Inc.
www.madawaska-doors.com
(800) 263-2358

AREA DOORS

Wooden Screen Door Company
www.woodenscreendoor.com
(207) 832-0519

YesterYear's
Vintage Doors and Millwork
www.vintagedoors.com
(800) 787-2001

Upstate Door
www.upstatedoor.com
(800) 570-8283

Touchstone Woodworks
www.touchstonewoodworks.com
(330) 297-1313

Phantom Screens
www.phantomscreens.com
(604) 855-3654

Vintage Woodworks
www.vintagewoodworks.com
(903) 356-2158

Hull Historical
www.hullhistorical.com
(817) 332-1495

Great Northwest Door Company
www.greatnwdoors.com
(800) 895-3667

Victoriana East
www.victorianaeast.com
(856) 546-1882

DOOR HARDWARE

Charles Locksmith, Inc.
www.charleslocksmith.com
(866) OLD-KEYS

Ball and Ball
www.ballandball.com
(800) 257-3711

Australian Global Services
www.aussieglobe.com
(888) 222-8940

Old Rose Hardware
www.oldrosehardware.com
(800) 508-0022

Al Bar Wilmette Platers
(hardware restoration)
www.albarwilmette.com
(800) 300-6762

Bungalow Metal
(hardware restoration)
www.bungalowmetal.com
(888) 205-3444

Cabin 26
www.cabin26.com
(800) 264-2210

Crown City Hardware
www.crowncityhardware.com
(800) 950-1047

Craftsmen Hardware
Company, Ltd.
www.craftsmenhardware.com
(660) 376-2481

Vintage Hardware
www.vintagehardware.com
(408) 246-9918

Eugenia's Antique Hardware
www.eugeniaantique
hardware.com
(800) 337-1677

Liz's Antique Hardware
www.lahardware.com
(323) 939-4403

Van Dyke's Restorers
www.vandykes.com
(800) 787-3355

Arts and Crafts Hardware
www.arts-n-
craftshardware.com
(586) 772-7279

Baldwin Hardware
www.baldwinhardware.com
(800) 566-1986

Rejuvenation
www.rejuvenation.com
(888) 401-1900

House of Antique Hardware
www.houseofantique
hardware.com
(888) 223-2545

Web Wilson
www.webwilson.com
(800) 508-0022

Knob Gallery
www.knobgallery.com
(888) 921-KNOB

WOODEN TRIM (see also: All About Eaves, p. 62)

Architectural Millwork
www.archmillwork.com
(800) 685-1331

Victorian Architectural
Millworks, Inc.
www.victoriantrim.com
(773) 237-6272

T and H Industries
www.tandh.com
(727) 573-7989

COMPOSITE TRIM

Axylon Industries
www.axylon.com
(973) 473-3878

CAST STONE

Stromberg Architectural
www.stromberg
architectural.com
(903) 454-8682

Classic Cast Stone
www.classiccaststone.com
(972) 276-2000

Continental Cast Stone
www.continentalcaststone.com

STONE

Stone is heavy and should be
bought locally, if possible.

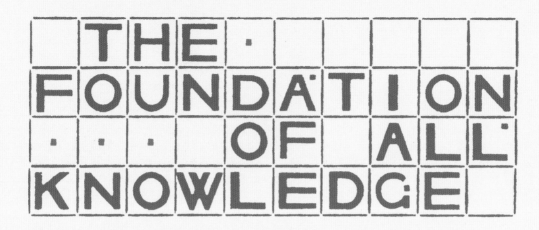

CHAPTER SIX

THE FOUNDATION OF ALL KNOWLEDGE

"Nothing, indeed, could be more flimsy than their method of construction. Their owners rarely indulge in the luxury of a foundation, and when a foundation is provided the stones are as often as not laid directly upon the grass. Generally, however, it is the sills, and not the stones, which are placed with mathematical precision upon the turf, and throughout the structure the timbers are made as light as possible for a one or two story building . . . The cheapness of these houses, is, of course, the direct result of their flimsiness of construction, and both are conditioned on the mildness and for the greater part of the year the dryness of the California climate. In the East even the cheapest house, except when it is occupied only for a couple of months in the summer time, requires a cellar and a comparatively substantial foundation and as this foundation is one of the chief sources of expense the tendency is to make it cover as small an area as possible . . ."

— Fred T. Hodgson, in Practical Bungalows, 1906

MOTIVATED CELLARS

I think I detect just a hint of jealousy. You know, they don't call it "laying the groundwork" for nothing.

The foundation is the first part of any building to be built. The foundation ties the house to the earth and keeps it there. As Mr. Hodgson said, although a foundation may be as simple as some flat rocks just sitting on the ground, permanent foundations were generally set below the ground.

Brick, stone, poured concrete, or concrete block were and are the most commonly used foundation materials.

FOOTING THE BILL

The foundation starts with *footings,* an area wider than the wall above it that spreads the load of the house over a wider area so it won't sink into the ground (kind of like the theory of snowshoes). The main reason that homes in cold climates

OPPOSITE: Even the basement window of this Chicago bungalow is a tripartite window, and an arched window at that, with proper wooden storm windows. The bricks forming the walls are textured in a waffle pattern not unlike a sugar cone. The corbels above have lost the window box they were meant to support, which could have had tulips as well.

have basements is that the footings have to be below the *frost line* (however far down the ground freezes in winter), otherwise the foundation walls will be subject to *frost-heaves* (which is not what happens after you eat too many sno-cones . . .). You know how water expands when it freezes, like when you overfill the ice tray? Well, when it freezes in the earth and expands, it can actually lift up whatever's on top, be that a road or the wall of your house. By keeping the footings below the frost line, the house will stay put. For a similar reason, bungalows in areas with a high *water table* (the level below the ground where the ground is completely saturated with water) are often built on poured concrete slabs that sit on top of the ground or raised up on piers above the ground. Conveniently, most areas with high water tables seem to be warm-weather areas or else it might be a problem. But, despite the opinion of Mr. Hodgson, most bungalows, in California and elsewhere, had full perimeter foundations.

PIER INTENTLY

In some areas, mostly in the South, bungalows were built on brick, stone, or concrete *piers* (really short structural columns) rather than continuous foundations to allow ventilation underneath the structure (and give the animals somewhere to hang out on hot days). Bungalows with perimeter foundations also had piers as secondary structural support within the perimeter foundation. Even the smallest bungalow had a beam down the center, supported either by posts resting on piers or on a continuous piece of foundation, and possibly other posts and piers for additional structural support.

JOIST THE FACTS, MA'AM

However tall the foundation happens to be, the *sill plate* (generally a 2 by something like 8, 10, or 12 inches) sits on top of it. The horizontal joists (usually 2 by 10 or 12 inches) that hold up the floor may sit directly on the sill, or there may be a *cripple wall* between the top of the foundation and the first floor with the joists sitting on top of that. They are attached to the *rim joist* (sometimes called a *ribbon joist*). Down the center of the bungalow, the other ends of the joists rest on the beam held up by the aforementioned piers. The ceiling joists generally run in the same direction as the floor joists. Upstairs in the house, any interior partition wall that is at right angles to the direction of the joists is known as a *load-bearing* wall. Joists may have diagonal or straight *blocking* or *bridging* in between to keep them from bowing to one side or the other. Often pieces of tin were placed between the joists and over the sheathing to prevent rodents from getting in.

WRIGGLE ROOM

In warm climates where basements are not common, there is likely to be a *crawl space,* which is sometimes a misnomer because in a few of them it's impossible to crawl—slithering is more like it. Some are tall enough that it's possible to sort of stand up in them, if you're the Hunchback of Notre Dame. And they are dirt, which means they can easily become a litter box for cats and other neighborhood animals if measures aren't taken to keep them out. Sometimes part of the foundation area was dug out deeper and had a concrete floor and some retaining walls, making a *partial basement*. These areas were used for laundry, storage, coal bins, the furnace, sometimes even an extra half-bath. A bungalow built on a sloping lot might also have a partial basement by virtue of the slope (sometimes called a *daylight* or *walkout* basement). A partial basement could be accessed from the outside or occasionally had an interior staircase. Crawl spaces were usually ventilated with wood or metal vents to allow air circulation. Metal vents commonly had a decorative grille, while wooden vents were screened with anything from simple latticework to decorative *balusters*. In addition, crawl spaces or partial basements could have fixed or operable windows to allow the passage of light and air.

It's a good idea to cover the dirt in a crawl space with plastic sheeting (4 or 6 mil polyethylene—comes in big rolls at the hardware store or home center)—this keeps moisture in the earth from condensing on the foundation framing. You can staple the edges to the sill if you want and weight the rest of it down with bricks or rocks or what have you. As an added bonus, it makes it a little more pleasant to crawl around under there.

A full basement was usually given a concrete floor, although I am sure there were exceptions. This essentially doubled the available space of the house, and many owners took advantage of that to add bedrooms, bathrooms, workshops, offices, and even ballrooms in the cellar. Depending on the depth of the frost line, basements could have quite high ceilings, although often the ceilings were somewhat lower than those in the house, especially after allowing for plumbing, heating ducts, and so on. There was normally a staircase leading to the basement from somewhere inside the house, often near the kitchen. In many places, builders took advantage of the chimney's foundation in the basement to put in a basement fireplace.

Depending on the slope of the lot and the design of the bungalow, very little or a lot of the foundation walls might show. A California bungalow on a flat lot might only have 6 or 8 inches of foundation showing, or it might have a *raised basement,* which is basically like building a basement above ground, which means it's not really a basement at all, but, hey, I don't make up the terminology. In this case, the outside walls will be covered with some kind of siding, which may or may not be different from the siding above it. This is also true for full basements, because often the top of the foundation wall is above *grade* (the ground). A visible poured concrete or non-decorative concrete block foundation wall may be faced with something more attractive like stucco, brick, or stone. Brick or stone foundations could also be faced, using more-expensive brick or stone for the outside layer.

Basement windows were often included for light and ventilation. These could be above ground level or below the surface in drained *window wells,* which still allowed some light to get in.

If you're lucky, whoever built your house will have done a good job of waterproofing the outside of the basement walls, and your basement will be dry. If not, you have the option of digging all the way down to the footings on the outside in order to waterproof it properly and add drainage to make the water go somewhere else. This will be tedious and expensive, to say the least. The other option is to deal with the water after it gets in by using perimeter drainage and a sump pump to pump the water back outside (a sump pump should not be connected to the sewer line), hopefully far enough from the house that it doesn't come right back in.

Basement or crawl space cripple walls should also be insulated (if you're going to insulate), and insulation should be installed between the floor joists as well.

■ ■ ■

CHAPTER SEVEN

LET'S PORCH THE PLACE

"You have the right to remain indolent, any chair in which you lay may be used against yews, you have the right to insult an attorney, if you can not afford a tourney, one will be disappointed for you . . ."

VERANDA RIGHTS

The original Indian bungalows had porches; therefore, all bungalows should have porches. Or they should have a veranda, terrace, deck, portico, stoop, entry, loggia, gallery, balcony, patio, lanai, piazza, or portal—these are all different words that mean, essentially, porch. A prominent porch is a feature of almost all bungalows. A bungalow without a porch is hardly a bungalow at all.

A FRONT TO DECENCY

". . . It is impossible to live upon one's lawn in privacy. The veranda offers a compromise between indoors and outdoors, and has developed into a species of open-air room, the furnishing of which is quite as important as that of any other room in the house."
—*Esther Singleton in* American Homes and Gardens, *May 1907*

In the time of the bungalow, people were sociable. They actually liked to interact with their neighbors and the community at large, and they did so from their front porch. The porch was probably second only to the hearth in the pantheon of bungalow mythology. Front porches were often generously sized, enabling them to be used as outdoor rooms. Like their predecessors in India, many front porches wrapped around the bungalow on two or three sides. Often French doors from other rooms would open onto this expanded porch.

The front porch might be sheltered under the sweep of a side-gabled bungalow's roof, or it might have a roof of its own, echoing the main roof or different from it, such as a shed roof. Not everyone approved of this sort of thing. Charles White, an architect writing in the December 1911 *House Beautiful*, had this to say: "Nothing is in poorer taste than one style for the main roof and another for porches." Poor Charles, no one listened to him. Part of the porch might be covered with a pergola (an arbor or trellis) rather than a roof, perfect for growing the climbing roses or wisteria that would help the bungalow be a part of nature. (In reality, it's not really a good idea to grow wisteria on your porch since it will eventually destroy the pergola, unless you're extremely vigilant about pruning it.) Or the porch might not have had a roof at all, maybe just a small one to shelter the door. The porch might be deep or shallow, curved or straight, small or large. There might be another porch on top of it that was accessed from upstairs.

OPPOSITE: The porch of a Seattle home combines stone, river rock, brick, concrete, and wood for its pillars and porch railing. It also has some impressively ornamental rafters.

Or a porch on top of it that couldn't be accessed from upstairs—just another old-house mystery.

The roof covering for a porch was usually the same as for the house, although a flat roof on a porch would have built-up roofing or metal. Inside the roof, the structure could be visible, or it could be boxed in and covered with bead board, board and batten, or a plastered ceiling. The porch ceiling was (and still is) frequently painted sky blue, and there are various rationales floating around as to why that was done, including:

- *It keeps spiders and bugs from nesting there.*
- *It repels flies.*
- *It keeps birds from nesting there.*
- *It is reminiscent of the sky.*
- *Ghosts who came out at night mistook the blue paint for the sky and thought it was daylight at that particular house, and thus passed it by. In some places in the South it was called "Haint Paint."*

What these all seem to have in common is they relate to the sky.

In warm climates, the porch might have ceiling fans to provide a breeze when there was none.

Gabled porches could have an open gable filled with elaborate openwork decoration and beams, or a closed gable with siding and decoration that sometimes repeated the design on the main gable of the house, and sometimes didn't. Every so often the gable was just plain.

ABOVE: The wide wraparound porch of a Seattle bungalow has a board-and-batten ceiling instead of the more usual bead board and is supported by robust square pillars. The ceiling has been painted a light color to reflect more light since the porch is so deep.

RIGHT: The front porch stretches all the way across the front of this bungalow, with the zigzag beam of the porch gable supported by four sturdy square pillars sitting on concrete block piers. A concrete block railing echoes the shape of the piers (obviously this builder had bought the "porch molds" with his concrete block machine), though unfortunately all the concrete has been painted white. The undulating shape of the beam is picked out in dentil molding, though the gable décor is fairly subdued compared to others in Los Angeles' West Adams neighborhood.

A shingled bungalow shown in Keith's magazine has a small, mostly open front porch, with only a small roof over the front door, supported by knee braces. The side porch is covered and looks to have another open porch on top, accessed by a door to the right of the chimney.

The colossal tapered pillars found on many bungalows were often called "elephantine," but the gigantic piles of clinker brick on this bungalow from the Herrick Improvement Company of Seattle really take the concept to its illogical conclusion. Even the chimney base looks like it's melting and spreading across the lawn. But I digress. This bungalow also has a rather large pergola over its brick porch. The pillars and pergola are actually not so out of scale, given the very wide front-facing gable of this home, most of which isn't even shown in the photo. The advertisement, from the May 1912 *House Beautiful,* mentions that special attention is paid to "the convenient arrangement of rooms—no long dark hallways." I guess that would be important in Seattle in the winter.

These two covered porches, or verandas, are furnished like rooms, with chairs and rockers, tables, and even carpets. The top porch has a striped canvas awning, while the bottom one has bamboo shades. Both have bead board ceilings, probably painted blue, though it's hard to know from a black-and-white photo.

A long porch with a low concrete block railing and round concrete columns has been enclosed with simple wooden screens. Striped canvas roll-up shades can be seen just inside the screens. The porch was obviously seeing a lot of use—besides the tables, chairs, and wicker porch swing, there is an easel near the wall of the house, as well as books, magazines, and a needlework project on the table in the foreground.

The porch of this Memphis bungalow has an arched bead board ceiling and lattice screening in the gable.

The front porch on another Milwaukee bungalow has been enclosed with multi-light wooden windows above wood panels. A wooden storm door completes the enclosure. Sometimes this is done in such a way that the wooden windows can be traded out for screens in the summer. Unfortunately, this kind of enclosure distorts the proportions and relationships between different architectural elements of a bungalow, even though it may have some practical value in cold climates.

The porch gable on this gold-brick Milwaukee bungalow shows a lot of Prairie School influence, both in the wooden gable decoration and the design of the small niches and half-round shelves on the pillars. The front windows have art glass with touches of metallic gold, and the shed dormer has round top windows. The porch, though small, is still large enough for a couple of wicker chairs, the backs of which can just be seen above the railing.

PILLARS OF THE COMMUNITY

The outside edges of the porch roof were supported by *pillars* (columns). If there is one architectural detail that really screams "bungalow," it's the pillar. We're not talking understated neoclassical columns here, we're talking pillars humongous enough to hold up many tons of multi-story building, employed instead to hold up a porch roof, a pergola, or sometimes nothing at all. The key thing here is that they are completely out-of-scale with the building, yet somehow they look right anyway. Constructed of rock, brick, stucco, or wood, or varying combinations of these, and sometimes referred to as "elephantine" (for obvious reasons), there are as many variations of pillars as the designers and builders could come up with, and then some. Designs range from fairly understated square, round, or tapered to the completely zany, asymmetrical, or just plain weird. Playing with scale can also be part of the pillar itself: sometimes a huge pillar will be separated from the roof it is holding up by a small piece of wood which, in this context, looks totally incapable of bearing the load it has been assigned to carry. . . . This amusing practice is one of the great joys of bungalows—a total disregard for Louis Sullivan's famous rule that

form should follow function. In reality, the average porch roof could be held up by four-by-fours, and in modern buildings it often is, but where's the fun in that? This is not to say that all bungalows have exaggerated pillars. Many have quietly understated columns (generally Doric or Tuscan, the latter of which is a plain, round, tapered column), and keeping in mind that there's no such thing as architectural purity, they may even be Ionic (with a spiral scroll at the top) or Corinthian (with acanthus leaves at the top).

Wood pillars may be made of solid wood like tree trunks or large timbers (some as large as 12 by 12 inches), but more often were built up as hollow boxes or columns. Round columns that are hollow are composed of staves (like barrels). Square columns could be built up with boards around the actual structural support or they could be structural themselves. Some pillars were faced with wood siding or shingles. Some pillars were multiple—there might be three small columns or two eight-by-eights, or some other thing the builder dreamed up. Wood pillars were either left natural (especially if they were tree trunks), stained, or painted.

Brick pillars were either built as solid masonry or as a facing over a wooden understructure, and this was also true

Zany architecture is rampant in bungalows all over the country, but I think that the West Adams district of Los Angeles wins the prize for the biggest concentration of zaniness in one neighborhood. This is almost a parody of an Ionic column, with a bulbous base that's too short and a caricature of an Ionic capital that's so big the column barely seems capable of supporting it. And we haven't even gotten to the bracket and dentil molding. I can't help it. The whole thing reminds me of Elmer Fudd. I can't even explain why. And this is only one bungalow on this block; there are probably forty houses on this block, and thirty of them are nearly as weird as this one.

A substantial tapestry brick pillar alone apparently wasn't enough to hold up the porch roof on this Memphis bungalow; two more twisted plaster columns with Egyptian-style papyrus capitals were needed as well.

A Vancouver home presents a pillar with more piercings and expressed structure than you can shake a stick at, combined with some chunky X-shaped railings and a few notches thrown in for good measure.

OPPOSITE: Brawny sandstone block columns with a matching railing are illuminated by the low rays of the winter sun falling across the front of an Eagle Rock, California, home. The porch floor is concrete, and on the railing is a banana plant, this being southern California.

PILLAR RESTORATION

OBSESSIVE RESTORATION

If you know what the old pillars looked like (from a historic photograph or other source), then they can be rebuilt in the same way. If you don't know what they looked like, look at some other houses in the neighborhood or around town to get ideas. But don't go overboard and replace it with something really elaborate that may not be appropriate to the house. When in doubt, err on the side of understatement.

Wood pillars or columns tend to rot at the bottom, because the end grain soaks up water like a sponge. This can often be repaired with epoxy consolidants. Many wood columns had a plinth—a small platform for the column to sit on that is both decorative and also protects the vulnerable end grain. Of course the plinth has end grain as well—but it can serve as a sacrificial object that is more easily replaced than the column. If the pillar can't be consolidated it may have to be rebuilt in some way—it's difficult to be specific on this because there are so many different designs for pillars. The wood structure of a stucco column can also rot if water has been allowed to get in. To repair this requires taking off the stucco, replacing the damaged wood, and re-stuccoing.

Huge timbers of the twelve-by-twelve variety are hard to come by these days, except as salvage. I would urge you to go the salvage route—it will be cheaper, and you won't be using up scarce resources, given that a salvage timber is taken from a tree that is long since dead. It will probably be a higher-quality timber as well.

Brick or stone columns need to be re-pointed occasionally in the same way as walls. Sometimes brick or stone is painted in order to avoid re-pointing. The thinking goes: if it's painted, deteriorating joints can be filled with caulk instead of mortar. Just a slight problem with that—caulk isn't really strong enough to hold up masonry. Anyway, first you'll be looking at paint-stripping before you can even continue on to re-pointing.

Repairing ornamental concrete such as rock-face blocks may require molds to be made to cast new matching blocks.

Sometimes the builder will have done something that we, with the advantage of 20/20 hindsight, can clearly see was bound to fail. Something like, oh, running a downspout through the middle of a pillar. That's all fine and dandy until it starts to leak, which of course it will; then, over a period of time, it will destroy the column, either by wood rot or by undermining the mortar. Or both.

Here's another example. I mentioned earlier that Frank Lloyd Wright didn't like downspouts, so when he designed the Robie House in Chicago, there were no downspouts, only a few holes at the edge of the eaves. The splashback from all that water eventually undermined the foundation and the terraces. As part of the restoration, downspouts were added.

Just because you're obsessive doesn't mean you have to rebuild things that are that blatantly stupid in the same ridiculous way, unless you really want to. In the case of the downspout inside the pillar, if you insist on putting it back inside instead of rerouting it, at least use copper so it won't rust out.

COMPROMISE SOLUTION

If the house is supposed to have pillars, then it's gotta have pillars. If the existing pillars are falling apart to the point that they really can't be saved, then they should be replaced with something similar in style, scale, and proportion. This doesn't mean you can replace a brick pillar with wood on a brick house, but it might mean you can replace a brick and wood pillar with all wood on a wood-sided house. Or with less brick. Or with a brick facing on a plywood box. It might be okay to put a stucco pillar on a wood house or a brick house. This is an aesthetic decision that is hard to dictate since it depends on so many factors.

If new wood pillars are being installed, painting them may allow the use of less-expensive wood or several different wood species together (which wouldn't match otherwise) on the same column. A box pillar made of flat boards around the actual load-bearing structure would certainly be an acceptable substitute for a large timber.

If the originals are long gone and replaced with a pipe column or some lovely wrought iron, here's the good news. If whatever is there is structurally sound and doing its job, just build a box around it that's more in scale with what a bungalow should have, and cover that with appropriate siding or boards.

Although "cultured stone" has improved from the Permastone days, I would still choose cultured stone very, very carefully to make sure it greatly resembles real stone. It does weigh somewhat less than real stone, which can be an advantage in earthquake areas.

I have to keep saying this: no commercially manufactured "used" brick—this is not the same thing as actual used brick, which you can get at the salvage yard. If there is other brick on the house, either try to match it or get something which contrasts but still blends in. This is, of course, trickier than it sounds.

If one giant tapering pillar is good, wouldn't two be even better, especially if they were connected by an arch and were a different color of brick at the bottom, like they are on this bungalow in Denver? Sometimes you wonder what the designers were smoking.

A round concrete pillar with textured bands supports an openwork porch gable. The pier it sits on has crown and dentil molding as well as chamfered corner accents. The balusters of the porch railing are also concrete. Evidently this Denver builder ordered the really deluxe concrete block molds.

On this pillar in Victoria, clinker bricks are used only as accents, the rest of the bricks being fairly normal.

The granite pillar of this Victoria, British Columbia, bungalow has an interesting mortar treatment.

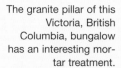

"Y"? "Y" not? Angled timbers support an openwork gable on a Victoria bungalow, with help from a few brackets and beam ends.

The bark-covered log pillars of a home in Berkeley, California, seem almost conservative. The house has recently been reshingled.

for stone. Stucco pillars usually had a wooden understructure as well, though stucco could also be applied over masonry.

Some pillars combined more than one material, such as stone and brick; brick and stucco; stucco and wood; brick, stone, stucco, and wood; stone, bacon, sausage, and spam . . . . Pillars could also have decorative tiles set into them.

On top of the pillar, there may be more corbels, beams, or other mysterious pieces of wood before you ever arrive at the beam(s) it is holding up. Actually the thing the pillars are holding up is called an *architrave* (this all has to do with classical Greek architectural concepts which I won't go into here), but it's really a beam.

Here's the worst thing you can do to a pillar—rip it out and replace it with a four-by-four post, steel pipe, or wrought-iron column (surely not ALL of the people who do this can be homesick for New Orleans!). Any of these things are structurally adequate and will probably hold up the roof, but visually they are wrong, wrong, wrong.

LONG WALK OFF A SHORT PIER

Short pillars are often called piers and may or may not be holding something up. On a porch, often the only thing they

Largish (though not by bungalow standards) river rock pillars "pierced" by 8-inch square timbers of the porch railing suddenly shrink to relatively small timbers that are actually holding up the porch roof. Although in reality the eight-by-eight timbers are plenty large for the load they bear, in contrast to the pillars they seem like tiny sticks that could snap at any second under the weight.

are holding up is a planter or maybe a railing. The piers often match the taller pillars, or they may be different. Sometimes piers are used to support the porch from underneath, rather than a continuous foundation. Or they may start at the level of the floor. They can also be found alongside the stairs, or as part of a fence (also true of taller pillars). How short does a pillar need to be to be considered a pier? Knee-high to a caterpillar? Waist-high to a wombat? Beats me. As with their taller brethren, piers can be understated and demure, or oversized and ridiculous. The rules for restoration or replacement of pillars also applies to piers.

If the porch is supported on piers, rather than having a continuous foundation, the spaces between the piers were traditionally filled with panels of lattice between the porch floor and the ground. The lattice could be square or diagonal. Because it is near the ground, lattice is vulnerable to rot. This does not mean you can replace it with vinyl lattice. You can either buy redwood or cedar lattice, or buy pressure-treated lattice and paint it. Yes, I know that painting lattice is a pain in the rear. Those are still the choices.

River rocks and clinker bricks combine to form "peanut brittle" piers and pillars on the front of a Denver bungalow. Part of the porch is open and covered only by a pergola. The bricks of the walls are the same color as the clinkers, allowing the whole thing to blend together.

The piers on the front of this Denver bungalow are topped with slabs of red sandstone. Check out the angular planter, which is probably original. The two-tone brick either helps tie this house to the ground or makes it look like someone dipped it in burgundy stain—you decide which.

RAILING AGAINST FATE

In between the pillars and/or piers, there may be a railing. I say "may" because sometimes there isn't, or there may only be a heavy chain, or maybe one wide board that is wide enough to sit on, or maybe a four-by-four that's not wide enough to sit on, made to look as though it is piercing the pillars and coming out on the other side. Not quite what one could define as a railing. Among things one could define as a railing, the wealth of options in any one material is staggering. In wood, for instance, there were flat boards with or without cutouts, of different sizes, vertical, horizontal, diagonal, alternating sizes, alternating cutouts; boxed-in railings covered in siding, shingles, or panels; railings made from dimensional lumber like two-by-fours, two-by-sixes and larger; railings made from logs or saplings; horizontal, vertical, diagonal, made into patterns, combined with flat boards; turned balusters of various diameters from skinny to rotund; railings made of lattice in various spacings and directions; planter boxes on top of railings, and combinations of all of the above. Built-in benches may be part of a railing as well.

TOP: A bungalow from the Lewis Homes 1925 catalog features an interesting porch railing with uprights that go all the way to the ground, with cut-outs at the bottom (which can barely be seen behind the greenery). This home also sports an attention-grabbing ribbed pattern in the wood shingled roof, accomplished by doubling up on every sixth row of shingles.

Wood railings could be left natural or treated with a clear oil finish (linseed oil combined with turpentine was the usual thing), or they could be stained or painted.

Railings of brick, concrete block, or stone had a similar multiplicity of treatments, although flat boards are a little difficult to do with masonry. A "lattice" treatment using spaced bricks or blocks was the most common.

Ceramic tiles of various persuasions could be inserted into every kind of railing. These were usually decorative flat tiles, but sometimes more structural pierced tiles were used.

I'm sure that somewhere there are a couple of bungalows with wrought-iron railings, perhaps ones with a Spanish influence. These would not,

ABOVE: More cutouts resembling router bits in wider boards alternate with plain narrow boards in another Milwaukee railing. This railing is probably high enough to meet modern code. A concrete block base holds a tapered wood column with corbels that support the porch roof.

BELOW: Inverted "exclamation point" cutouts in wide boards alternate with pairs of narrower boards in the railing of a Milwaukee bungalow.

Wide boards with a cutout design form a low railing over the arroyo stone porch base of a Pasadena bungalow.

The solid low porch railing of a Victoria bungalow has had a more open top piece, constructed of two-by-two lumber added to the top, although the uprights are still much too far apart to meet code. The porch retains its clear-finished fir floor.

RAILING RESTORATION

OBSESSIVE RESTORATION

Because of their exposure to the weather, wooden porch railings are one of the first things to go if they are not maintained. The horizontal parts are the most vulnerable due to the fact that water tends to pool on the flat areas. If the original railings are still present, they will be easy enough to repair, whether that involves epoxy consolidants or replicating missing parts. It's generally easier to paint epoxy, since it doesn't look like wood. It can be tinted to a wood color, and then faux-grained to blend with the existing wood. If the railing is missing altogether, as with pillars, historic photos may provide clues; otherwise other homes in the neighborhood that still have their original railings can provide inspiration. If the entire neighborhood has been remuddled, then you may have to resort to copying a railing out of an old house-plan catalog, of which there are several available as inexpensive reprints.

The biggest problem you are likely to encounter in rebuilding a historic railing is the building code. Bungalow railings were often nonexistent or much shorter than current building code requires, which is at least 36 inches high and up to 42 inches in some jurisdictions, and requires balusters with no more than a 4-inch opening between supports so that small children can't fall through or get their heads stuck in the railing (of course, this just means that cats can get their heads stuck in the railing, but cats don't have anyone lobbying on their behalf). If your house is on some register (local, state, or national), you may be able to invoke the State Historic Building Code, which allows more flexibility in meeting code requirements. If not, the best you can do is to try to minimize the impact of a higher railing. The best way to do this is to build the railing at the historic height, then add a separate top section which is different but still compatible to bring the railing up to the correct height. If the railing is to be painted, this part can be painted a different color (possibly matching the siding), which will make it visually disappear. Unfortunately, a higher railing often destroys the scale of the porch. If you want to practice civil disobedience in the fight for architectural purity after the inspector leaves, that is entirely up to you.

If you want to keep the historic baluster spacing you might be able to—if the original railing was made of flat boards that were more widely spaced

A porch railing in Vancouver has been subtly raised by about 6 inches, but the added height isn't obvious because the top rail has been painted dark blue, making it mostly disappear.

Still pretty craftsman-like for 1925, this complicated bungalow in the Lewis Homes catalog has many interesting features, but in particular, the porch railing with the X-shapes below and the three horizontal cross pieces above would easily lend itself to becoming a high railing that would meet modern code while still maintaining proper bungalow proportions. And that doesn't even get into the openwork beam of the porch, the complex interaction between the dormer, the inset porch, and the asymmetrical gable to the left of it, the peanut brittle chimney, or the other fine features of this bungalow.

Although this Vancouver railing is probably modern, the impact of its two-by-two uprights has been lessened by grouping them in threes and painting them the same color as the house siding, which allows the horizontal emphasis of the lighter-colored top and bottom rails to be more apparent, visually making the railing appear shorter than it really is.

The hefty uprights of the railing on a Santa Barbara, California, bungalow featured in *House Beautiful* were constructed of 4-by 4-inch timbers, with deeply chamfered corners giving them the look of flaring at the top and bottom. The beefy corner posts (probably 8 by 8 inches) were also deeply chamfered. The flare of the posts is mirrored by the similar flare on the concrete block chimney.

than modern code allows, the spacing could be left, and the spaces filled in with safety glass applied to the back of the boards (which would still give the illusion of actual spaces between). The glass can be treated with an anti-reflective coating to make it less obvious. Glass should be installed so that individual panes can be easily removed and replaced if they get broken. Or you could try to charm the building inspector.

An even thornier problem will be encountered if the house never had a railing at all. If you don't do anything to the house, the lack of railing will be grandfathered in, but the minute you do anything major, you may be forced to bring it up to code. It's probably impossible to do so without having a major impact on the authenticity of the porch. The best solution is never to do anything that will force you to bring it up to code but lacking that, possibly the best option is taut wire cables strung horizontally between the pillars. Tempered glass panels, often used for deck railings in modern construction, are too reflective for a bungalow; unless, maybe if you had an anti-reflective coating put on them, but it would still be pushing it.

Repair of masonry railings is similar to repairing walls. The code issue is a bigger problem with masonry—a stone, brick, or concrete wall 36 inches or more in height is really obtrusive. It might be better to add a wood railing that's a bit more open to the top of the masonry—it will have less visual impact.

COMPROMISE SOLUTION

Here are a few things *not* to use for railings: cheap diagonal lattice (wood or vinyl); plywood (unless it's part of a paneled railing, and the edges are covered by molding); the abovementioned steel "wrought iron"; two-by-twos nailed or screwed to the outside of the horizontal rails (ugly even on a modern deck); pressure-treated anything; fiberglass anything; vinyl anything; used brick; large panels of tempered glass; or fancy turned balusters unless you have proof that the house originally had fancy turned balusters.

Existing wood railings can be painted in situations where epoxy has been used for repairs, such as to blend the repairs with the existing railing, if a different species of wood had to be used for the repairs, or to blend a repair using the same species, because old wood will have darkened with age and weathering.

If existing masonry railings have been painted and stripping is just going to be too labor-intensive, the railing can be repainted in a color that mimics brick, stone, or concrete, depending on the composition of the railing. You can even fauxfinish it if you want to.

however, be cheap black-painted steel railings from the home center with curlicues on them! Nonetheless, many people have replaced their real railings with these. Get rid of them.

This may seem really low-rent and just the thing to go with asphalt siding, but actually some bungalows, even fancy ones, had railings made out of one-inch galvanized pipe.

FLOOR AND AFT

Front porch floors were customarily wood or concrete. Concrete floors might be covered with ceramic tile, stone, or brick. Wood floors were tongue-and-groove one-by-four (or sometimes one-by-six) boards. Woods like fir, cedar, redwood, cypress, and heart pine were the most popular. These were laid at right angles to the house walls and sloped slightly so that water would run off the edge. If the porch railing was

Con-Ser-Tex, advertised here in a 1915 *American Carpenter and Builder,* was apparently some kind of treated canvas (possibly rubberized, although it seems like they would have said so if that were the case). Their claim that it wouldn't rot or leak was probably only true in the short term. Traditionally, canvas used to cover a porch floor was tacked down with copper nails and then painted.

FLOORING RESTORATION

OBSESSIVE RESTORATION

Any horizontal surface exposed to the weather is vulnerable if not maintained. The end grain of wood floorboards is particularly susceptible to rot because it sucks up water (think of a board as being pretty much a bundle of straws). Original floorboards, because they used old-growth timber, were much more rot-resistant than anything that is available now, but they will go eventually if not kept well-sealed. And if the floorboards fail, the structure underneath may be rotten as well and have to be repaired. There are a few different options for repair. Epoxy consolidants are one choice. Another is to replace only the rotted ends and have a joint a foot or two from the end, although this joint is also vulnerable to water getting in and damaging the wood. A third choice is to take all the boards off the porch and turn them around, placing the splice near the house where it may be less visible, and, in the case of a covered porch, less prone to water infiltration. Or the damaged boards can be wholly replaced with salvaged boards. These will need to be the same thickness as the old boards, which may be 1 or $3/4$ inch. If new boards are used, they probably won't be as thick as the old ones and may have to be shimmed up to match. And prepare yourself to repaint them often and probably replace them within fifteen years, because the second-growth wood that is used now just doesn't hold up as well. Oil-base paint holds up better than latex for this purpose.

There doesn't seem to be any agreement regarding whether tongue-and-groove flooring should be back-primed (coated on the back). Proponents of back-priming maintain that it protects the underside from moisture and keeps the boards from cupping. The anti-back-priming camp insists that the underside should be left unsealed so that moisture that does get in can get back out, and that back-priming won't have any effect on cupping. Everyone seems to agree that the joints between boards should not be caulked.

Concrete may crack due to settlement or other movement or due to structural problems. Small cracks may be filled, but larger cracks may be due to structural problems that need to be dealt with first. Cracks can allow water to get into the framing below, so they should be dealt with.

A common problem with the omnipresent red-stained concrete is that after some number of years, it fades to about the color of a pencil eraser, that is to say, pink. What should be done at this point? One of two things: learn to love patina and leave it pink, or get some concrete stain. So what do people actually do? They paint it red. This is a bad idea. Paint lasts a maximum of about two years on concrete that is exposed to the weather, then it starts peeling, water gets underneath, it peels even more, and it becomes a vicious cycle of repainting. This might not be so bad if it was only the porch, but they usually also paint the steps, the front sidewalk, and sometimes the driveway as well. The only really obsessive thing to do is strip the paint, which will be unbelievably tedious. Feel free to curse the previous owners (or yourself, if you were the one who mistakenly painted it) while doing so. Another option is to have a thin surface coating of polymer-modifed concrete put over the paint. There is a new cementitious product that sprays on in a thin layer like paint, which preserves any texture that might be underneath. Tiling over it with mosaic or terra-cotta tile is a slightly less obsessive option. Or you could have all new concrete put in. Even concrete that wasn't initially stained gets painted. The options for that are the same.

If the wooden structure under the concrete has rotted due to moisture problems, it can usually be repaired from underneath without removing the concrete, unless it's so bad that the porch has collapsed. In which case you will have to replace the whole thing, or at least a great deal of it.

Surface coverings on top of concrete, such as tile, stone, or brick, may only need re-pointing or regrouting. Missing pieces may have to be filled in. If you are unable to find anything that matches, you may have to figure out a way to make the replacements look like they were put there on purpose, as part of a pattern. This is, of course, easier said than done. If the covering is terrazzo, it may require professionals to do the repairs.

Mosaic tiles in black, white, and gray form a design on the floor of a covered porch in Memphis, Tennessee.

A canvas-covered porch obviously doesn't last forever. Canvas was customarily either glued down or just tacked around the edges with copper nails (they don't rust), then varnished or painted or given some kind of rubberized coating. Unless this has been obsessively maintained for the last eighty-odd years, it has probably rotted away, if it's even still there at all. But canvas is still available and can still be installed the same way. It might be worthwhile to consider some other options for coating it—a marine supply store is a good place to find various sorts of waterproof coatings. If they hold up under the harsh conditions on a boat, they'll probably hold up on your porch.

COMPROMISE SOLUTION

Here's a few things *not* to use as a floor: two-by-something decking with spaces in between, composite decking (sawdust and plastic), plywood, pressure-treated anything (okay for structure underneath), vinyl decking, or aluminum decking. And don't cover a concrete porch with multi-colored slate. There is one exception allowed, a new product called *Tendura,* which is a composite product made from polyethylene and sawdust that is molded into tongue-and-groove boards that look remarkably like real wood flooring. It has to be painted, and they don't warrant it for use on uncovered porches, only sheltered ones. It comes in one-by-four and one-by-six widths.

Another option which would actually allow the use of ply-wood is covering it with a non-slip decking material. There are several proprietary systems involving fiberglass or polypropylene sheets with coatings and texturing compounds. There are also some others that don't involve reinforcing sheets. There is even a product that involves tiny pebbles set in epoxy. There are many vinyl products, too, but those should be avoided. Any of these make a decent substitute for canvas on an open porch. Another alternative to canvas is EPDM—they make a special kind that's meant to be walked on.

Covering a wood porch with concrete might be okay as a last resort.

If you don't want to keep repainting painted concrete, the options are pretty much as outlined above.

STAIR RESTORATION

OBSESSIVE RESTORATION

Stairs are one of the most vulnerable parts of the porch, being out in the open and exposed to the weather and having numerous horizontal surfaces. Wood is of course more susceptible to rot than masonry or concrete, particularly the treads. If the rot isn't extensive, it can be repaired with epoxy consolidants; otherwise, the tread can be replaced, though the little suckers are expensive. It's best to use redwood or cedar or some other rot-resistant wood, and make sure it is angled so water will run off. Widespread rot may have also affected the structure underneath.

Cracked concrete should be repaired, after first ascertaining whether there is a structural problem that needs to be repaired before the cracking and checking for rotting wood structures underneath. Repairs to coverings such as ceramic tile or terrazzo are the same as for porch flooring.

Brick stairs may require re-pointing in the same way as walls or anything else. Clinker bricks have a tendency to crack. It may be easier to fill the crack with mortar, but if there's a source of replacement bricks, the cracked brick can be removed and a new one installed in its place.

COMPROMISE SOLUTION

Replacing wooden stair treads with treads made from two two-by-sixes or one two-by-twelve is not allowed. Changing wooden steps to concrete might be okay, although you could buy a lot of wooden replacement treads for the price of having concrete stairs built. Covering concrete stairs with brick or tile would be acceptable provided it's not some currently trendy kind of tile such as glass, or something really glossy, which would be a bad idea on steps anyway. Nor are you allowed to cover the stairs with slate or tumbled marble, or any other current fad in stone. If you want to set a couple of nice reproduction art tiles into the risers, I would certainly not be opposed to that.

But you absolutely cannot have those open riser concrete stairs where the treads are set into a central steel support—you know the ones they have at every motel in America? And if you do have them, get rid of them.

solid, there would be a cutout at the bottom to allow the water to exit, or else there would be a gutter at the outside edge of the porch. Floorboards were sometimes varnished, but usually painted. Sometimes wood floors would be covered with painted, varnished, or rubberized canvas for waterproofing, especially on an open porch.

Concrete porches usually had a wood understructure because that required less material—the concrete would only have to be a few inches thick. Concrete could be left plain, colored with concrete stain, painted, or covered with something

The treads on the steps of this Victoria bungalow are made up of multiple boards but are still properly bullnosed on the front edges. The risers have decorative diamond cutouts for ventilation. This home has both Tuscan columns at the top of the stairs and shingle-covered rectangular pillars at the corners. It's conceivable that one or the other of them might have been replacements.

like tile, stone, brick, or even terrazzo. Stained concrete was common, especially in the 1920s, when the favored color was red. If tiles were used, the most common varieties were small mosaics (like the ubiquitous 1-inch hexagons) or red quarry tile types. Stone might also appear as mosaic or larger tiles, or as flagstones or honed (smooth but not polished) slabs. Various materials might also be combined—for example, brick and concrete. Terrazzo was used for porch floors as well, though only sporadically.

TREAD LIGHTLY

The usual method of getting from the ground to the porch is steps, which may be made of wood, concrete, brick, or stone. Steps may be flanked by piers, which may also be stepped down, depending on the height of the porch. Bungalow steps often did not have railings. A flight of steps may be wide or narrow or may widen at the bottom. Stairs may also be curved. A long flight of steps may have one or more landings before it arrives at the porch. The stairs didn't always match the house—a wood-sided house could have concrete stairs, or a stucco house could have wooden stairs, and so forth.

OPPOSITE: The deep wraparound porch attached to this Victoria, British Columbia, bungalow has a clear-finished tongue-and-groove floor. The traditional wood for porch floors in many areas of the country was Douglas fir (sometimes known as Oregon pine). The reddish color of the floor is a nice contrast with the dark green stain of the shingle siding.

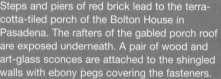

Steps and piers of red brick lead to the terra-cotta-tiled porch of the Bolton House in Pasadena. The rafters of the gabled porch roof are exposed underneath. A pair of wood and art-glass sconces are attached to the shingled walls with ebony pegs covering the fasteners.

Stone piers and steps direct visitors up onto the wooden front porch of a Vancouver bungalow, where the welcoming front door with its leaded-glass sidelights awaits. Notice to everyone: although they are festive, your holiday lights should not still be up in March.

OPPOSITE: Concrete steps that widen toward the bottom are flanked by river rock (or in this case, probably beach rock) piers. The porch floor itself is wood. Low rock railings between the pillars are topped by wooden planter boxes. The house is stained a deep charcoal color, which is characteristic of Vancouver homes. Bright white trim is apparently typical everywhere, even though it shouldn't be.

Wooden steps almost invariably had thick bullnose (rounded edge) treads, which are slanted toward the outside edge to allow water to run off rather than pooling up on the wood. The risers (the vertical part) were also wood, and were solid or decoratively pierced (no, they did not have nose rings . . .) for ventilation. Wire screening behind the cutouts kept out small animals and bugs. The treads and risers sit on stringers, angled pieces of dimensional lumber with cutouts that the stair parts fit into.

The flanking piers usually matched the house—a stucco house would have stucco piers, a shingled house would have shingled piers, and so on, except for the houses where the piers didn't match at all.

Concrete steps usually had a wood framework underneath. Concrete steps generally led to concrete porches, but not always. On many bungalows, the bottom step was concrete even if the rest were wooden. Concrete also served as the base for tile, terrazzo, or stone mosaics.

Brick steps could be built entirely of brick or have a wooden or concrete understructure. Clinker brick was utilized for stairs, although making use of the less-distorted bricks to keep them relatively flat while the more-distorted bricks were used on the piers. The mortar joints on brick stairs were made flush to keep the treads even. Brick was often combined with concrete on the finished surface of the stairs.

Stone stairs were constructed in much the same way, although slabs of stone were sometimes employed. Sporadically, big hunks of stone were used for stairs.

SCREENED PORCHES

OBSESSIVE RESTORATION

Because bungalows worked their way across the country from California, and because California has very few insects, most bungalows were designed with open porches. Because of that, an enclosed porch kind of destroys the way the front is supposed to look. Certainly a screen porch is a practical thing in most parts of the country—when I was a child in Indianapolis, we pretty much spent the entire summer on the screen porch. Nonetheless, because this *is* obsessive restoration, I urge you to think about un-enclosing the front porch, unless there is definitive proof that it was built that way originally.

There was such a thing as a sun porch, and these were built on the front of a lot of houses, but a glassed-in porch that's not a sun porch and that isn't heated in the winter—how useful is it really?

If there was a screen porch, the screens were obviously wooden, so stick to that.

Canvas shades are still available, as are various kinds of bamboo, reed, and other plant-based shades. As noted under "Awnings," canvas awnings are still available as well.

COMPROMISE SOLUTION

There's a lot of talk about having a "three-season" porch, this talk coming primarily from northern climates. (There's not a lot of talk about that sort of thing in Florida or Arizona.) I guess the idea is that it will be usable in spring and fall as well as summer. And maybe it is. It's hard for me to judge, being a Californian. Even during my childhood in Detroit and Indianapolis, we never had a glassed-in front porch, though in Detroit we had a sun porch on the side and in Indianapolis we had the aforementioned screened porch, which was on the front (although the front door was on the side). But when I think about it, even in the fairly benign climate of Oakland, I only have a two-season porch. (We do actually have four seasons in California, in spite of what you might think. They're just extremely subtle.) I generally take the porch furniture inside in November and don't put it out again until June, though I may drag out a folding chair on a nice day in February. However, this being the compromise part, if you want to have an enclosed porch, go ahead, provided the windows are wood, and the screens as well. And the door.

There are some modern systems for screening porches involving crosspieces and uprights made of aluminum or vinyl. I could maybe accept the aluminum kind if it's a dark color (not white!), but vinyl is out.

ACCESSIBILITY ISSUES

Among the differently abled, the rest of us are known as TABs, which stands for Temporarily Able-Bodied. Most of us are in denial about that, but someday we will (hopefully) be old and less able to deal with stairs than we are now, or we may break a leg skiing. And suddenly a simple set of steps will become Mount Everest. The steps on a majority of bungalows do not have railings, so you might want to (sensitively) add some, if not for yourself, then perhaps for your aging parents. A lot of bungalows have had wrought-iron (or fake wrought-iron) railings added to the steps at a later date—if these are not too objectionable, you can just paint them a nice color and let it go at that. Otherwise, put in a simple wood railing—a wooden clothesrod works well. Whatever it is, it has to be "grippable," so don't use a two-by-six.

Depending on the design of the porch and steps, it may be easy or difficult to put in a wheelchair ramp. The ramp has to be a certain width, it can't be overly steep, and it has to have a railing. If not well-designed, these can be quite obtrusive. Sometimes the ramp can be put at the side or back of the house instead. A more expensive option is a wheelchair lift, though this may involve removing a section of railing.

Once a wheelchair is on the porch, it may still be necessary to have a small ramp in order to get it over the door threshold and into the house.

SCREENING ROOM

In climates where there are lots of insects, provisions were often made to screen the porch. Often the screens could be changed out with windows for the winter months, although sometimes it was strictly screens, and the porch wasn't used in the winter. Or the porch was simply glassed in with operable windows and screens, essentially making it into a room, albeit a room that generally wasn't heated. It will be obvious, I hope, that the screens and/or windows were made of wood. Various methods were employed for changing the windows and screens. The whole porch might be screened or only a portion of it.

A glassed-in porch often served as a sunroom, usually with a concrete, tile, or masonry floor to soak up the heat and radiate it back. Fill it with plants, and you've got a conservatory.

Porches that weren't screened instead made use of roll-up shades made out of canvas, bamboo, or reeds, which could be unrolled for privacy or shade. Open porches may also have had canvas awnings for shade and to keep the rain out during summer rainstorms. As with window awnings, canvas shades were solid colors or stripes, while bamboo or reed shades were either left natural or dyed (green was a favored color).

AN EXERCISE IN UTILITY

Bungalows also had porches in back, which were generally used for utilitarian purposes such as the icebox and the laundry. They may have been glassed in or screened in, depending on the climate, although a few were completely open. Some were more like an anteroom, with only a few windows and possibly with a small bath (sink and toilet, or just a toilet) in one corner. Every so often there would be a *kitchen porch,* which was kind of like a giant cooler cabinet—it would be screened, and there would be storage for various foodstuffs. Some of these were large enough to serve as an eating area, or as a

work area that could be used in the summer when it was too hot to be in the kitchen. Back porches were simpler than front porches, usually lacking the pillars and other accoutrements of a front porch. A back porch might have a separate roof, and it might have wood siding even if the rest of the house had stucco or brick or stone. A screened porch might only have a screen door, or it might have a regular door, commonly with a single pane. A glassed-in or walled-off porch would have a normal door. From time to time, the back porch would have French doors leading to the outside. Generally there was only a small stoop and a set of steps, which could be wood or concrete. Frequently there was a window between the kitchen and

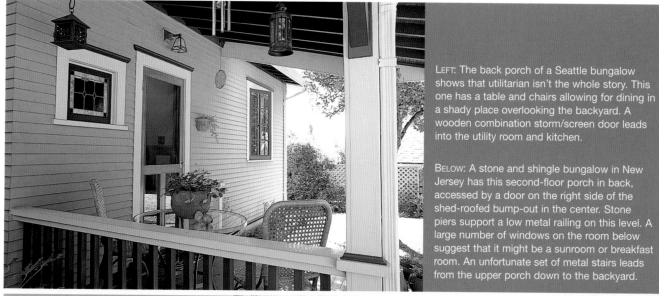

LEFT: The back porch of a Seattle bungalow shows that utilitarian isn't the whole story. This one has a table and chairs allowing for dining in a shady place overlooking the backyard. A wooden combination storm/screen door leads into the utility room and kitchen.

BELOW: A stone and shingle bungalow in New Jersey has this second-floor porch in back, accessed by a door on the right side of the shed-roofed bump-out in the center. Stone piers support a low metal railing on this level. A large number of windows on the room below suggest that it might be a sunroom or breakfast room. An unfortunate set of metal stairs leads from the upper porch down to the backyard.

the back porch to allow more light into the kitchen. A stairway leading to the basement might also be located on the back porch.

Sometimes there were also side porches or back porches accessed from the dining room or the bedrooms, often through double French doors. These could be quite large, and the dining porch might be a continuation of the front porch, or they could be small, like a shallow porch off a bedroom just big enough for a couple of chairs.

For all the Arts and Crafts talk about merging the inside with the outside, and the famous quote "landscape gardening around a few rooms for use in case of rain," one has to be clear that bungalows were oriented toward the front yard. The backyard was reserved for functional purposes like the vegetable garden, the clothesline, and the incinerator. In the majority of bungalows, access to the backyard is through the utility porch or laundry room, not through wide doors onto a deck that is typical in contemporary houses.

TO AIR IS HUMAN

"Under ideal conditions it is nothing short of the perfect way to sleep; at worst, it is infinitely better than sleeping indoors."
— *Elizabeth Conover Moore*
in House Beautiful, *May 1912*

At the time bungalows were being built, there was a lot of belief that "bad air" was responsible for disease. Tuberculosis was prevalent, and it was believed that fresh air would cure it or prevent you from getting it. An almost-religious fervor had developed around the idea of fresh air, and in particular, of sleeping outside in it, no matter the season. Thus was born the sleeping porch. Normally a sleeping porch was off the bedroom, with a door between. But sometimes that didn't work with the layout, so the porch would be accessed from an upstairs hallway. In a big house, normally each bedroom would have its own sleeping porch, though not always.

When sleeping porches were all the rage, they were added to homes that didn't previously have them. "The Home," a supplement to *Women's Weekly,* showed a simple sleeping porch addition in the 1923 issue. Featuring bi-fold casement windows, it also had decorative shaped "look-outs" where the 2 by 6-inch ceiling joists ostensibly came through the outer walls (which is amusing because the joists were 24 inches apart and only came out the front, not the

sides, not to mention that the visible look-outs appear to be more like 16 inches apart). Although the roof appears flat in the photo, it was actually sloped. The interior ceiling was to be finished in bead board, and the floor in canvas. The two openings that are visible just above the lower molding near the corners are there to drain any rainwater that might get inside the porch.

California Redwood

Resists fire and rot

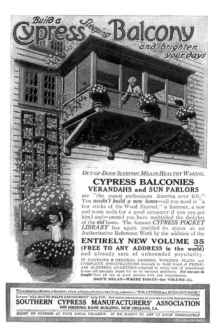

A somewhat smaller cantilevered sleeping balcony was promoted in this advertisement from the Southern Cypress Manufacturers' Association. For once, the knee braces are actually structural.

LEFT: A cantilevered redwood sleeping balcony at one end of this Berkeley home is balanced visually by a covered upstairs porch with casement windows at the other end (on top of the board-and-batten section). A lower open terrace is partially covered by an extension of the cantilevered pergola that holds up the sleeping balcony and is enclosed by a stucco wall. The home was designed by Maybeck (as in Bernard) and White (as in John Maybeck's brother-in-law) and featured in an ad in the July 1918 *House Beautiful*. This was, unfortunately, one of the many houses that burned in the 1923 Berkeley Fire.

Sometimes one porch would serve two different bedrooms. A sleeping porch was generally covered with a roof, although in climates where it didn't rain a lot the porch might be open to the sky. Generally there was a solid railing for privacy. Usually the porches were on the sides or back of the house for more privacy and were usually on the second floor, although a first-floor sleeping porch wasn't unheard of. It was recommended that the porch be put on some side other than the east, so the sun wouldn't wake you up. Above the railing it might be open but with canvas or bamboo roll-up shades for privacy. Sometimes there would be "porch curtains," or the porch would be enclosed by sliding, casement, folding, or even double-hung windows that could be opened or closed according to the weather. Every so often, pocket windows that could be slid down inside the wall by opening a hinged slot in the sill, or slid into an adjoining wall like a pocket door, were used, making the sleeping porch completely open. Clever bungalow designers also invented things like beds that slid out from the wall or used Murphy beds (beds that fold down out of the wall). Sleeping porch floors were primarily wooden, although a sheltered porch might have a linoleum or felt-base rug or possibly even a carpet of some sort. On open porches, by and large, the floors were covered with waterproofed can-

vas or composition roofing.

Sleeping porches were added to houses that hadn't originally been built with them as the craze grew. Later on when people came to their senses and realized that sleeping outside when it's freezing cold is insane, many of the open porches were glassed in. It's still lovely to sleep out there in the summer, although many cities have become too noisy to do this.

BALCONY SCENE

There were other porches as well, on either the first or second floor. These could be anything from a small balcony barely large enough to stand on, to a full porch big enough for several pieces of furniture. Sometimes it was unclear whether a porch was meant for sleeping or merely intended to be a porch, since it was quite common for a porch to be off a bedroom. I suspect that many were used for both purposes. Balconies were often cantilevered (sitting on projecting beams or members that are only anchored at one end—that end being somewhere inside the house) and held up by decorative brackets or corbels. Many times there would be a second-floor porch on the roof of the first-floor porch. Dormers of all shapes were also frequently accompanied by a porch.

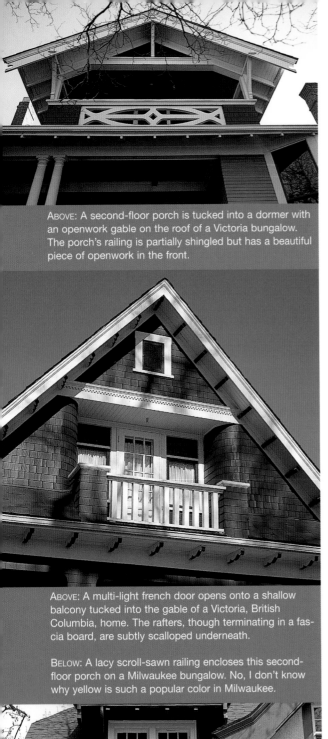

ABOVE: A second-floor porch is tucked into a dormer with an openwork gable on the roof of a Victoria bungalow. The porch's railing is partially shingled but has a beautiful piece of openwork in the front.

ABOVE: A multi-light french door opens onto a shallow balcony tucked into the gable of a Victoria, British Columbia, home. The rafters, though terminating in a fascia board, are subtly scalloped underneath.

BELOW: A lacy scroll-sawn railing encloses this second-floor porch on a Milwaukee bungalow. No, I don't know why yellow is such a popular color in Milwaukee.

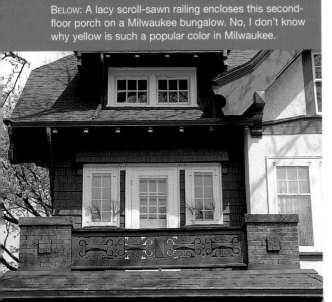

RULING FROM THE BENCH

Benches were built into some porches, either as part of the railing, along the wall or on one or both sides of the door, though that was usually on a small porch. For the most part, these were constructed of wood. They may or may not have had seats that lifted up for storage underneath.

IT DON'T MEAN A THING IF IT AIN'T GOT THAT SWING

A porch swing is a cliché, and it became that way by being installed on practically every front porch in America if there was room for it. Even after they were no longer being hung from the ceiling they lived on in the glider, a kind of self-supporting porch swing that could also be put out in the yard. Porch swings were traditionally made of wood or wicker, and some of them were actually more like suspended beds, perfect for napping on a warm afternoon.

LEFT: The front porch of the Bolton House in Pasadena includes built-in benches with a cloud-lift design integrated into the backs.

The Charles Limbert Company advertised their porch swings as "Inexpensive-Practical-Serviceable." They also offered a "most interesting booklet" about Arts and Crafts furniture "made famous by William Morris," which was a "tale of craftsmanship, utility, and beauty."

Two ladies appear to have fallen asleep over their reading because their Queen Hammock was so comfy.

If not swinging on a porch swing, one could always sit quietly in a willow chair to work on one's embroidery out on the porch.

DO YOU URN A LOT?

Since a bungalow had all those piers and railings, one of the ways to bring nature closer to the house was through the use of planters, window boxes, pots, and urns. Planters could be built into piers or solid railings, either as a metal-lined box or a concrete-lined recess. Window boxes were supported on projecting beam ends (most likely fake ones), brackets, or corbels, and might be made of wood (with drainage holes), metal-lined wood, or cast concrete. More often than one might think, someone would put a window box below a gable vent or a fixed attic window, although exactly how you were supposed to plant or water this box was unclear. (But I'm thinking drip irrigation and evergreen plants if you want something up there. It will mystify the neighbors too.)

Pots and urns of various sorts were set on assorted flat surfaces, the piers on either side of the front steps being a popular location. These pots could be made of cast concrete, glazed or unglazed terra-cotta, or even stone.

ILLUMINATING CONVERSATION

"Outside of a dog, a book is man's best friend.
Inside of a dog, it's too dark to read."
— Groucho Marx

Which is why you need a light. Also so you don't trip on your front steps in the dark, people can find your house at night, and the moths have something to do. The bungalow porch invariably had a light near the front door, either wall-mounted or ceiling-mounted, and depending on the size of the porch, it might have had other light fixtures elsewhere. Decorative lights might have been found at the entry gate, the driveway, at points along a perimeter wall or fence (if there was one), on the sleeping porch or other porches, or along the front walkway. Other areas, such as the back porch, the garage, the basement door, etc., would have had more utilitarian light fixtures.

Decorative light fixtures ranged from the simple ceiling-mounted canopy (the metal part that holds the shade) with a frosted shade, to cast-iron or hammered copper lanterns with colored art-glass shades, which might be flush-mounted on the wall or ceiling and hung from a short chain off an arm or bracket. If the porch had a high ceiling, then pendant fixtures could be used. These hung on chains or tubing (round or square). On top of piers or posts, post-mount fixtures were used. A lantern might also hang from a pergola or arbor over the front gate or over the driveway.

The more serviceable fixtures ranged from bare light-bulbs in porcelain sockets to simple canopy or wall-mounted fixtures with frosted glass shades.

Since most bungalows were built during the era of electricity, the fixtures tended to be electric. They used incandescent bulbs, invented by several people, none of whom were Thomas Edison. Henry Woodward and Matthew Evans of Toronto took out a patent for a lightbulb in 1875 but were unable to garner enough financial backing to commercialize their invention. Meanwhile, in 1878, English physicist Joseph Swan received a patent for an incandescent bulb with a carbon filament, though he had actually publicly unveiled his invention for the first time in 1869. Edison bought the rights to Woodward and Evans's invention, and after messing with it for a few years, unveiled his carbon filament vacuum bulb in 1879. It burned a whole thirteen hours. Nonetheless, Edison decided to electrify his laboratory. Lewis Howard Latimer, a member of Edison's team, made improvements to the carbon filament, for which he took out patents in 1881

Stepped brick corbels project from the porch railing of a Denver bungalow and hold small concrete planters.

Metal planter boxes are built into the piers that border the steps of this Victoria bungalow. Low-voltage lighting has been recessed into the sides to light the stairs in the evenings.

Sixteen brackets in descending sizes are apparently necessary to hold up a railed plant shelf on the front of a West Adams bungalow. Barely visible above are the four very short Tuscan columns holding up the dormer's roof.

WINDOW BOXES

OBSESSIVE RESTORATION

Probably nine out of ten bungalows that formerly had window boxes have lost them, and often the supports are gone as well. (Take a look at my previous house on the cover of *Bungalow Colors: Exteriors*—it once had a wooden window box extending the full width of the window, supported by "beams" with pyramid-shaped ends. These probably rotted and were removed and the holes carefully stuccoed over by some previous owner. All the houses on that street were built by the same builder and most had window boxes, but only one of them still had an extant window box.) I suppose it's too much trouble for some people to keep them planted, and the wooden ones do tend to rot eventually. Put them back. You'll probably have to conjecture (boy, that was a two-dollar word) as to what the box might have looked like, unless there are historic photos to go by.

A surprising number of concrete pots or urns have remained intact—perhaps they're just too heavy to steal. Fewer terra-cotta pots remain—they break more easily than concrete, but they don't weigh as much. Replacement concrete pots will be harder to come by than terra-cotta and may have to be custom-made, especially to match an original. Companies like Gladding-McBean, producers of many of the original terra-cotta pots and urns, are still in business. And many of the shapes that were used for bungalows are still being made by many manufacturers of terra-cotta. It may be difficult, even if you have a historic photo showing the urns, to figure out what color they were (if glazed), so you may have to wing it.

An unfortunate modern problem with pots is theft. The green pots on my porch, shown on the cover of *Bungalow Colors*, were stolen a week after that photo was taken. I would not suggest putting a valuable piece of art pottery out on the front porch. You can try using some thin-set mortar or hot glue to attach a pot to the porch—it probably won't stop a really determined thief, but it might discourage an adolescent kid. You can also try bolting them down through the drainage hole, although that has a few drawbacks like wicking water into whatever you're bolting it to. I could argue for just getting some fairly inexpensive pots (some of the ones that come from China are quite decent) that can be easily replaced if stolen. And I wouldn't put any rare plants in them, either.

Planters set into piers or railings may have caused the railing or the pier to deteriorate due to the failure of a metal liner, allowing water to penetrate the structure. That will have to be repaired first. Then it would be best to line the recess with copper, either with a watertight liner (put a layer of pebbles in the bottom) or one where the drainage has been routed to the exterior in some way (use some copper tubing, perhaps, or some copper pipe). It probably wouldn't hurt to line a concrete planter in the same way.

Naturally, a really obsessive person will look into what plants were used historically (no impatiens) and use only those.

If you're not the sort of person who remembers to water plants, an unobtrusive drip irrigation system hooked to an automatic timer might be a good idea.

COMPROMISE SOLUTION

You still have to put your window boxes back, and you're not allowed to use plastic (okay, plastic liners will be all right). Fiberglass might be okay. Even those metal-banded redwood or cedar ones are better than nothing, though try to get some that are big enough—they only come in certain sizes. Drip irrigation—not a problem. But you do have to plant them. If you don't want to fuss with them, you can plant evergreens.

It's important that your pots be big enough that they go with the scale of the porch and aren't dwarfed by the massive piers they may be sitting on—so a 6-inch flowerpot is not going to do the trick. There are a lot of imported pots that are relatively inexpensive, and a large unglazed terra-cotta flower pot doesn't cost all that much. There are various sorts of fake terra-cotta pots made of plastic or fiberglass, but try to get one that doesn't look too fake. The fiberglass ones can also be painted with glossy paint for a glazed look. Big square redwood or cedar planter boxes may also be appropriate—they'd look pretty good on a bungalow with big, square, wood pillars.

LIGHTING FIXTURES

OBSESSIVE RESTORATION

Original light fixtures may need to be rewired or have broken or missing glass replaced. If the original fixtures are missing, salvaged fixtures are readily available, and fine reproductions are being made as well.

Reproduction incandescent bulbs that cost twice as much and give off half as much light as regular bulbs are available for the truly fanatical. Naturally, these are known as "Edison bulbs."

COMPROMISE SOLUTION

Many reproduction fixtures are available, and even a home center may have a few decent "Craftsman" or "mission" fixtures that are reasonably priced, though these will be pretty generic. Stay away from things like brass coach lamp fixtures and other "colonial" lights. They generally didn't have outdoor chandeliers, either—maybe a two-light fixture, but if you want to have a chandelier, what the heck. But for everybody's sake, don't use those mercury vapor security lights. Ever.

Compact fluorescent bulbs save a lot of energy and last a long time (particularly important if there's a fixture that's hard to get to), but they are kind of pinkish. Which is still better than how they used to be, which was kind of bluish or greenish. A fixture with art glass does a pretty good job of hiding the weird light of fluorescents, and you can even get a compact fluorescent bug light (yellow bulb) for that amber Arts and Crafts glow. Plus it will discourage bugs.

Probably a reproduction, a hipped-roof copper post light tops an arroyo stone column in the front yard of a Los Angeles home.

Henry Greene designed this wood-and-glass sconce for the Gould House in Ventura, California.

A round lantern of black iron is attached to the limestone wall of a Memphis bungalow.

An art-glass lantern over a door at Stickley's Craftsman Farms home appears to hang from chains but also has a bracket.

Hammered copper is the material for this mailbox in Berkeley, which either now or previously belonged to someone named C. W. Christiansen. The bevel siding it sits on has been laid in alternating wide and narrow exposures. The plaque above reads, "There's music in the sighing of the reed; there's music in the gushing of the rill; there's music in all things, if men had ears; their earth is but an echo of the spheres."

A black iron mailbox in an owl design sits on a Seattle porch.

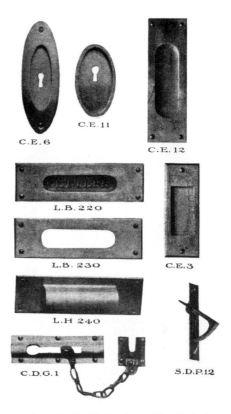

A page from the Pacific Hardware Manufacturing Company's 1912 catalog showed three mail slots, as well as a chain lock and some recessed pocket door hardware.

and 1882. In 1903, Willis R. Whitney invented a treatment for the filament so that it wouldn't darken the inside of the bulb, and in 1910, William David Coolidge invented a longer-lasting tungsten filament, which is what we're still using.

But it wasn't just the bulb. The bulb was not going to be practical for home use without a system to make it safe, economical, and widely available. What Edison did (and should get credit for) was invent a more durable lightbulb (Edison bulbs would eventually last 1,200 hours), then safety fuses and insulating materials, followed by light sockets with on/off switches, plus the parallel circuit, and then he basically invented the power grid. This had to include the invention of devices for maintaining constant voltage, improved dynamos for generating the electricity, and a system of distribution for the electricity.

In 1901, Peter Cooper Hewitt invented the mercury vapor lamp, used for years in streetlights until it began to be phased out in favor of sodium vapor lights (the orange ones). Mercury vapor lives on as a dreadful form of security light that no one should be allowed to have.

In 1911, Frenchman Georges Claude invented the neon light, which was far more amusing but still unlikely to be found on a bungalow.

In 1927, the first fluorescent light was invented in Germany, which was less amusing.

MAIL BONDING

A bungalow that's out in the country probably has a standard rural mailbox out by the road, but this is also true for some city bungalows, often those that are on a sloped lot, where the mailbox is down at street level. But most bungalows had mailboxes or mail slots on the porch. A mailbox was commonly attached to a pillar or pier, or to a wall. These might be made of steel, brass, copper, or wood. They were generally small by modern standards—people mostly received letters and postcards, not the umpteen catalogs, magazines, and large envelopes that most of us receive these days. There was no junk mail either.

Mail slots were installed either in the front door or through an outside wall. With a front-door slot, the mail would just be laying on the floor inside when you got home, as there was rarely a receptacle on the inside. A through-the-wall slot typically had a receptacle of some sort, often with a small door on the inside. This might be in the living room, the entry, or inside a closet.

FIGURE SKATING

To assist friends, the mail carrier, and the fire department in finding one's bungalow, there were usually house numbers somewhere. This might be somewhere along the front gate, fence, or wall, but more likely the numbers were somewhere on the porch. Numbers could be attached to a pillar or pier, the mailbox, the front door, the screen or storm door, a small plaque which hung on the wall or from the architrave (remember the architrave? it's the horizontal beam), or on the wall itself. The plaque could be wood or metal, or sometimes back-painted glass was used. Back-painted glass could also be illuminated from behind with a low-wattage lightbulb. Sometimes the house number was incorporated into the design of the light fixture. Attached numbers were normally brass or wrought iron, though the occasional ceramic house number plaque was found—often these were art tiles with the numbers integrated into the design.

Along with the jagged bark-themed door hardware, Pacific Hardware could provide matching house numbers, door knockers, or doorbells.

CHIME IN

When arriving at some bungalows, you just had to knock on the door with your bare knuckles. But at most homes, there was a doorbell or a door knocker. Doorbells were either electric or mechanical. A mechanical doorbell was mounted directly on the door and involved turning a knob or other protrusion that activated the bell on the inside of the door. Electric doorbells ran on low voltage, so there was a trans-former installed somewhere (the attic was a common place for it). The transformer converted alternating house current to the low-voltage direct current used by the doorbell. Often the transformer served both front and back doorbells, and the chime or buzzer was installed in the kitchen. Electric doorbells were mounted in the door trim or on the wall next to the door. The push-button itself was encircled by a brass, copper, or wrought-iron surround and often had a decorative back plate as well.

Do I need to say that plastic doorbells are out? Doorbells aren't expensive—get a metal one.

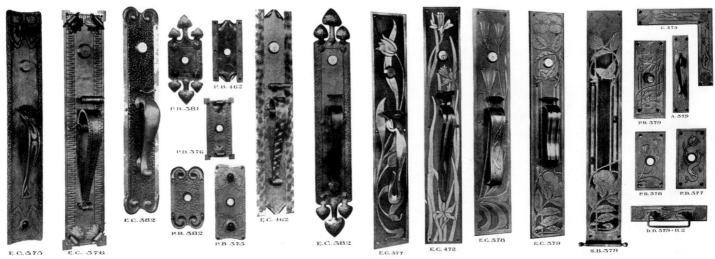

Several different doorbells, as well as their matching thumb latches, were offered on this page of the Pacific Hardware catalog.

Art Nouveau–inspired door hardware with companion doorbells and hinges filled this page of Pacific Hardware's catalog.

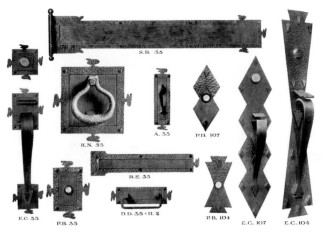

If your preference was for overlapping diamonds or hardware with strange little feet sticking out of the sides, they had that too.

Perhaps something in an Art Nouveau repoussé pattern that was vaguely owl-like was desired. Or a thumb latch with the doorknocker right next to it? That was available as well.

A round wall sconce, mailbox, and doorbell, all decorated with a "Franciscan monk" casting, were made by Waterglass Studio, the lighting and hardware company that belongs to the home's owners.

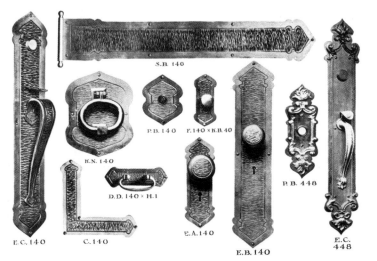

Door hardware with a kind of "Tudor arch" motif, perhaps appropriate for a more English influenced bungalow, was presented alongside a somewhat fancier thumb latch set with "beading" on the handle.

If you needed a complete set of matching hardware, Pacific could supply it, including this bunch with strange little motifs sticking out of the corners.

KNOCKING AROUND

Door knockers were the precursors of the doorbell, but they were still being used at the time and still are. Mounted on the door, with a hinged portion that lifted up so it could be banged against the fixed piece, a knocker saved one's knuckles from being bruised. Traditionally made of cast brass or cast iron because they needed to be heavy, door knockers ranged from simple to elaborate. The more elaborate versions involved things like animal heads and such.

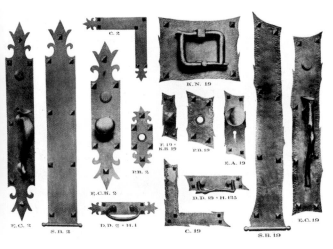

ABOVE: On the right, asymmetrical "bark" hardware with hammered edges and "twig" handles, and on the left, early Wicked Witch of the West.

BELOW: Possibly these motifs are meant to represent California oak trees, which are vaguely this shape; or maybe it was just some whimsical idea in the mind of the designer.

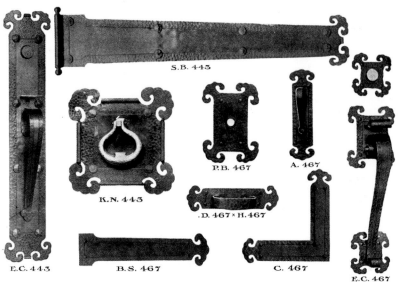

Here's some of Pacific's hardware in the flesh (the pattern with strange little motifs sticking out of the corners) on the door of a Los Angeles bungalow. Pacific Hardware was located in Los Angeles, so it all makes sense.

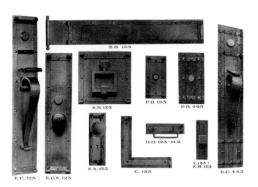

ABOVE: This set was outlined with riveted straps.

BUILT TO LATCH

Doors and windows would just be flapping in the breeze unless some provision was made for keeping them closed, and thus was born the latch. The earliest latches were surface-mounted, and this kind was still used on the interior of some doors for a very rustic look. This kind of latch was activated by a thumb latch on the exterior, which raised a small bar on the interior, releasing it from its resting place on a U-shaped metal catch that was attached to the door frame. Most bungalows have a doorknob or lever. Turning the knob or pressing the lever activated a spring-loaded bolt, pulling it back from the *strike plate,* which was recessed into the door jamb, or from the catch of a *rim lock,* which was surface-mounted. The mechanical parts that made this work were mounted inside a flat metal box, which could either be surface-mounted, in the case of a rim lock, or inserted into a mortise (recess) in the door. The doorknob or lever fit over a square *spindle* and was held on by a *set screw.* Later spindles were fluted in different ways and had threads that allowed the knobs to screw onto the spindle (though these still had set screws to immobilize the knob once you got it where you wanted it). The same bolt mechanism could also be activated by a thumb latch. Often a large mortise lock would have both a spring-loaded bolt and a deadbolt, which required a key for locking and unlocking from the outside, and usually had a thumb-turn on the inside. Separate deadbolts were also made, as they still are. Old deadbolts do not have the same *throw* (how far the bolt penetrates the jamb) as modern ones—an original deadbolt may only have a half-inch throw, as opposed to a one-inch throw for a modern deadbolt. Early locks used skeleton keys, which are still available at well-stocked

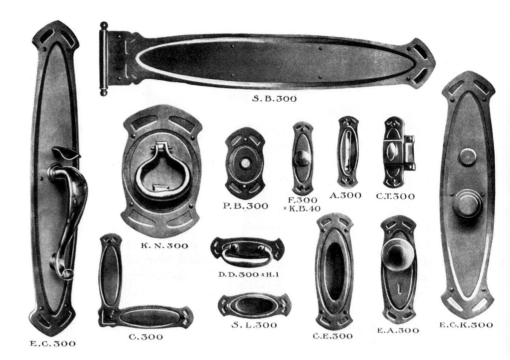

Not all hardware was square, as evidenced by this elliptically shaped set.

More Pacific Hardware featuring oak leaves, twigs, and acorns is perhaps a bit overdone but highly amusing. Acorns even adorn the screw heads that hold the hardware to the door.

A hammered brass doorplate and ring pull at Craftsman Farms bears the shop mark of the Craftsman Workshops, which can be seen inside the ring.

locksmiths. Mortise locks usually had push-buttons on the door edge, which could be used to lock or unlock the knob without requiring a key. This feature is handy to avoid locking oneself out when going out to fetch the newspaper. Pin tumbler locks were invented by the Egyptians 4,000 years ago.

In 1833, a man named J. A. Blake patented the grandfather of today's tubular lock, but it was Walter Schlage (it's pronounced *shlāg*) who took Blake's idea and came up with a different spring-loaded mechanism for doorknobs in 1920. It only required a couple of round holes instead of a full mortise and is the more common door lock or doorknob sold today. The door could be locked using a push-button that was part of the knob. This kind of lock had a *rosette* (small round back plate) rather than the larger back plates of mortise locks, and a separate small plate for the keyhole. These were used more often on interior or secondary doors, while front doors continued to use mortise locks. Mortise locks are still commonly available, though, and are the standard for high-end entry sets.

Mortise locks had *back plates* attached to the door on both sides. These ranged from extremely simple to extremely elaborate. Brass, copper, bronze, or iron were the favored materials, and the plates might be cast or stamped from sheet metal, or they might be hand-hammered. Less-expensive entry sets might have plated steel or plated *pot metal* (metal of unknown pedigree). Plated hardware could be had in different finishes such as lacquered brass, brushed brass, or what was known as *japanned,* which was a tiger-striped copper and black finish. Large mortise lock sets with deadbolts were used for the front door, while side or back doors had the simpler mortise locks or sometimes used rim locks. Screen or storm doors, especially those that didn't use spring hinges, had small mortise lock sets of their own, and these often had a button allowing one to lock the screen door from the inside.

The main nationwide lock companies at the time were Russell and Erwin (known as Russwin—they used to be two separate companies), Corbin, Yale, Schlage, Simpson, and Stanley.

And just so you know, the key-duplicating machine was invented in 1909. Before that, keys had to be filed by hand.

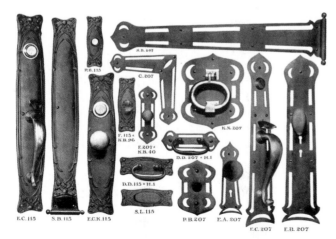

The sinuous Art Nouveau curves of the hardware on the left is reminiscent of the Paris Metro, while the set on the right with its elongated cutouts has more of a traditional Arts and Crafts look.

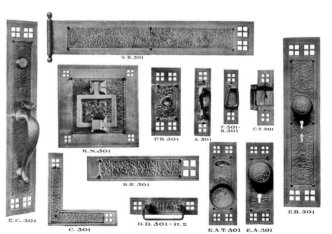

Some very rectangular hardware with hammered insets is set off by quatrefoil (four squares) designs, which were a popular Arts and Crafts motif.

LEFT: A jagged bark back plate with a "twig" thumb latch on a Vancouver, British Columbia, bungalow is similar to a Pacific Hardware's E.C. 13 model.

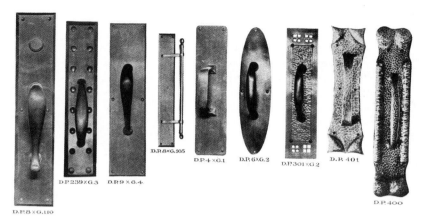

D.P.239 × G.3   D.P.9 × 6.4   D.R.8 × G.105   D.P.4 × G.1   D.P.6 × G.2   D.P.301 × G.2   D.P. 401

D.P.8 × G.110

D.P. 400

Several varieties of handles without accompanying locks were also offered.

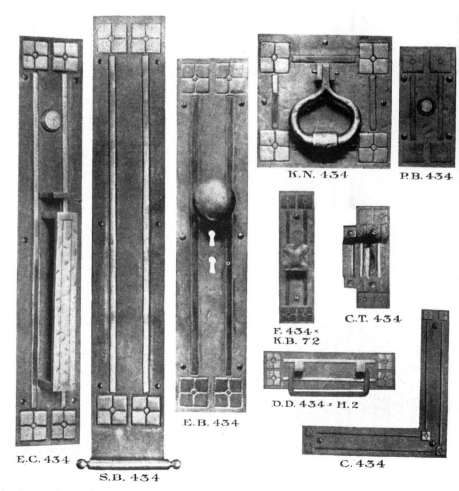

K.N. 434   P.B. 434

E.C. 434   S.B. 434   E.B. 434   F. 434 × K.B. 72   C.T. 434   D.D. 434 × H.2   C. 434

Another set featured conventionalized (simplified and abstracted) flowers in repoussé.

KNOB HILL

Doorknobs were made of spun or cast metal that matched the rest of the lock set, and could be solid or hollow. One exception is glass knobs, which were molded and attached to a metal base for strength. Glass knobs came in various shapes, either plain, fluted, or faceted. Metal knobs were round or oval, and some featured beading, hammering, or other ornamental features. Arts and Crafts door hardware was far simpler than its Victorian antecedents. Thumb latches were generally quite simple, though the handle that accompanied the thumb latches could be fancier.

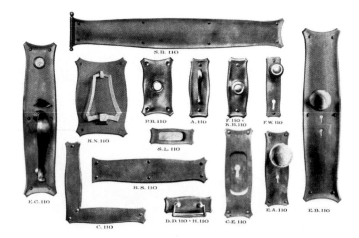

DOOR LOCKS

OBSESSIVE RESTORATION

An original lock that is broken may be able to be fixed—take it to a local locksmith who is experienced with old locks, if there is one. Sometimes the lock may be beyond hope unless custom parts are replicated by casting or other methods. It's conceivable that the lock guts may be able to be replaced; otherwise, you'll have to buy a whole new lock set, or at least the part that goes in the mortise. For simple mortise locks these are readily available; for a more elaborate front door lock, they may be harder to come by. Often an old lock that doesn't work may simply need a shot of lubricant (like WD-40).

Contrary to popular belief, a skeleton key will not open every kind of lock—there are actually different shapes for different locks. If none of the standard ones fit your locks, you can have one custom-made. If the existing locks use modern keys, a locksmith can also rekey them. If this is being done, you can have all your locks rekeyed so that one key will open all of them.

Locks had a certain backset—meaning the distance from the edge of the door to the center of the bolt mechanism. Generally this was 2 3/8 inches (then and now), but on some locks it can be as much as 4 inches.

If the knobs are missing, salvage doorknobs are widely available, so unless the knob is unusual, it shouldn't be too much trouble to find a replacement. Glass knobs that have detached themselves from the metal base are difficult to repair—it may be easier to get a new one. No doubt the truly obsessive will try melting the glass near the base with a torch to try to reunite the two parts. It might work. Reproduction knobs are also being made, both in metal and glass.

Salvaged back plates are also widely available, though reproduction styles are more limited than what was available at the time. They can be custom-made as well, for a price. A mortise lock that requires a skeleton key does allow air infiltration through the keyhole. If you're not using the key, this can be plugged by removing the lock from the mortise, opening it up (there's a screw to remove—take the top off carefully because if the spring goes sproing, it will be hard to put it back together), and covering the holes with a thin piece of cardboard or sheet metal held down with small pieces of foil tape.

Antique lock sets are also available, though it would be a good idea to make sure the lock actually works before buying one. An antique lock can be paired with a modern deadbolt for extra security.

COMPROMISE SOLUTION

There are many fine reproduction lock sets to be had, and even a home center will have a few that are simple enough to be acceptable. Try to avoid really shiny lacquered brass, and stay away from "colonial" or very contemporary lock sets. As noted above, an antique lock set can be paired with a modern deadbolt (in a matching finish) for more security. Many modern lock sets utilize modern spring-loaded bolts while still having the appearance of a mortise set, especially useful if the door itself is new and has been predrilled for a modern lock set rather than having a mortise.

There is one modern doorknob that has a concave face—this is probably the ugliest doorknob ever invented. Don't buy a set that has this knob, and if it's already on the house, remove it. Often you can replace just the knobs. If the front door has modern knobs and a separate deadbolt, it would be better to replace these with a lock set that looks like it's mortised, since the separate knob and deadbolt were usually reserved for secondary doors.

PIVOT HEDGE

One generally doesn't want to pick up the entire door and shove it aside, which is why hinges were invented. Doors had either mortise hinges or strap hinges. Mortise hinges were set into a shallow recess chiseled in the doorjamb. These hinges were invariably ball-tipped, with one ball attached to the bottom of the hinge and the other one fastened to the end of the pin, which slipped through the knuckles attached to each leaf of the hinge to hold the hinge together (these are called loose-pin hinges). Each door had at least two hinges, and the larger the door, the more hinges would be required. Front doors usually had at least three. Exterior doors traditionally opened inward, with the possible exception of French doors. Hinges were made of brass, bronze, or plated steel.

Surface-mounted hinges were customarily strap hinges, with the exception of spring hinges for screen doors. Brass, copper, bronze, or wrought iron were the usual materials. The shape of the strap could be simple or exceedingly complex. Frequently the straps would be adorned with decorative nailheads or screws. These may or may not have had a structural purpose, like fastening the strap to the door. Strap hinges were used when a more rustic effect was desired.

Honesty of structure notwithstanding, there were a lot of fake strap hinges attached to doors that actually had mortise hinges.

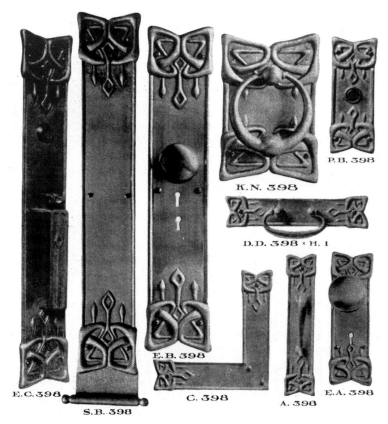

There are two keyholes on the back plate of this hardware—one for the deadbolt above and one for the door latch below. The repousse' design is kind of an Art Nouveau take on Celtic knotwork designs.

DOOR HINGES

OBSESSIVE RESTORATION

If the original door is still there, the hinges are usually there with it—people rarely bother to replace the hinges unless they're replacing the door. Hinges can pull away from the jamb over time if the screws work their way loose. Sometimes the fix for this is as simple as jamming a few pieces of wooden matchstick (do I really have to point out that you shouldn't use the matchhead for this?) into the screw hole so that the screw threads have something to grab onto. If that doesn't work, longer screws of the same diameter can be substituted—these will be capable of reaching through the jamb and into the studs of the door frame. Hinge pins can bend, especially on a heavy door but can be straightened in a vise, or if that doesn't work, replaced with new ones.

The fake part of faux strap hinges may have been removed. If so, there should be ghosts or a pattern of holes where the nails or screws were that may give some idea of the shape (assuming there is no historic photo or original drawings to go by). Conjecture may still be involved.

Hinges were made of brass, bronze, cast iron, or plated steel. As with other plated hardware, finishes such as brushed brass or japanned finish were used on hinges. Although the finish usually doesn't wear off hinges, they can always be replated if it does.

Only slotted screws were used—although Phillips screws were around at the time, they weren't used residentially.

COMPROMISE SOLUTION

Okay, you can use Phillips screws. But you still have to get ball-tip hinges.

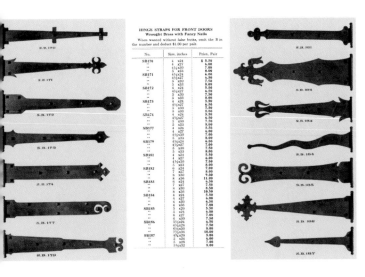

HINGE STRAPS FOR FRONT DOORS
Wrought Brass with Fancy Nails
When wanted without false butts, omit the B in the number and deduct $1.00 per pair.

No.	Size, inches	Price, Pair
SB170	4 x24	$ 5.50
"	4 x27	6.00
"	4½x30	7.00
"	5 x33	8.00
SB171	4½x24	6.00
"	4½x27	6.50
"	5 x30	7.50
"	5 x33	8.00
SB172	4 x24	5.50
"	4½x27	6.50
"	5 x30	7.50
"	5 x33	8.00
SB173	4 x24	5.50
"	4½x27	6.50
"	5 x30	7.50
"	5 x33	8.50
SB174	4 x24	5.50
"	4½x27	6.50
"	5 x30	7.50
SB177	5 x60	8.00
"	4 x24	5.50
"	4 x27	6.00
"	4½x30	7.00
"	5 x55	8.00
SB179	4½x24	6.00
"	4½x27	7.00
"	5 x30	7.50
"	5 x33	8.00
SB181	4 x24	5.50
"	4 x27	6.00
"	4½x30	7.00
"	5 x33	8.00
SB182	6 x24	7.00
"	7 x27	8.00
"	8 x50	9.50
"	8 x56	11.00
SB183	6 x24	6.50
"	7 x27	7.50
"	8 x30	8.50
"	8 x56	10.50
SB184	4 x24	5.50
"	4 x27	6.00
"	4½x30	6.50
"	4 x20	5.50
SB185	4 x24	6.00
"	4 x27	7.00
SB186	6 x20	7.50
"	5½x24	6.50
"	6½x28	7.50
"	6½x30	8.00
"	7½x36	10.00
SB187	4½x24	5.00
"	5 x24	6.00
"	5½x32	9.00

ABOVE: Fake strap hinges were popular enough that Pacific Hardware offered a whole page of them, not counting the ones that were available to match various styles of door hardware. As noted in the center text, "when wanted without false butts (hinges) . . . deduct $1.00 per pair."

BELOW: Though generally considered a neoclassical motif, the Greek key designs on this hardware are angular enough to fit in on a bungalow.

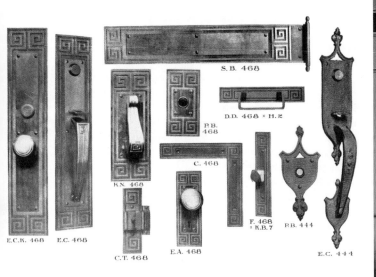

BELOW: A somewhat medieval-looking set of hardware, including a matching mail slot, decorates the door and sidelights of a Victoria, British Columbia, bungalow. The brass numerals above the door are a standard typeface that is still available.

RESOURCES

PORCHES
(See also Eaves)

Victoriana East
www.victorianaeast.com
(856) 546-1882

Ryan Wholesale
www.ryanwholesale.com
(800) 799-3237

Hennis Enterprises
www.hennisenterprises.com
(888) 643-2879

Architectural Millwork
www.archmillwork.com
(800) 685-1331

PILLARS

Melton Classics
www.meltonclassics.com
(800) 963-3060

Fine House, Ltd.
www.finehouse.net
(540) 436-8080

Columns and Carvings
www.columnsandcarvings.com
(866) 453-4034

H.B. and G. Products
www.hbgcolumns.net
(800) 264-4424

Chadsworth
www.columns.com
(800) COLUMNS

PORCH RAILINGS

Victorian Wood
www.victorianwood.com
(715) 573-1990

Hoffmeyer's
www.hoffmeyersmill.com
(877) 644-5843

Forester Moulding and Lumber
www.forestermoulding.com
(800) 649-9734

McCoy Millwork
www.mccoymillwork.com
(888) 236-0995

WOODEN FLOORING

Jefferson State Forest Products
www.jeffersonstate
products.com
(530) 628-1101

Hoffmeyer's
www.hoffmeyersmill.com
(877) 644-5843

Bear Creek Lumber
www.bearcreeklumber.com
(800) 597-7191

Manomin Resawn Timbers
www.mrtimbers.com
(888) 207-6072

TerraMai
www.terramai.com
(800) 220-9062

Windfall Lumber
www.windfalllumber.com
(362) 352-2250

Duluth Timber Company
www.duluthtimber.com
(218) 727-2145

Fine House, Ltd.
www.finehouse.net
(540) 436-3180

COMPOSITE FLOORING

Tendura
www.tendura.com
(800) TENDURA

Terralastic
www.terralastic.com
(800) 878-5788

Crossfield Products
www.crossfieldproducts.com
(908) 245-2800

URNS AND POTTERY

Gladding McBean
www.gladdingmcbean.com
(800) 776-1133

Window Box.com
www.windowbox.com
(888) 427-3362

Garden Furnishings
www.gardenfurnishings.com
(866) 318-3300

Garden Artisans
www.gardenartisans.com
(410) 451-9535

Arizona Pottery
www.arizonapottery.com
(800) 420-1808

World Pottery.com
www.worldpottery.com

Flower Framers
www.flowerframers.com
(800) 315-1805

Fair Oak Workshops
www.fairoak.com
(800) 341-0597

Craftsman Homes Connection
www.crafthome.com
(509) 535-5098

LIGHTING FIXTURES

Craftsmen Lighting, Ltd.
www.craftsmenhardware.com
(660) 376-2481

Rejuvenation
Lamp and Fixture
www.rejuvenation.com
(888) 401-1900

Arroyo Craftsman
www.arroyocraftsman.com
(626) 960-9411

Old California
Lantern Company
www.oldcalifornia.com
(800) 577-6679

Mica Lamp Company
www.micalamps.com
(818) 241-7227

Brass Light Gallery
www.brasslight.com
(800) 243-9595

Revival Lighting
www.revivallighting.com
(509) 747-4552

Cherry Tree Design
www.cherrytreedesign.com
(800) 634-3268

Luminaria Lighting
www.luminaria.com
(800) 638-5619

Waterglass Studios
www.waterglassstudios.com
(250) 384-1515

Turn of the Century Lighting
www.tocl.on.ca
(888) 527-1825

Vintage Hardware
www.vintagehardware.com
(408) 246-9918

Victorian Revival
www.victorian-revival.com
(416) 789-1704

Historic Lighting
www.historiclighting.com
(626) 303-4899

Aamsco Lighting
(reproduction
antique bulbs)
www.aamsco.com
(800) 221-9092

MAILBOXES

Waterglass Studios
www.waterglassstudios.com
(250) 384-1515

Craftsman Homes Connection
www.crafthome.com
(509) 535-5098

Fair Oak Workshops
www.fairoak.com
(800) 341-0597

ADDRESS NUMBERS

Rocheford Handmade Tile
www.housenumbertiles.com
(612) 824-6216

Craftsman Homes Connection
www.crafthome.com
(509) 535-5098

Craftsmen Hardware
www.craftsmenhardware.com
(660) 376-2481

Fair Oak Workshops
www.fairoak.com
(800) 341-0597

DOOR KNOCKERS
AND CHIMES

Waterglass Studios
www.waterglassstudios.com
(250) 384-1515

Craftsmen Hardware
www.craftsmenhardware.com
(660) 376-2481

Craftsman Homes Connection
www.crafthome.com
(509) 535-5098

CHAPTER EIGHT

OUTSIDE CHANCES

COUPE UP

Depending on when the bungalow was built, it may or may not have a garage. The word *garage* comes from the French word *garer,* meaning "to protect." During the first decade of the twentieth century, automobiles were not that common, though a bungalow built at that time may have had a carriage house that has since become a garage. Initially people used to put the car in the carriage house along with the carriage and the horses, but the horses didn't think much of that idea.

The first garages were portable garages, starting in about 1908. These came prefabricated or as kits, much like the precut houses. By the 1910s and afterward, garages were standard with most bungalows. As a rule, garages were detached from the house, which mostly had to do with the fear of exploding gasoline, a pretty legitimate fear at the time, because gasoline initially had to be stored at home before the invention of filling stations. For this same reason, the garage was often built of brick, concrete block, or hollow clay tile, rather than wood, even if the house itself was wood-framed and had wood siding. Sometimes pressed tin was used for siding, similar to the pressed tin that was used on ceilings. In the 1920s, as people became more comfortable

with cars and filling stations opened up, garages started to sometimes be built underneath the house, particularly if the bungalow was on a sloping lot that made this easy to do. Garages were seldom attached on the side as garages are today, though that probably happened on occasion. A detached garage might be connected to its bungalow by a pergola or roofed breezeway. And the garage itself often had an attached pergola or trellis for growing vines.

At times, the garage was built in a style that matched the house, and other times it wasn't. The garage often had completely different siding from the house. So a shingled bungalow could have a stucco garage, or a house with bevel siding could have a garage that featured tongue-and-groove siding, etc. The garage might even be stucco on the front and wood-sided on the sides, or vice versa. Garages generally didn't have sheathing—the siding was applied directly to the studs. Garages were more likely to have rolled roofing or metal roofing, regardless of what kind of roofing was on the house.

Some garages had dirt or gravel floors, but most had a concrete slab. This was generally not reinforced concrete and usually wasn't that thick either, which means that it's probably cracked by now. Frequently there would be a *grease pit* in the center, which was sometimes covered by

OPPOSITE: A rather tall porte cochere is supported by brick pillars into which random chunks of local New Jersey brown stone have been inserted. It's easy to see that the bottom portions have been re-pointed with lighter colored mortar that unfortunately doesn't match the old mortar at the top.

boards and sometimes not. "Grease pit" is kind of a misnomer, since its function was to allow one to get underneath the car to do repairs (and to do them standing up or sitting, unlike now when you have to lay on your back). A loft was a common feature at the far end, utilizing the space above the car's hood for storage. If the garage was large enough for it, there might be a workshop area, some built-in storage, and even a toilet and sink.

Many garages were built with an apartment on the side or back or with a second-floor apartment. While this was built for the chauffeur if it was a fancy house, many bungalow owners would first build a garage with a small apartment, which they would live in while the house was being built, and then could rent out for income after they moved into the house. These were often called *garlows*.

In dense urban areas with narrow lots, the garage was built right on the property line. In places where alleys were used, the garage door faced the alley, or the

A single-car garage with outswinging doors has been tucked underneath the back porch of a bungalow on a corner lot in this photo from *American Homes and Gardens*.

A more traditional apartment on the upper floor tops a three-bay garage with a hipped roof. Three bays was a lot in a time when there weren't a lot of cars and generally would be found with a larger house, as is the case with this New Jersey garage.

garage might be at right angles to the alley. Alleys are a civilized thing—it gives the bungalow more yard because that space isn't taken up by the driveway (though the cynical would say that it allowed the developer to make the lots narrower), and all the garbage cans, recycling, and such can stay back there. If there was no alley, the garage was still placed at the back of the property, at the end of a driveway. Sometimes the garage had a turntable so that the car could be turned around and driven out frontwards. Another option involved having a drive-through garage with doors at both ends.

Although a single-car garage was typical (this was before the two-car family), many two- (or more) car garages were also built. There is a correlation, though not direct, between the size of the house and the number of stalls in the garage. Many single-car garages were later expanded with another bay if there was room. Unlike a modern two-car garage, there was a center support in the middle of the front wall, dividing the garage into two separate doorways. Each bay of the garage measured about 12 by 18 feet, and the door opening was about 8 by 8 feet. This has led to the fairly common "garage extension"—a lean-to added onto the front or back to accommodate the larger cars of the 1940s and 1950s. (And probably the oversize SUVs of today.) Twelve feet wide is a little tight, even for a compact car. If you want to get out of the car, that is.

ABOVE: Four decorative vertical panels are topped by eight lights, each on the swing-out doors of a textured brick garage behind a Milwaukee bungalow.

RIGHT: A flat-roofed brick garage in Denver has bypass sliding doors with six-light windows and diagonal bead board panels. The doors slide on a metal track mounted above the door opening.

ABOVE: *The Home* presented a deluxe two-bay brick garage with a dormer and a tile roof in the 1923 issue. The dormer supposedly helped to "allow smoke and gases to escape." In addition to the dormer, three windows were provided, two on the side and one on the back. On the front, each set of doors was divided into three panels. The outer panels were bi-fold, and the two inner panels were hinged to the central brick pillar, allowing them to be opened separately for entry into the garage without folding back the other doors.

RIGHT: A rather fancy side roof supported by two Tuscan columns protects a porch at the side door of a stone garage in New Jersey. A wavy-topped fence adds another decorative element.

GARAGES

OBSESSIVE RESTORATION

Hardly anyone takes care of their outbuildings, so the garage may be halfway falling down, if not gone altogether. Many are being held up only by ivy or climbing roses. If the garage is still there, even if it's falling down, it's important to repair it. Especially a garage that is built on the property line, because most jurisdictions will not allow garages to be built on the property line anymore. So even if there is only one wall left, call it a repair and rebuild the rest of it.

Outswinging doors are often long gone, because in places where it snows, they're kind of hard to open in the winter. In spite of this, they were the most popular door style. You have to decide just how obsessive you want to be about this. You could certainly put them back if you want. A slightly more practical option is to have a tilt-up door made that looks like two separate doors, that way you'll only have to clear the snow for maybe two feet in front of it. They did have roll-up doors, so if the house is fancy enough that it might have had an expensive garage door, that would be a perfectly legitimate option. And I guess you could have an automatic opener, provided you mount it on a post by the driveway.

Since garages are often neglected, there may be rot in various places, particularly at the sill plate and the bottom of the studs. The best solution might be to remove the rotten sill, cut off the studs above the rot, build a small concrete curb, attach a new sill, and sister the rotten studs (put a new stud right next to the old one and nail them together). Naturally, provision must be made to prop up the wall while doing this. It probably wouldn't hurt to pour a new reinforced slab while doing this (concrete is reinforced with a grid of *rebar*, which stands for reinforcing bar). Rot may also have caused the garage to lean—this can sometimes be reversed by attaching cables to one side and using winches to pull it back upright (creative types have been known to use a pickup truck for this purpose). No fair widening the garage, though—this is the obsessive part. Get a smaller car instead.

COMPROMISE SOLUTION

As noted in "Obsessive Restoration," a garage on the property line should be repaired, unless you've got a huge lot and want to rebuild from scratch elsewhere. If the garage faces an alley, it doesn't matter so much what the door looks like, although a really ugly door is kind of insulting to your neighbors. But if the door faces the street or towards the house, it would behoove you to get a decent-looking door. Solid wood would be preferable. But expensive. There are various kinds of composite wood, which feature plywood or hardboard panels and solid wood stiles and rails. Doors also come in steel, aluminum, fiberglass, and vinyl. Just forget about vinyl right now.

Solid wood doors are available as tilt-up doors and sectional overhead doors. I'm assuming you wouldn't be interested in swing-out or bi-fold doors, given that this is the Compromise Solution section. Although much has been made of the fact that roll-up doors that look like swing-out doors are being manufactured, the reality is that when you get close you can see the horizontal lines, unless the panel style is chosen very carefully and has horizontal rails to disguise the lines. If you want the look of outswinging doors, get the tilt-up model instead. (Yes, you can still have an automatic opener on a tilt-up door.) Composite doors are fine, though the plywood ones will last longer than the hardboard ones. The hardboard panels have a tendency to become rippled after several years. Doors should have flat panels, not raised panels like so many modern garage doors have. The cheapest wood door available is a tilt-up door with a plywood skin. These are easy to tart up by nailing on some one-by-whatever boards in an interesting pattern, and you can end up with a pretty good-looking door this way.

All kinds of window options are available on garage doors—everything from restoration glass to stained glass to plastic. Try to avoid the fake brass "leading," if possible.

Steel, fiberglass, and aluminum doors tend to suffer from the "embossed wood grain" disease so common to fake siding, so if you're going to go that way, try to find one that's smooth. As with wood, look for flat panels, not the raised panels that are common today. These doors usually have some kind of foam insulation as part of their makeup, which means they can dent easily.

There is a particular kind of ribbed aluminum door that I absolutely hate. It seems to be very popular in Los Angeles. If you have one, do me a favor and get rid of it.

The Stanley Works advertised their garage door holder in a 1918 issue of *House Beautiful*. It locked the door in an open position, preventing the wind from slamming the door into your car.

The side walls were built both with and without windows. Windows could be fixed or operable and may have even matched the windows of the house. Often a side door was provided so that it wouldn't be necessary to open the main doors to get into the garage. Garage doors were wooden and came in different styles. Some opened outward like a pair of French doors, some were bypass sliding doors, some folded up accordion-style, and some ran on a J-shaped track that allowed them to slide along one inside wall of the garage. The sectional roll-up door that we are familiar with began to be manufactured shortly after the turn of the century, though it was more expensive and therefore not that common. Spring-loaded tilt-up doors were also around but didn't come into widespread use until later. Some doors had a separate *wicket door* set into the main door so the garage could be accessed without opening the main door.

The doors were assembled using board-and-batten or paneled construction, with or without windows. Outward opening doors hung on large strap hinges or ball-tip mortise hinges. Sliding doors generally hung on an outside mounted track using barn door hardware, as did the J-track doors. Accordion-fold doors usually had pins set into the tops of the doors, and those ran in a track at the top of the door opening. Sectional roll-up doors ran on tracks on each side, the way they do today. Tilt-up (sometimes called *swing up*) doors were counterbalanced by heavy springs to make them easier to lift.

And lest you think that electric garage door openers are a recent invention—they first began to be available in the 1920s. They were operated by using a key to activate a switch mounted on a pole next to the driveway.

DRIVE TO SUCCEED

If the garage doesn't face an alley, then there's probably a driveway. A typical driveway for an urban bungalow on a narrow lot would run alongside the house and consist of two concrete tracks about eighteen inches wide and as far apart as the wheels on a car. The space in between was supposed to be grass but invariably is now weeds. Sometimes this part was filled in later with more concrete because some owner was tired of dealing with the weeds. Full concrete driveways were also used, as well as gravel driveways and occasionally brick. The driveway concrete might be tinted to match the porch or front path. As noted earlier about stained concrete, somebody may have painted it—this is really annoying. A bungalow on a larger lot might have a curved driveway. Or it might not. Asphalt wasn't used much for driveways then, not as much as it is now.

It's likely that an old driveway is cracked, as the concrete

The curved driveway of a Memphis twin-gabled bungalow leads to an angled porte cochere that still retains its original limestone piers and tapered wood columns.

was rarely reinforced. If you decide to replace it, the option is pretty much: concrete. Don't use those interlocking pavers they sell for this purpose—they are inappropriate. The kind you can plant grass in are also not a good idea on many levels. Driveways that aren't too far gone can also be coated with a thin layer of polymer-modified concrete on top, called *concrete resurfacing,* which may also be a solution to the afore-mentioned paint problem. This can be used to make the drive-way look like flagstone, brick, etc., but try not to get too carried away. You can also have it engraved with your initials or your company logo. Amusing, but very wrong. It is better to keep the existing driveway if at all possible—sending a whole bunch of concrete to the landfill isn't a good idea. If you have to take the driveway out, see if you can use the pieces to build a retaining wall or something.

ANY PORTE COCHERE IN A STORM

Seems a little hoity-toity, but a remarkable number of bun-galows sported a porte cochere (literally, "coach door"), a roofed structure extending out from the house over the adja-cent driveway to shelter those getting in and out of vehicles. While this brings to mind the eighteenth-century upper class alighting from coaches and being helped by footmen, a porte cochere is actually a civilized invention that allows you to unload your groceries during a rainstorm without getting wet. As with porches, the porte cochere was held up on the outside end by a pair of sizeable pillars, usually matching the ones on the porch. Because a lot of these structures were built during the era of the Model A Ford, the passage is often

much too narrow for a large American car, and this has led to the pillars being replaced with the dreaded "wrought iron," or with four-by-fours or steel pipe columns (and even these sometimes are bent to allow a larger car through). I suspect much of this pillar removal was done quite recently by people who had bought gigantic sport utility vehicles. As with porch pillar replacement, just because a pipe column is strong enough to support the roof doesn't mean it looks right.

WALK LIKE AN EGYPTIAN

No doubt there were bungalows where you just had to walk across the lawn to get to the house, but most of the time there was some sort of path. This could be anything from a dirt path (which was often what you ended up with when people were walking across the lawn) to a gravel walk, stepping stones, or a path of brick, concrete, or stone. And contrary to contempo-rary landscape thought, these paths were nearly always straight, not amusingly curved. The standard path for an urban bungalow on a flat lot was a straight shot from the side-walk to the front steps. Or from the driveway to the front steps. Concrete was standard, plain, or stained. A sloped lot might have a straight or curving path interrupted by short flights of stairs or the occasional landing. Sometimes the path was brick, set in either sand or mortar. And although it seems a bit down-scale, a sloping path often had a handrail made from galva-nized pipe. A wrought-iron railing might be used instead.

A brick path can become slippery with moss—resist the urge to sandblast it. Pressure-wash it instead, and then put on a sealer.

RIGHT: A twin-gabled bunga-low highlighted in 1923's *The Home* includes a per-gola porte cochere resting on wooden piers that match the porch piers. More deco-rative than protective, it would be a lovely place to grow vines. This bungalow is set on top of a small bank, so the driveway includes steps up the middle between the two concrete tracks for the car's tires.

OPPOSITE: The welcoming entry to an Eagle Rock, California, bungalow is through a rustic arbor built of saplings with the bark left on and covered with vines. Rocks from the arroyo edge the planting beds to either side.

SHACK UP

Though they are even less likely to be standing than the garage, many bungalows had other out-buildings, like tool or potting sheds, summer houses, gazebos, bathhouses, and so forth. A rural bungalow (or one that was once rural) may have had a barn, stable, chicken coop, etc. I have friends whose grounds include a one-room schoolhouse, two greenhouses, and a cattery (a building for raising cats; this particular one has windows on all four sides with a foot-deep platform running all the way around at sill height, which is a cat's idea of heaven). These were customarily built of wood. Restoring these outbuildings is similar to restoring a garage. Must I mention that those prefab metal sheds that are bolted together are not appropriate?

POOL YOUR RESOURCES

Yeah, like I'm an expert on historic swimming pools. They were probably either concrete or gunite, and concrete resurfacing will probably work wonders. Many of them were tiled, at least around the edges. And unlike modern pools, they were usually all one depth.

But there was the occasional fountain, pool, or pond. A fountain might be freestanding, or it might be built into a wall. Often art tile was involved. A pool or pond was generally integrated into some sort of terrace or patio and might either be formal (rectangular, round, or some other shape) or more naturalistic, possibly involving river rock and/or a small waterfall.

The problem with all of these things after ninety-odd years is that they probably leak. Concrete resurfacing or an EPDM pond liner will fix that. If the pump is broken, get a new one.

Okay, being a Californian, I do have to address this. If you're actually installing a swimming pool, an irregular shape and a dark bottom will make it look less like a pool and more like a pond. Unless you actually want to build a rectangular gunite pool that's all six feet deep.

They did not have hot tubs or spas. But since I've already said that no whirlpool tubs are allowed in bathrooms, disguise the spa in your backyard as a pond or tiled fountain, or build a lovely Craftsman gazebo around it.

IF YOU PICKET IT'LL NEVER HEAL

One aspect of the informal nature of bungalows was the lack of fences. Arts and Crafts landscaping was much more naturalistic than what had preceded it, and boundaries were often not defined at all or defined by hedges or lattice screens. This was particularly true in the front yards. In some urban bungalow neighborhoods you can look all the way down the block and there will be nary a fence. In some neighborhoods this was even true of the backyards. Even the backyard fences tended to be short and see-through, not like today's 6-foot walls. Sometimes the more utilitarian areas were fenced off, like the vegetable garden, but just as often they weren't.

LEFT: A shingled playhouse complete with fireplace was obviously a hit with these children, as shown in a photograph in *House Beautiful*. A small porch on the back has lattice pillars and overlooks the river.

RIGHT: Water bubbles out of a ceramic vase set in a fountain, surrounded by a wisteria-covered pergola outside a southern California bungalow. Low boxwood hedges surround a patio formed of rectangular slabs of concrete separated by plantings of a low-growing groundcover. A wooden bench and table provide a pleasant place to sit outdoors and enjoy the fountain.

LEFT: Another "Berkeley fence" with a somewhat Asian look is located just down the street from the previous fence. Though it may be viewed as somewhat unfriendly to enclose a front yard with a high fence, it does provide privacy for the front yard, especially important on a small lot with limited yard space, as is often the case in dense urban neighborhoods.

BELOW: A high fence, made less wall-like by spaces between the two-by-two uprights, surrounds the front yard of a Berkeley brown shingle. The solid paneled gate is flanked by two art-glass lanterns. The house itself shows a certain Greene and Greene influence, especially the sleeping porch at the upper right side.

Fences were most often made of wood or wire. Simple kinds of lattice or pickets (originally a pointed stake, but eventually a flat, thin board with a pointed top) were used in wood fences. The lattice used was more likely to be the right-angle sort rather than the diagonal that is more common today. A lattice fence provided an ideal support structure for the flowering vines that were *de rigeur* for a bungalow garden.

BEYOND THE PALE

Okay, I really only put this in a separate section so I could use that pun. A somewhat more substantial fence board (6 to 8 inches wide) is known as a *pale*. These were usually about 5 feet tall. A common design in the Arts and Crafts era utilizing wider boards was board and batten. Also used as bungalow fences were rustic designs made from saplings, influenced by the rustic Adirondack style.

There has been a distressing trend since the late 1980s of building a 6-foot solid fence around *the front yard*. Apparently this is both for security and privacy in an increasingly crowded environment. Locally this is known as a *Berkeley fence*, although I don't think Berkeley deserves all the blame. This is so antithetical to everything that bungalows stand for that I am nearly rendered speechless by the mere existence of these fences. A fence of this sort is essentially giving the finger to passersby and to the neighborhood.

THROWN FOR A LOOP

Probably the most universal fence was the double-loop wire fence, made from twisted galvanized wire. This was attached to wooden or metal fence posts, and theoretically kept (other people's) children and pets out of the garden while keeping your own children and pets in. I say theoretically because the fence was only 4 feet high, which would hardly deter a

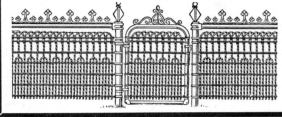

Cheaper Than Lumber!
and Pays You Bigger Profits—
GLOBE SANITARY FENCING

It's a fact that you can buy Globe Sanitary Yard Fencing direct from us at a lower price than the lumber needed to fence the same space—put it up considerably cheaper and offer your customers a durable, ornamental, all-around better fence at a saving to them and at a greater Profit for yourself.

Write for views of Houses fenced both back and front with Globe Fencing together with our Catalogue showing our large variety of styles.

GLOBE FENCE COMPANY, North Chicago, Ill.

ABOVE: Globe Sanitary Fencing shows the most typical double-loop pattern in this advertisement from the 1915 *American Carpenter and Builder,* although in the bottom illustration they've added some fancy cresting as well.

BELOW: The Rossman Wire Fence Company showed their version of a double-loop wire fence in an advertisement in *House Beautiful.* According to them, it had "all the advantages of any other form of fence without their disadvantages."

Protect Your Home

by inclosing your grounds with the strongest, most ornamental and durable fence on the market. This illustration can give you but a faint idea of the beauties of

Rossman WIRE FENCE
STEEL AND IRON

It has all the advantages of any other form of fence without their disadvantages, and is made in several sizes and styles to meet all requirements. Complete illustrated catalogue mailed on request. Kindly ask for Catalogue E.

SLEETH-BROOK & SEAMAN CO.
253 BROADWAY   NEW YORK CITY

resolute child or pet from getting over it. Matching gates were made as well. Even during the years when the tall version was not being made, this fence lived on as a commonly available flowerbed edging. The tall kind is once again available.

CHAIN OF FOOLS

Another kind of woven wire fencing, which we know as chain-link fencing, began to be available in the first decade of the twentieth century, so it would actually be historically correct. That doesn't mean you can have it. No, not even if you live where there are hurricanes. Get the double-loop stuff instead.

PERCENTAGE OF THE GATE

A fence was often accompanied by a gate, as was a wall. The gate might be of metal or wood and could be quite elaborate or simply functional. A double-loop wire fence came with a matching gate, while a wooden fence might have a gate that matched or something more elaborate. Almost any gate design that could be dreamed of was probably used. Wooden gates consistently used ornamental strap hinges, as they mostly still do. The front gate was frequently made into an elaborate entry that could involve a pergola, an arbor, or even a roof, hanging or post lanterns for lighting, house numbers, benches, fancy gate hardware, inset decorative tiles (often pierced), and whatever else the builder could think of.

WALL STREET

Some bungalows had walls instead of, or in addition to, fences. Walls were made of stone, brick, concrete block, or stucco (over wood or masonry), or combinations of the above. These were more likely to be

A double gate with a wisteria-covered arbor above has been built using two salvaged doors set into a black steel frame. The six-light doors feature stained glass with an Arts and Crafts–stylized rose design. The gate and accompanying shingled fence provide some privacy and sound control to the front of this Seattle bungalow, which is on a relatively busy street.

FENCES

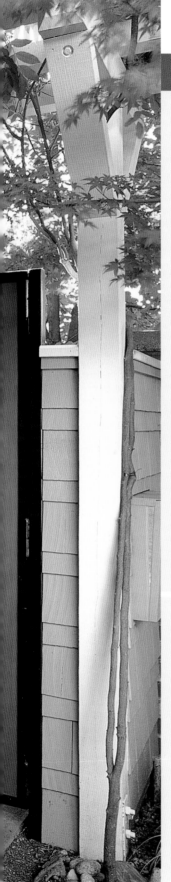

OBSESSIVE RESTORATION

Historic wooden fences are unlikely to have lasted this long, unless they were actually maintained (rare) or they were made out of really big rot-resistant timbers. Nonetheless, if the fence or any parts of it are still there, it should be saved and restored. Lattice is the first thing to go—being made of thin strips of wood, even rot-resistant lattice will eventually bow to the hand of time. Unless there are historic photos, replacement lattice will have to be based on supposition, although some sort of square or rectangular grid would be a good bet. Remaining fence parts can be repaired with epoxy consolidants or *dutchmen* (wood patches). The posts often rot below ground level, as posts were not usually set in concrete and may also need replacing. It's a good idea to put new posts on top of concrete footings with an embedded metal connector that keeps the vulnerable end grain above grade. Post tops are end grain and were often beveled on four sides into a pyramid shape to shed water—even so, it's still end grain. Sometimes post caps were used, more or less solving the end grain problem. If the posts happen to be big timbers, salvaged timbers may be the best option, as huge pieces of wood are hard to come by these days. Another option is to build up a larger post around a four-by-four. The rails, which are generally two-by-fours, may also need replacing. Rot-resistant woods such as redwood, cedar, or cypress are usually the best bet.

Some hardwoods also work well for posts, though that is an expensive option. The Brazilian hardwood known as *ipe* or *pau lope* is one of the less-expensive hardwoods. Pressure-treated wood is toxic, not to mention ugly, although there are some alternatives that employ less toxic treatments such as ACQ (alkaline copper quaternary). Lumber treated with this would be a less toxic, though not completely non-toxic, alternative to use as a support post inside a built-up post.

The gate is the most vulnerable part of a fence, since it moves. Gates are prone to sagging because they are only attached on one side. Traditional sag prevention methods include diagonal bracing or a metal rod or cable with a turnbuckle. But a better method, which is also very true to the Arts and Crafts style, is to construct the gate using pegged mortise-and-tenon joinery. Gustav Stickley would be proud.

Wire fences tend to rust out once the galvanizing wears off. About the only solution at that point is paint. I would recommend spray painting for obvious reasons.

Masonry piers or pillars that are part of a fence can deteriorate even faster than the same materials in a house wall since all sides of them are exposed to the weather. The usual stuff about re-pointing, patching stucco, etc., would apply here.

COMPROMISE SOLUTION

Here are some kinds of fences you can't have: split-rail fences, fancy cast-iron fences, grapestake fences (it was practically the state fence of California when I was growing up, and it is amusingly rustic, but no), chain-link fences, vinyl fences, barbed-wire fences (well, maybe if your bungalow is on an actual ranch), rail fences (like the white ones that all horse farms are apparently required to have), or a fence with dog-eared boards (a personal prejudice, I admit), and any of those prefab picket fences you can buy at the home center. It's not that hard to build a picket fence, and the pickets are always too far apart on the prefab ones. In the front, there's always the option of no fence at all. It's a cheap option too.

There is also a sort of fence that seems to be growing in popularity, consisting of brick (often "used" brick) pillars with pointy wrought-iron fencing in between, which often curves or swoops and sometimes has gold accents. These are often installed by the same people who cover their wood-sided bungalows with stucco. Sometimes the pillars are topped with statuary—lions are popular, but classical Greek statues also make an appearance. Sometimes these are so over-the-top as to be amusing, but mostly they're an affront to the neighborhood.

Most sorts of simple wooden fences will do, even the ones you can buy in 6-foot sections at the home center, though they are kind of generic. Simply alternating wide and narrow boards will make for a nice Arts and Crafts look.

OPPOSITE: A pergola made of heavy timbers covers a gravel walkway that leads from a southern California bungalow to the guest house next door. Timbers this large are sturdy enough to stand up to the wisteria that covers them, which could easily destroy a pergola made from lighter-weight materials.

ABOVE: The curved arbor over this gate in Berkeley has real expressed structure—the curved pieces actually go through slots in the uprights and are held in with triangular wedges at the top and bottom. The uprights in the fence and gate are grapestakes, albeit with the traditional pointed tops cut off.

BELOW: Pink climbing roses cover a pergola over the front walk of a bungalow in Ojai, California. Some Swiss influence is seen in the wide gables and scalloped fascia boards of this home, as well as the shutters with heart-shaped cutouts that frame the windows.

low and decorative rather than high and utilitarian. Often the wall sections were broken up by taller piers or pillars. Sloping lots or raised bed planting areas often required retaining walls, which were integrated into the landscape.

CUTTING HEDGE

Informal hedges (as opposed to more formal clipped hedges) were also used to define the boundaries of the lot. Flowering shrubs like spirea, mock-orange, rosa rugosa, forsythia, and hydrangea were popular for this purpose. The occasional formal hedge was found gracing a bungalow whose owner had decided to go for the classical Italian garden look, probably accompanied by cypress trees and statuary.

OVERWROUGHT IRON

There was not a whole lot of wrought ironwork, but there might be a wrought-iron gate in a masonry wall, especially on a high-dollar bungalow. The other place that wrought iron commonly appeared was in hardware, either door hardware or gate hardware.

ABOVE: Many stone walls in Vancouver, British Columbia, feature these pointed stegosaurus-like tops. The mortar on this one has been tooled in a convex manner so it stands out from the surrounding stones.

BELOW: A low wall of clinker brick and stone from the arroyo caps a low concrete foundation and serves as a welcoming entrance to a Pasadena bungalow court. Unfortunately, a modern-looking wrought-iron fence has been added on top for security purposes.

OPPOSITE: Iron is less common for bungalow fences, but this lovely version, with yin-yang symbols at the top and an extremely stylized flower worked into the uprights, surrounds a large bungalow in Denver, Colorado.

RESOURCES

GARAGES

Moulton Custom Door of
  Vermont
  www.moultoncustomdoor.com
  (802) 244-5357

Hahn's Woodworking Company
  www.hahnswoodworking.com
  (908) 793-1415

Artisan Custom Doorworks
  www.artisandoorworks.com
  (888) 913-9170

Sections, Inc.
  www.sections.com
  (877) 707-8810

Raynor
  www.raynor.com
  (800) 472-9667

Designer Doors
  www.designerdoors.com

Northstar Wood Works
  www.northstarww.com
  (360) 384-0307

Clopay Building Products
  www.clopay.com
  (800) 225-6729

Summit Door, Inc.
  www.summit-door.com
  (888) 768-3667

Gunnison Garage Door, Inc.
  www.garagedoorsrus.com
  (970) 641-2769

Amarr Garage Doors
  www.amarr.com
  (800) 503-3667

Vintage Garages
  (plans for vintage garages
  and other outbuildings)
  www.vintagegarages.com

DRIVEWAYS

Perma-Crete
  www.permacrete.com
  (800) 607-3762

Concrete Solutions
  www.concretesolutions.com
  (800) 232-8311

Engrave-A-Crete
  www.engraveacrete.com
  (800) 884-2114

Pebblestone Decking
  www.pebblestone.net
  (800) 341-2734

Grail Coat
  www.grailcoat.com
  (877) 472-4528

OUTBUILDINGS

Spirit Elements
  www.spiritelements.com
  (800) 511-1440

Pine Harbor
  www.pineharbor.com
  (800) 368-7433

Garden Sheds
  www.gardensheds.com
  (717) 397-5430

Visscher Specialty Products
  www.visscherspecialty.com
  (877) 795-7423

FENCES

Fence Factory
  www.fencefactory.com
  (818) 889-2240

Bear Creek Lumber
  www.bearcreeklumber.com
  (800) 597-7191

Jimmy's Cypress
  www.jimmys-cypress.com
  (888) 245-1050

Museum Resources
  www.museum-resources.com
  (804) 966-1800

WIRE FENCES

Hutchison Western
  www.hutchison-inc.com
  (800) 525-0121

GARDEN GATES

Deckway
  www.deckway.com
  (877) 332-5929

Walpole Woodworkers
  www.walpolewoodworkers.com
  (800) 343-6948

Fine House, Ltd.
  www.finehouse.net
  (540) 436-8080

Garden Arches
  www.gardenarches.com
  (800) 947-7697

Bow Bends
  www.bowbends.com
  (978) 779-6464

BUNGLE-ODE

Irving Gill
  (for Alfred Heineman's
  response to the Bungle-Ode)
  www.irvinggill.com

Opposite: The high stone wall of a hillside bungalow in Seattle is
capped with redwood and features two different masonry patterns,
one for the wall and a different one for the pillars.

·FINAL· CONFUSION

I thought I'd let Ernest Freese have the last word. This was published in *The Architect and Engineer of California* in March 1918. In no way do I mean this to suggest that I'm not serious about bungalows, because I am. It's just that it was too amusing to pass up.

A BUNGLE-ODE

A Bungalow is a species of inhabitable mushroom that springs up over night on vacant lots. It might be more comprehensibly defined as the manifestation of a peculiar style of Western domestic architecture that causes lady tourists from the two-storied East to be precipitated into involuntary and rapturous comments, such as "Oh! How cute!"

Architecturally speaking, the bungalow is a composite of Swiss chalet, Japanese tea-house, Frank Lloyd Wright leaded glass, Spanish hacienda, Chinese influence, Mission furniture, monstrous originality, disappearing beds, and disillusioning appearance.

What? You are incredulous? Listen, then. Allow me to describe one of these bungalows as I hypothetically view it from where I sit. No, I shall first describe the whole flock.

Flock is the proper term. They appear to have just lit, or as if flight were imminent. That is the first impression; restlessness and impermanency, created by the multiplicity of flattened-out gable roofs and enormous flapping eaves, all abristle with fantastically fashioned rafter ends. However, on further survey, it is realized with a jolt that if the bungalow proper takes to flight, at least a part will remain eternally anchored to earth. I refer to the huge piles of masonry-brick, cobblestones, concrete—that constitute the porch piers. For, behold, even though a bungalow has no foundation upon which to rest other than a two-by-six redwood plank, yet in the porch piers must there be at least ten tons of solid masonry to support the two-by-four raftered roof. Why mention the mysteries of ancient Egypt? Imagine future antiquarians discoursing as follows of the days in which we live:

Huge piles of masonry still stand upon the sites of those ancient Western cities. The origin and purpose of these great and numerous Cobble-Isks are shrouded in mystery. The only rational theory by which we can account for their existence is that the people of that Peculiar Era did start to build what were then known as Skyscrapers, but that Land Values changed over night and the project was abandoned because there was no Money in it.

One bungalow in particular attracts my attention. The porch piers of this one are of cobblestone. And the

---

OPPOSITE: A clinker-brick pier (unfortunately, painted) holds up a complex variety of wooden timbers and cross members in the open porch gable of a Victoria, British Columbia, home.

cobblestones are studded with brick—for effect. The effect is that you wonder why the contractor neglected to furnish enough cobbles to finish the job. The rivers are full of them—not contractors: cobbles. They are a dominant note in the scenic grandeur of far Western rivers. These rivers are peculiar; they are upside down most of the time. That is to say, the water is underneath, the sand and cobbles on top! You simply drive down the river and pluck them.

Well, as I have said, the porch piers of this particular bungalow are studded with brick—for effect. You have noted the effect—upon me. Wait. There are four of these great piers, all in a row. At the ground line they are perhaps six feet square, and they rise roofward in sweeping curves of the fourth or fifth dimension to the dizzy height of about seven feet. At this point, the sweeping curves have swept into tangency with the vertical. And here they terminate, two feet square, capped with a chunk of concrete half a foot thick. But the end is not yet. There still intervenes a space of two feet between the top of each pier and the overhead roof-beam. And now—O ye of little understanding—I beseech ye to behold the monstrous originality of the bungalow builders! This intervening space of two feet is occupied by a four-by-four stick of timber that rests in supreme and supercilious stability upon its enormous base of stone. This construction is artistic. What? I repeat—artistic. It is moreover delightfully frank—not Frank-Lloyd-Wright: frank. For it acknowledges the fact that instead of a tonnage of masonry to support that paper roof, all that is actually required is a four-inch stick of Oregon pine!

In the end-spaces between these piers are described graceful catenaries. A Catenary is no part of cat or canary. It is the curve described by a hanging chain. Perhaps I should have said that between these piers hang chains, describing catenaries. Then describing on my part would end into the eternal masonry of the piers. They replace the antiquated classic balustrade—and they serve a useful purpose (beauty and utility should be co-existent)—they serve as swings for children. Not necessarily the bungalow-dwellers' children, but your children, my children, the children of the next-door neighbors, and the children of generations yet unborn. The chains are procured from the manufacturers or harbor dredges and also from the builders of steel derricks.

Farther along on bungalow row is what is technically known as an "aeroplane." This particular aeroplane is a bi-plane—that is to say, it has two sets of white planes—two paper roofs, one above the other. The upper roof hovers over a second-floor sleeping apartment. The walls of the sleeping apartment are set back, all around, from the walls of the story beneath. This is an aeroplane of the bungalow army. It is also a highly successful combination of freight-train—caboose and Japanese pagoda. And the Chinese influence is decidedly marked in the jig-sawed, tip-tilted rafter ends. Other influences are also in evidence.

Another bungalow exhibits a melee of original and startling timber work. The starting point of it is that it does not crash to earth of its own weight. Mighty timbers—with ends cut into every conceivable form of curve known to higher geometry, planing—mill mechanics and jigsaws—are piled up this way and the other ways in a bewildering and

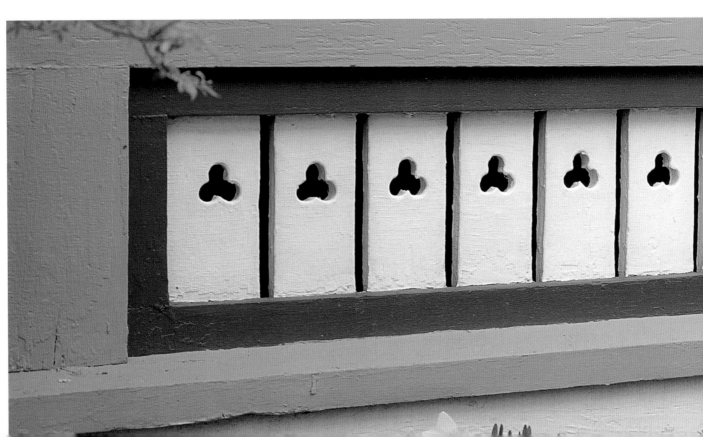

spiked-together intricacy that causes the beholder to gasp in unbelief. Theoretically, this bewildering intricacy is the "support" of the over-hung roof. Theories are flexible and nebulous things. But the law of gravitation is an undisputed fact. Wherefore, these flapping, wing-like, overhanging eaves of two-by-four rafters sag under the very weight of their aforementioned "supports," and a typical bungalesque down-drooping roof curve manifests itself just beyond the wall line.

Have patience. Not yet have you learned all the wonders of the bungalow. Enter. Grasp the ponderous store-front handle of that four by six by eight slab of solid oak, and come in. Solid oak? Ah-vain and for the nonce are the front doors of the bungalow builders, for the paper veneer on that door is already wrinkling its back where the sun hits it. But come in.

Look out! Don't open the door too wide—twill crash into the Mission rocker. And if the rocker starts rocking, twill smash the leaded glass of the book-case doors. Now look at the mantelpiece and the beamed ceiling. All of solid mahog—Oh!—one-by-six Oregon pine boards nailed together and stained—stained out of all semblance to Oregon pine boards.

You are curious as to the meaning of that lowered ceiling-beam occurring midway between the front door and the kitchen. Ho! Ho! Surely you are from the far, far East—mayhap from Massachusetts. Listen. That particular beam is the dividing line between this and that, "this" being the living-room and "that" being the dining-room.

Follow the path into the kitchen. Careful. Don't bump your shins on that seat-end. Oh, I nearly forgot—that built-in seat conceals the head-end of a perambulating bed. The feet-end projects into the bedroom closet. The roof of the bed-space is the floor of the closet, and the floor of the closet is three steps above the floor of the bed-room. If you stand up straight in the closet you bump your head on the ceiling.

Isn't this kitchen a wondrous thing! In comparison, a dining-car kitchen becomes a vast and immeasurable space. Stand there by the sink. You can reach everything in the room.

And this is the bed-room. Where is the bed? In the wall behind that mirror. Step back in the kitchen and I will let the bed down. There! That's how it works. But now if you insist upon seeing the bath-room, I shall have to fold up the bed again or we shall have to crawl over it—we are on the wrong side!

Enough. I would a confession make.

Once upon a time, a very dear friend of mine casually remarked that she would "just love to live in a bungalow." Her casualness was affected. For she thereupon confided to me that she had one "all picked out," and that it was "the dearest thing." She had an acute attack of bungalomania. But, as I have said, she is a very dear friend of mine. Would I go with her and see that bungalow? I would. And I did. "Isn't it just adorable?" she pleaded.
I repeat, she is a very dear friend of mine. So I didn't kill her outright.

I let her live and suffer.

We rented that bungalow.

A front porch in Milwaukee is vented with these spaced boards that have had holes drilled in a clover pattern in each board.

BIBLIOGRAPHY

Aladdin Company, The. *Aladdin Homes: "Built in a Day" Catalog #29*. Bay City, Michigan, 1917. Reprint by Mineola, New York: Dover Publications, 1995.

American Technical Society. *Cyclopedia of Architecture, Carpentry, and Building, Volume I*. Chicago, Illinois, 1916.

Building Brick Association of America, The. *One Hundred Bungalows*. Boston, Massachusetts: 1912. Reprint by Mineola, New York: Dover Publications, 1994.

Duchscherer, Paul and Douglas Keister. *The Bungalow: America's Arts and Crafts Home*. New York, New York: Penguin Books, 1995

Duchscherer, Paul and Douglas Keister. *Outside the Bungalow: America's Arts and Crafts Garden*. New York, New York: Penguin Books, 1999.

E. C. Young Company. *Young's Garages and Bungalows*. Randolph, Massachusetts, n.d.

Gordon-Van Tine Company. *Gordon-Van-Tine Homes*. Davenport, Iowa, 1923. Reprint by Mineola, New York: Dover Publications, 1992.

Graham, Frank D. *Audel's Carpenters and Builders Guide*. New York, New York: Theo. Audel and Company, 1923.

Grimmer, Anne E. and Paul K. Williams, *The Preservation and Repair of Historic Clay Tile Roofs*. Washington, D.C.: National Park Service, 1992.

Grimmer, Anne. *The Preservation and Repair of Historic Stucco*. Washington, D.C.: National Park Service, 1990.

Hodgson, Fred T. *Practical Bungalow and Cottages for Town and Country*. Chicago, Illinois: Frederick J. Drake and Company, 1906.

House Beautiful Publishing Company, The. *The House Beautiful,* May 1908, December 1911–May 1912. Chicago, Illinois.

House Beautiful Publishing Company, The. *The House Beautiful*, June–December 1918. Boston, Massachusetts.Hull, Brent. *Historic Millwork*. Hoboken, New Jersey: John Wiley and Sons, Inc., 2003.

Jester, Thomas C. *Twentieth Century Building Materials*. Washington, D.C.: McGraw-Hill Companies, 1995.

Keith, M. L. *Keith's Magazine on Home Building*, July 1918. Minneapolis, Minnesota.

King, Anthony D. *The Bungalow: The Production of a Global Culture*. London, England: Routledge and Kegan Paul plc, 1984.

Lancaster, Clay. *The American Bungalow*. New York, New York: Abbeville Press, 1985. Republication by Mineola, New York: Dover Publications, 1995.

Levine, Jeffrey S. *The Repair, Replacement, and Maintenance of Historic Slate Roofs*. Washington, D.C.: National Park Service, 1992.

Lewis Manufacturing Company. *Lewis Homes: Homes of Character*. Bay City, Michigan, 1923.

Loizeaux Lumber Company. *Loizeaux's Plan Book #7*. Plainfield, New Jersey, 1927. Reprint by Mineola, New York: Dover Publications, 1992.

Lowndes, W. S. and Boyd, D. Knickerbacker. *Plastering and Stucco Work*. Scranton, Pennsylvania: International Textbook Company, 1931.

Magazine Circulation Company. *The Home*, 1923. Chicago, Illinois, 1922.

Meany, Terence. *Working Windows*. Bothell, Washington: Meany Press, 1997. Republication by Guilford, Connecticut: Lyons Press, 1998.

Morgan. *Building with Assurance*. Chicago, Illinois: Morgan Woodwork Organization, 1921.

Munn and Company. *American Homes and Gardens*, January–December 1907. New York, New York.

Pacific Hardware and Manufacturing Company. *Builders Hardware*. Los Angles, California, 1912.

Park, Sharon C. *The Repair and Replacement of Historic Wooden Shingle Roofs*. Washington, D.C.: National Park Service, 1989.

Prentice, Helaine Kaplan and Blair, and City of Oakland Planning Department. *Rehab Right*. Oakland, California: City of Oakland, 1978. Reprint by Berkeley, California: Ten Speed Press, 1986.

Radford Architectural Company. *Radford's Cyclopedia of Construction: Carpentry, Building, Architecture, Volumes IV, V, VI*. Chicago, Illinois, 1923.

Radford, William A. *Architectural Details for Every Type of Building*. Chicago, Illinois: Radford Architectural Company, 1921. Reprint by Mineola, New York: Dover Publications, 2002.

Radford, William A., Editor-in-Chief. *American Carpenter and Builder,* March–December 1915 issues. Chicago, Illinois: The American Carpenter and Builder Company.

Radford, William A. *Radford's Artistic Bungalows*. Chicago, Illinois: Radford Architectural Company, 1908. Reprint by Mineola, New York: Dover Publications, 1997.

Radford, William A. *Radford's Details of Building Construction*. Chicago, Illinois: Radford Architectural Company, 1911.

Ray H. Bennett Lumber Company. *Bennett Homes: Better-Built Ready-Cut*. North Tonawanda, New York, 1920. Reprint by Mineola, New York: Dover Publications, 1993.

Sears Roebuck and Company. *Honor-bilt Modern Homes*. Chicago, Illinois: 1926. Reprint by Mineola, New York: Dover Publications, 1991.

Springfield Manufacturing Company. *Springfield Portable Houses*. Keene, New Hampshire, 1914.

Stickley, Gustav. *Craftsman Homes*. New York, New York: Craftsman Publishing Company, 1909. Reprint by Mineola, New York: Dover Publications, 1979.

Stickley, Gustav. *More Craftsman Homes*. New York, New York: Craftsman Publishing Company, 1912. Reprint by Mineola, New York: Dover Publications, 1982.

Sweetser, Sarah M. *Roofing for Historic Buildings*. Washington, D.C.: National Park Service, 1978.

Wilson, Henry L. *A Short Sketch of the Evolution of the Bungalow: From Its Primitive Crudeness to Its Present State of Artistic Beauty and Cozy Convenience*. Los Angeles, California, n.d. Reprint by Mineola, New York: Dover Publications, 1993.

Winter, Robert. *The California Bungalow*. Los Angeles, California: Hennessey and Ingalls, Inc., 1980.

WEB ARTICLES

DeLorenzo, Josephine. *Historic Metal Roofing*. roofingcontractor.com. September 2003.

Faragher, John Mack. *Bungalow and Ranch House: The Architectural Backwash of California*. Western Historical Quarterly Summer 2001. http://www.historycooperative.org/journals/whq/32.2/faragher.htm.

Morris, William. *The Lesser Arts of Life. An Address Delivered in Support of the Society for the Protection of Ancient Buildings*. London, 1882. http://www.burrows.com/morris/lesser.html.

National Park Service. *From Asbestos to Zinc, Roofing for Historic Buildings*. Washington, D.C., 1999. http://www2.cr.nps.gov/tps/roofingexhibit/asbestoscement.htm.

Paquette, John. *What's Wrong with Vinyl Windows?* City of Newport, Kentucky. http://www.eastrow.org/articles/vinylwindows.htm.

Phillips, Kerry. *What is a Bungalow?* Sacramento Bungalow Heritage Association, 2003. http://www.sacbungalow.org/whabunga.htm.

Turrell, Colleen. *Storm Windows Save Energy*. Home Energy Magazine Online, July/August 2000. http://www.homeenergy.org/archive/hem.dis.anl.gov/eehem/00/0007contents.html.

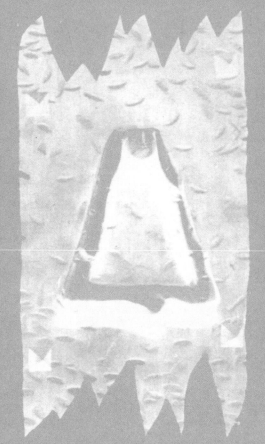

S.B. 13

P.B. 13

K.N. 13

C. 13

E.C. 13